TEXT BOOK OF PHARMACOLOGY – II

[According to latest syllabus of B. Pharm of Pharmacy Council of India]

Mr. Nitin Chauhan

Ph. D. Scholar

Amity University,

Gurugram (Haryana)

Dr. Mekha Monsi Chenthiyethu

Assistant Professor

NIMS University,

Jaipur (Rajasthan)

Ms. Rashmi Dorai

Assistant Professor

NIMS Institute of Pharmacy,

Jaipur (Rajasthan)

Ms. Anjali Saini

Assistant Professor of Pharmacology

Vaish Institute of Pharmaceutical

Education and Research,

Rohtak (Harayana)

Mr. Vipin Sharma

Assistant Professor

Deen Dayal Rustagi College of

Pharmacy,

Faculty of Pharmacy

Gurugram (Haryana)

Notion Press

TEXT BOOK OF
PHARMACOLOGY – II

First Edition 2024

Published by:

NOTION PRESS

Publisher and distributor

Head office: Notion press Media Pvt. Ltd.

7, Red cross Road,

Egmore, Chennai, Tamil Nadu 60008

Website: www.notionpress.com

TEXT BOOK OF PHARMACOLOGY – II
NOTION PRESS

PREFACE

The authors feel great pleasure in presenting the first edition of the book **"Text Book of Pharmacology – II"** for graduate and post graduate students. The present book on **Text Book of Pharmacology – II** has been written according to the syllabus of B. Pharm of Pharmacy Council of India and covers full course of the subject.

THE SALIENT FEATURES OF THE BOOK ARE: -

- *Easy to understand style of writing* which makes the book a self-study material.
- *Each new concept has been introduced through day-today problem of interest* to the students which makes the subject matter interesting.
- *The language of the book, on the whole, is lucid and easy to understand.*
- Wherever needed *neatly labeled figures have been drawn?*

The authors hope that the students, teachers and other readers will find the book interesting and to the point covering the course. We hope that the students will receive the book warmly.

I express a sincere thank you to the Management of Amity University, NIMS Institute of Pharmacy, NIMS University, Vaish Institute of Pharmaceutical Education and Research and Deen Dayal Rustagi College of Pharmacy, Faculty of Pharmacy for their support during the writing of this book.

Every effort is made to keep the book error free. The author will gratefully acknowledge the suggestions to improve the book to make it more useful.

Wishing our readers success in examination and life ahead. The authors feel that their efforts will be fully rewarded if the book serves the purpose for which it is written.

TEXT BOOK OF PHARMACOLOGY – II
CONTENT

CHAPTER – 1

PHARMACOLOGY OF DRUGS ACTING ON CARDIO VASCULAR SYSTEM – I

INTRODUCTION:

The cardiovascular system is a complex network comprising the heart, blood vessels, and blood, responsible for transporting nutrients, oxygen, and waste products throughout the body. Pharmacological agents targeting the cardiovascular system are designed to manage a wide array of cardiovascular diseases such as hypertension, heart failure, ischemic heart disease, arrhythmias, and hyperlipidemia.

Categories of Cardiovascular Drugs

1. **Antihypertensive Agents**

    a. **Diuretics**: Promote the excretion of water and salts to reduce blood volume and lower blood pressure. Examples include thiazides (e.g., hydrochlorothiazide), loop diuretics (e.g., furosemide), and potassium-sparing diuretics (e.g., spironolactone).

    b. **Beta-Blockers**: Decrease heart rate and contractility, reducing cardiac output and blood pressure. Examples include propranolol, metoprolol, and atenolol.

    c. **Calcium Channel Blockers**: Inhibit the influx of calcium ions into vascular smooth muscle and cardiac cells, leading to vasodilation and decreased heart rate. Examples include amlodipine, verapamil, and diltiazem.

    d. **Angiotensin-Converting Enzyme (ACE) Inhibitors**: Prevent the conversion of angiotensin I to angiotensin II, leading to vasodilation and reduced blood volume. Examples include enalapril, lisinopril, and ramipril.

e. **Angiotensin II Receptor Blockers (ARBs)**: Block the effects of angiotensin II, leading to vasodilation and decreased blood volume. Examples include losartan, valsartan, and candesartan.

2. **Antianginal Agents**
    a. **Nitrates**: Dilate coronary arteries and veins, reducing myocardial oxygen demand and relieving angina. Examples include nitroglycerin and isosorbide dinitrate.
    b. **Beta-Blockers**: Reduce myocardial oxygen demand by decreasing heart rate and contractility.
    c. **Calcium Channel Blockers**: Improve coronary blood flow and reduce myocardial oxygen demand.

3. **Heart Failure Medications**
    a. **Cardiac Glycosides**: Increase the force of myocardial contraction and reduce heart rate. The primary example is digoxin.
    b. **Beta-Blockers**: Improve survival and reduce hospitalization in heart failure patients.
    c. **ACE Inhibitors and ARBs**: Reduce morbidity and mortality by decreasing afterload and preload.
    d. **Diuretics**: Manage fluid overload and congestion.

4. **Antiarrhythmic Agents**
    a. **Class I (Sodium Channel Blockers)**: Slow conduction and reduce excitability. Examples include lidocaine and flecainide.
    b. **Class II (Beta-Blockers)**: Reduce sympathetic stimulation of the heart.
    c. **Class III (Potassium Channel Blockers)**: Prolong repolarization and refractory period. Examples include amiodarone and sotalol.
    d. **Class IV (Calcium Channel Blockers)**: Slow AV node conduction. Examples include verapamil and diltiazem.

5. **Anticoagulants and Antiplatelet Agents**

a. **Anticoagulants**: Prevent blood clot formation by inhibiting clotting factors. Examples include warfarin, heparin, and direct oral anticoagulants like dabigatran and rivaroxaban.

b. **Antiplatelet Agents**: Inhibit platelet aggregation to prevent thrombus formation. Examples include aspirin and clopidogrel.

6. **Lipid-Lowering Agents**

a. **Statins**: Inhibit HMG-CoA reductase to reduce cholesterol synthesis. Examples include atorvastatin, simvastatin, and rosuvastatin.

b. **Fibrates**: Reduce triglycerides and increase HDL cholesterol. Examples include fenofibrate and gemfibrozil.

c. **Niacin**: Lowers LDL cholesterol and triglycerides while raising HDL cholesterol.

d. **Cholesterol Absorption Inhibitors**: Reduce the absorption of cholesterol from the intestine. The primary example is ezetimibe.

Mechanisms of Action

1. **Modulation of Cardiac Output**

a. Drugs like beta-blockers and calcium channel blockers decrease heart rate and myocardial contractility.

b. Diuretics reduce blood volume, decreasing venous return and cardiac output.

2. **Vasodilation and Vasoconstriction**

a. ACE inhibitors, ARBs, and nitrates induce vasodilation, reducing blood pressure and myocardial oxygen demand.

b. Calcium channel blockers also promote vasodilation by relaxing vascular smooth muscle.

3. **Electrophysiological Effects**

a. Antiarrhythmic agents modulate ion channel activity, altering the electrical conduction properties of the heart to maintain normal rhythm.

4. **Antithrombotic Effects**

    a. Anticoagulants and antiplatelet agents prevent the formation of clots, reducing the risk of stroke and myocardial infarction.

5. **Lipid Regulation**

    a. Statins and other lipid-lowering agents reduce the levels of cholesterol and other lipids in the blood, lowering the risk of atherosclerosis and coronary artery disease.

Clinical Applications

1. **Hypertension Management**

    a. Comprehensive treatment often involves a combination of diuretics, beta-blockers, ACE inhibitors, and calcium channel blockers to achieve target blood pressure.

2. **Ischemic Heart Disease**

    a. Management includes the use of nitrates, beta-blockers, and antiplatelet agents to relieve symptoms and prevent myocardial infarction.

3. **Heart Failure**

    a. A combination of diuretics, ACE inhibitors, beta-blockers, and cardiac glycosides is commonly used to manage symptoms and improve survival.

4. **Arrhythmias**

    a. Antiarrhythmic drugs are selected based on the type and severity of the arrhythmia, with careful monitoring for potential adverse effects.

5. **Hyperlipidemia**

a. Statins are the first-line treatment, often combined with lifestyle modifications and other lipid-lowering agents as needed.

INTRODUCTION TO ELECTROPHYSIOLOGY OF HEART

Overview of Cardiac Electrophysiology

Cardiac electrophysiology is the study of the electrical properties and activities of the heart, including the generation and propagation of electrical impulses that regulate cardiac rhythm and function. Understanding cardiac electrophysiology is crucial for comprehending the mechanisms underlying various arrhythmias and the actions of antiarrhythmic drugs. Here's an overview of cardiac electrophysiology:

1. **Cardiac Action Potential**:
   a. The cardiac action potential is the sequence of electrical events that occur in cardiac cells during each heartbeat.
   b. It consists of several phases, including depolarization, plateau, repolarization, and resting membrane potential.
   c. The action potential is initiated by the opening of voltage-gated sodium channels, leading to rapid depolarization. This is followed by a plateau phase, primarily mediated by calcium influx, which sustains depolarization and allows for myocardial contraction. Repolarization occurs as potassium channels open, leading to the restoration of the resting membrane potential.

2. **Cardiac Conduction System**:
   a. The cardiac conduction system consists of specialized cells that generate and conduct electrical impulses throughout the heart, coordinating its rhythmic contractions.
   b. The sinoatrial (SA) node, located in the right atrium, serves as the heart's natural pacemaker, initiating electrical impulses that spread through the atria and stimulate atrial contraction.

c. The electrical impulse then travels to the atrioventricular (AV) node, where it is delayed before being transmitted to the bundle of His, bundle branches, and Purkinje fibers, which conduct the impulse rapidly through the ventricles, resulting in ventricular contraction.

3. **Automaticity and Excitability**:

   a. Automaticity refers to the ability of certain cardiac cells, such as those in the SA node, to spontaneously generate electrical impulses without external stimulation.

   b. Excitability refers to the ability of cardiac cells to respond to electrical stimuli by depolarizing and generating action potentials.

4. **Ion Channels and Membrane Potential**:

   a. Cardiac electrophysiology is governed by the activity of various ion channels, including sodium, potassium, calcium, and chloride channels, which regulate the flow of ions across the cell membrane.

   b. Changes in ion channel activity alter the membrane potential of cardiac cells, leading to changes in excitability and conduction velocity.

5. **Arrhythmias and Antiarrhythmic Drugs**:

   a. Arrhythmias result from abnormalities in the generation or conduction of electrical impulses in the heart.

   b. Antiarrhythmic drugs target specific ion channels or cellular processes involved in cardiac electrophysiology to restore normal rhythm and prevent arrhythmia recurrence.

   c. These drugs are classified based on their primary mechanism of action and their effects on cardiac action potentials, including sodium channel blockers, beta-blockers, potassium channel blockers, and calcium channel blockers.

The Cardiac Conduction System

The cardiac conduction system is a specialized network of cells responsible for generating and transmitting electrical impulses that coordinate the rhythmic contractions of the heart. Understanding the cardiac conduction system is essential for comprehending the physiological basis of cardiac rhythm and the pathophysiology of arrhythmias. Here's an overview of the components and function of the cardiac conduction system:

1. **Sinoatrial (SA) Node**:
    a. The SA node is located in the upper posterior wall of the right atrium, near the entrance of the superior vena cava.
    b. It serves as the primary pacemaker of the heart, initiating electrical impulses that trigger each heartbeat.
    c. The SA node generates spontaneous action potentials due to its intrinsic ability to depolarize spontaneously (automaticity).
    d. The electrical impulses generated by the SA node spread rapidly through the atria, leading to atrial contraction.

2. **Atrioventricular (AV) Node**:
    a. The AV node is located at the junction of the atria and ventricles, in the interatrial septum near the tricuspid valve.
    b. It acts as a gatekeeper, delaying the transmission of electrical impulses from the atria to the ventricles, allowing for coordinated atrial contraction and ventricular filling.
    c. The delay provided by the AV node ensures that the ventricles have adequate time to fill with blood before contracting.
    d. The AV node also conducts the electrical impulses to the bundle of His and the ventricles.

3. **Bundle of His**:

a. The bundle of His is a bundle of specialized cardiac muscle fibers that originates from the AV node and extends into the interventricular septum.

b. It divides into the left bundle branch and the right bundle branch, which transmit the electrical impulses to the respective ventricles.

c. The bundle of His conducts the electrical impulses rapidly through the ventricles, coordinating their contraction.

4. **Purkinje Fibers**:

a. Purkinje fibers are specialized cardiac muscle fibers that arise from the bundle branches and spread throughout the ventricles.

b. They transmit the electrical impulses quickly and efficiently to the myocardial cells of the ventricles, ensuring synchronized ventricular contraction.

c. Purkinje fibers play a crucial role in the rapid propagation of electrical impulses through the ventricles, coordinating their contraction from apex to base.

The cardiac conduction system ensures the coordinated and sequential contraction of the atria and ventricles, allowing for efficient pumping of blood throughout the circulatory system. Dysfunctions or abnormalities in the conduction system can lead to arrhythmias, which may result in impaired cardiac function and hemodynamic instability. Pharmacological interventions targeting specific ion channels or cellular processes involved in cardiac conduction can be used to restore normal rhythm and prevent arrhythmia recurrence.

Action Potentials in Cardiac Cells

In cardiac cells, action potentials are the series of electrical events that occur during each heartbeat, driving the contraction of the heart muscle. Understanding the cardiac action potential is essential for grasping the electrophysiological mechanisms underlying cardiac rhythm and the effects of pharmacological agents on cardiac function. Here's an overview of the action potentials in cardiac cells:

1. **Phases of the Cardiac Action Potential**:
   a. The cardiac action potential typically consists of five phases: phases 0, 1, 2, 3, and 4.
   b. These phases represent different stages of depolarization, repolarization, and restoration of the resting membrane potential.

2. **Phase 0: Rapid Depolarization**:
   a. Phase 0 is characterized by a rapid influx of sodium ions ($Na+$) into the cardiac cell through voltage-gated sodium channels.
   b. The rapid depolarization during phase 0 is responsible for initiating the action potential and triggering myocardial contraction.
   c. Phase 0 is relatively short-lived but essential for propagating electrical impulses through the heart.

3. **Phase 1: Early Repolarization**:
   a. Phase 1 is a brief period of early repolarization following phase 0.
   b. It is characterized by a transient efflux of potassium ions ($K+$) out of the cell, leading to a slight decrease in membrane potential.
   c. Phase 1 contributes to the termination of sodium channel activation and prepares the cell for subsequent repolarization phases.

4. **Phase 2: Plateau**:
   a. Phase 2 is a prolonged plateau phase during which the membrane potential remains relatively stable.
   b. It is primarily mediated by the influx of calcium ions ($Ca2+$) into the cell through voltage-gated calcium channels, balanced by the efflux of potassium ions ($K+$).
   c. The plateau phase sustains depolarization and allows for sustained myocardial contraction.

5. **Phase 3: Repolarization**:
    a. Phase 3 is the repolarization phase during which the cell membrane returns to its resting membrane potential.
    b. It is primarily mediated by the efflux of potassium ions (K+) out of the cell through voltage-gated potassium channels.
    c. Repolarization restores the cell's excitability and prepares it for subsequent action potentials.
6. **Phase 4: Resting Membrane Potential**:
    a. Phase 4 represents the resting membrane potential of the cardiac cell between action potentials.
    b. The resting membrane potential is maintained by the balance of ion concentrations across the cell membrane, with higher concentrations of potassium ions (K+) inside the cell and sodium ions (Na+) and calcium ions (Ca2+) outside the cell.

The duration and characteristics of the cardiac action potential vary depending on the type of cardiac cell (e.g., atrial, ventricular, or specialized conduction system cells) and the specific ion channels present in each cell type. Pharmacological agents that target ion channels or other cellular processes involved in the cardiac action potential can have profound effects on cardiac rhythm and function, making the understanding of cardiac electrophysiology essential for the development and use of antiarrhythmic drugs.

Mechanisms of Arrhythmogenesis

Arrhythmogenesis refers to the process by which abnormal cardiac rhythms, known as arrhythmias, are initiated and perpetuated. Understanding the mechanisms of arrhythmogenesis is crucial for developing effective treatments to manage these conditions. Here are some key mechanisms involved in arrhythmogenesis:

1. **Reentry**:

a. Reentry is one of the most common mechanisms underlying arrhythmias and occurs when a wave of depolarization circulates repeatedly within the heart, perpetuating the arrhythmia.

b. It typically arises due to conduction abnormalities or anatomical barriers that create pathways for reentrant circuits.

c. Reentry can occur in various cardiac structures, including the atria, ventricles, and accessory pathways (e.g., in Wolff-Parkinson-White syndrome).

2. **Triggered Activity**:

a. Triggered activity occurs when an abnormal cardiac action potential is initiated by afterdepolarizations, which are additional depolarizations that occur during or after repolarization.

b. Afterdepolarizations can be classified into two types: early afterdepolarizations (EADs), which occur during the plateau phase of the action potential, and delayed afterdepolarizations (DADs), which occur after repolarization is complete.

c. Triggered activity is often associated with conditions such as long QT syndrome, digitalis toxicity, and electrolyte imbalances.

3. **Automaticity**:

a. Automaticity refers to the ability of cardiac cells to spontaneously generate action potentials without external stimulation.

b. Abnormal automaticity can lead to the generation of ectopic beats, which disrupt the normal cardiac rhythm.

c. Automaticity is typically seen in pacemaker cells of the sinoatrial (SA) node but can also occur in other cardiac tissues under certain pathological conditions.

4. **Enhanced or Altered Conduction**:

a. Changes in cardiac conduction properties, such as slowing or block of conduction, can predispose to the development of arrhythmias.

b. Structural abnormalities, ischemia, scar tissue, and ion channel abnormalities can all contribute to altered conduction and arrhythmogenesis.

c. Examples include atrioventricular block, bundle branch block, and conduction abnormalities associated with myocardial infarction.

5. **Electrolyte Imbalance**:

a. Electrolyte disturbances, such as hypokalemia, hyperkalemia, hypocalcemia, and hypercalcemia, can disrupt normal cardiac electrophysiology and predispose to arrhythmias.

b. Electrolytes play a critical role in maintaining the membrane potential and ion gradients necessary for normal cardiac function.

6. **Structural Heart Disease**:

a. Structural heart disease, including cardiomyopathies, congenital heart defects, valvular heart disease, and myocardial infarction, can create substrates for arrhythmias by altering tissue architecture and conduction pathways.

b. Structural abnormalities can lead to reentrant circuits, abnormal automaticity, and triggered activity, contributing to arrhythmogenesis.

Pharmacology of Antiarrhythmic Drugs

The pharmacology of antiarrhythmic drugs is a critical component of understanding the management of cardiac arrhythmias. These medications target various ion channels and cellular processes involved in cardiac electrophysiology to restore normal rhythm and prevent arrhythmia recurrence. Here's an overview of the pharmacology of antiarrhythmic drugs in the context of cardiac electrophysiology:

1. **Classification**:

a. Antiarrhythmic drugs are classified based on their primary mechanism of action and their effects on cardiac action potentials.

b. The Vaughan-Williams classification system is commonly used to categorize antiarrhythmic drugs into four main classes (Class I, II, III, and IV), with additional subclasses based on more specific mechanisms of action.

2. **Mechanisms of Action**:

   a. **Class I (Sodium Channel Blockers)**: These drugs inhibit sodium influx during phase 0 of the cardiac action potential, reducing the rate of depolarization and conduction velocity. They are further subclassified into three groups (Ia, Ib, and Ic) based on their effects on conduction velocity and repolarization.

   b. **Class II (Beta-Blockers)**: Beta-blockers inhibit the effects of catecholamines (e.g., epinephrine, norepinephrine) on beta-adrenergic receptors in the heart, leading to decreased heart rate, myocardial contractility, and conduction velocity. They are primarily used to suppress ectopic pacemaker activity and reduce sympathetic tone.

   c. **Class III (Potassium Channel Blockers)**: These drugs prolong the action potential duration and refractory period by blocking potassium efflux during phase 3 of the cardiac action potential. They are often used to treat reentrant arrhythmias and atrial fibrillation.

   d. **Class IV (Calcium Channel Blockers)**: Calcium channel blockers inhibit calcium influx into cardiac cells during phase 2 of the action potential, leading to vasodilation, decreased myocardial contractility, and decreased conduction velocity. They are primarily used to control ventricular rate in atrial fibrillation and atrial flutter.

3. **Clinical Indications**:

a. Antiarrhythmic drugs are used to manage a wide range of cardiac arrhythmias, including supraventricular tachycardias (e.g., atrial fibrillation, atrial flutter), ventricular tachycardias, and atrioventricular nodal reentrant tachycardia (AVNRT).

b. The choice of antiarrhythmic drug depends on factors such as the type of arrhythmia, underlying cardiac pathology, patient-specific factors, and the presence of comorbidities.

4. **Pharmacokinetics and Adverse Effects**:

a. Antiarrhythmic drugs exhibit variable pharmacokinetic properties, including absorption, distribution, metabolism, and excretion.

b. Common adverse effects of antiarrhythmic drugs include proarrhythmia (the induction or exacerbation of arrhythmias), bradycardia, hypotension, QT interval prolongation, and various systemic side effects.

c. Close monitoring of patients receiving antiarrhythmic therapy is essential to assess drug efficacy, monitor for adverse effects, and adjust therapy as needed.

5. **Non-Pharmacological Treatments**:

a. In addition to antiarrhythmic drugs, non-pharmacological treatments such as catheter ablation, implantable cardioverter-defibrillators (ICDs), and cardiac resynchronization therapy (CRT) may be used to manage certain arrhythmias, particularly in cases refractory to medical therapy.

Clinical Implications

Understanding cardiac electrophysiology is crucial for the effective use of antiarrhythmic drugs. The selection of a specific agent depends on the type of arrhythmia, the underlying cardiac condition, and patient-specific factors such as comorbidities and potential drug interactions.

1. **Atrial Fibrillation**:

a. Commonly managed with beta-blockers, calcium channel blockers, and anticoagulants to prevent stroke.

b. Antiarrhythmics like amiodarone or flecainide may be used for rhythm control.

2. **Ventricular Tachycardia**:

a. Often treated with class I or class III antiarrhythmics.

b. Implantable cardioverter-defibrillators (ICDs) may be considered for high-risk patients.

3. **Supraventricular Tachycardia**:

a. Acute management may involve adenosine.

b. Long-term management may include beta-blockers or calcium channel blockers.

DRUGS USED IN CONGESTIVE HEART FAILURE

Overview of Congestive Heart Failure (CHF)

Congestive heart failure (CHF) is a condition where the heart is unable to pump sufficient blood to meet the body's needs. It can result from various cardiovascular diseases and often involves a combination of systolic dysfunction (reduced ejection fraction) and diastolic dysfunction (impaired filling). Pharmacological treatment aims to alleviate symptoms, improve quality of life, and reduce morbidity and mortality.

Pharmacological Agents in CHF

1. **Diuretics**

a. **Mechanism of Action**: Increase the excretion of sodium and water to reduce blood volume and relieve symptoms of fluid overload.

b. **Types**:

i. **Thiazide Diuretics**: Used for mild to moderate fluid retention. Example: Hydrochlorothiazide.

ii. **Loop Diuretics**: Used for severe fluid retention. Examples: Furosemide, Bumetanide, Torsemide.

iii. **Potassium-Sparing Diuretics**: Often used in combination with other diuretics to prevent hypokalemia. Example: Spironolactone (also has aldosterone antagonist properties).

2. **ACE Inhibitors (Angiotensin-Converting Enzyme Inhibitors)**

   a. **Mechanism of Action**: Inhibit the conversion of angiotensin I to angiotensin II, leading to vasodilation, reduced afterload, and decreased aldosterone secretion.

   b. **Examples**: Enalapril, Lisinopril, Ramipril.

   c. **Benefits**: Improve survival, reduce hospitalization, and slow disease progression.

3. **ARBs (Angiotensin II Receptor Blockers)**

   a. **Mechanism of Action**: Block the effects of angiotensin II at its receptor, causing vasodilation and reduced aldosterone effects.

   b. **Examples**: Losartan, Valsartan, Candesartan.

   c. **Indication**: Often used in patients intolerant to ACE inhibitors.

4. **Beta-Blockers**

   a. **Mechanism of Action**: Block beta-adrenergic receptors, reducing heart rate and myocardial oxygen demand, and inhibiting renin release.

   b. **Examples**: Carvedilol, Metoprolol Succinate (extended-release), Bisoprolol.

   c. **Benefits**: Improve survival, reduce hospitalization, and improve left ventricular function over time.

5. **Aldosterone Antagonists**

   a. **Mechanism of Action**: Block the effects of aldosterone, reducing sodium retention, potassium excretion, and myocardial fibrosis.

   b. **Examples**: Spironolactone, Eplerenone.

   c. **Benefits**: Improve survival in patients with severe heart failure or post-myocardial infarction.

6. **Vasodilators**
   a. **Mechanism of Action**: Dilate blood vessels to reduce preload and afterload.
   b. **Examples**:
      i. **Hydralazine**: Primarily dilates arterioles, reducing afterload.
      ii. **Isosorbide Dinitrate**: Dilates veins, reducing preload.
   c. **Combination Therapy**: Hydralazine and isosorbide dinitrate used together can be particularly beneficial in African American patients.

7. **Inotropic Agents**
   a. **Mechanism of Action**: Increase the force of myocardial contraction.
   b. **Examples**:
      i. **Cardiac Glycosides**: Digoxin (increases intracellular calcium and enhances contractility while also providing some vagal stimulation to reduce heart rate).
      ii. **Sympathomimetics**: Dobutamine (used in acute decompensated heart failure to provide temporary inotropic support).

8. **ARNIs (Angiotensin Receptor-Neprilysin Inhibitors)**
   a. **Mechanism of Action**: Combination of an ARB (valsartan) with a neprilysin inhibitor (sacubitril) which increases levels of natriuretic peptides.
   b. **Example**: Sacubitril/Valsartan (Entresto).
   c. **Benefits**: Shown to reduce cardiovascular death and hospitalization for heart failure more effectively than ACE inhibitors alone.

9. **SGLT2 Inhibitors (Sodium-Glucose Co-Transporter 2 Inhibitors)**

a. **Mechanism of Action**: Originally developed for diabetes, these drugs reduce glucose reabsorption in the kidneys and have beneficial effects on heart failure.

b. **Examples**: Dapagliflozin, Empagliflozin.

c. **Benefits**: Reduce hospitalization for heart failure and cardiovascular death.

Combination Therapy

a. **Guideline-Directed Medical Therapy (GDMT)**: Often involves a combination of the above agents to achieve optimal outcomes.

    i. **Initial Therapy**: Typically includes a beta-blocker and an ACE inhibitor (or ARB).

    ii. **Additional Agents**: Diuretics for fluid management, aldosterone antagonists for severe cases, and possibly ARNI or SGLT2 inhibitors.

Monitoring and Management

a. **Monitoring**: Regular follow-up is essential to monitor renal function, electrolyte levels, and signs of fluid overload or dehydration.

b. **Adjustments**: Therapy may need to be adjusted based on patient response, side effects, and progression of the disease.

ANTI-HYPERTENSIVE DRUGS

Overview of Hypertension

Hypertension, or high blood pressure, is a chronic medical condition in which the blood pressure in the arteries is persistently elevated. It is a major risk factor for cardiovascular diseases, including stroke, myocardial infarction, heart failure, and kidney disease. Effective management of hypertension often involves lifestyle modifications and pharmacological treatment.

Classes of Anti-Hypertensive Drugs

1. **Diuretics**

a. **Mechanism of Action**: Promote the excretion of sodium and water, reducing blood volume and, consequently, blood pressure.

b. **Types**:

    i. **Thiazide Diuretics**: Inhibit sodium reabsorption in the distal convoluted tubules. Examples: Hydrochlorothiazide, Chlorthalidone.

    ii. **Loop Diuretics**: Inhibit sodium reabsorption in the ascending loop of Henle. Examples: Furosemide, Bumetanide.

    iii. **Potassium-Sparing Diuretics**: Inhibit sodium reabsorption in the distal convoluted tubules and collecting ducts while sparing potassium. Examples: Spironolactone, Amiloride.

2. **Beta-Blockers**

a. **Mechanism of Action**: Block beta-adrenergic receptors, reducing heart rate and cardiac output, and inhibiting renin release from the kidneys.

b. **Examples**: Atenolol, Metoprolol, Propranolol, Carvedilol.

c. **Indications**: Particularly useful in patients with concurrent ischemic heart disease or heart failure.

3. **ACE Inhibitors (Angiotensin-Converting Enzyme Inhibitors)**

a. **Mechanism of Action**: Inhibit the conversion of angiotensin I to angiotensin II, leading to vasodilation and reduced aldosterone secretion.

b. **Examples**: Enalapril, Lisinopril, Ramipril.

c. **Benefits**: Improve outcomes in patients with heart failure and reduce the progression of diabetic nephropathy.

4. **ARBs (Angiotensin II Receptor Blockers)**

a. **Mechanism of Action**: Block the angiotensin II receptor, causing vasodilation and reduced aldosterone effects.

b. **Examples**: Losartan, Valsartan, Candesartan.

c. **Indication**: Often used in patients intolerant to ACE inhibitors.

5. **Calcium Channel Blockers**

   a. **Mechanism of Action**: Inhibit the influx of calcium ions into vascular smooth muscle and cardiac cells, causing vasodilation and reduced heart rate.

   b. **Types**:

      i. **Dihydropyridines**: Primarily affect vascular smooth muscle, leading to vasodilation. Examples: Amlodipine, Nifedipine.

      ii. **Non-Dihydropyridines**: Affect both vascular smooth muscle and the heart, reducing heart rate and contractility. Examples: Verapamil, Diltiazem.

6. **Alpha-1 Blockers**

   a. **Mechanism of Action**: Block alpha-1 adrenergic receptors on blood vessels, leading to vasodilation.

   b. **Examples**: Prazosin, Doxazosin, Terazosin.

   c. **Indication**: Often used in combination with other antihypertensives, particularly in patients with benign prostatic hyperplasia.

7. **Centrally Acting Alpha-2 Agonists**

   a. **Mechanism of Action**: Stimulate alpha-2 adrenergic receptors in the brain, reducing sympathetic outflow and decreasing blood pressure.

   b. **Examples**: Clonidine, Methyldopa.

   c. **Indication**: Methyldopa is particularly used in pregnancy-induced hypertension.

8. **Direct Vasodilators**

   a. **Mechanism of Action**: Directly relax vascular smooth muscle, causing vasodilation.

b. **Examples**: Hydralazine, Minoxidil.

c. **Indication**: Often used in severe or resistant hypertension, typically in combination with other drugs.

9. **Renin Inhibitors**

   a. **Mechanism of Action**: Inhibit renin, reducing the conversion of angiotensinogen to angiotensin I, leading to vasodilation.

   b. **Example**: Aliskiren.

   c. **Indication**: Used as an adjunct in patients who do not adequately respond to other treatments.

Combination Therapy

   a. **Rationale**: Combination therapy is often required to achieve target blood pressure, as different classes of antihypertensive drugs have complementary mechanisms of action.

   b. **Common Combinations**:

      i. ACE inhibitor or ARB with a diuretic.

      ii. ACE inhibitor or ARB with a calcium channel blocker.

      iii. Beta-blocker with a diuretic or calcium channel blocker.

Clinical Considerations

1. **Patient-Specific Factors**:

   a. Age, comorbidities, and risk factors influence the choice of antihypertensive therapy.

   b. Certain drugs are preferred in specific populations (e.g., ACE inhibitors in patients with diabetes).

2. **Side Effects**:

   Monitoring for adverse effects is crucial. For instance, diuretics can cause electrolyte imbalances, and beta-blockers can exacerbate asthma or chronic obstructive pulmonary disease (COPD).

3. **Adherence**:

Simplifying regimens and using combination pills can improve patient adherence.

4. **Lifestyle Modifications**:

    Pharmacological treatment should be accompanied by lifestyle changes, including dietary modifications, increased physical activity, and smoking cessation.

ANTI-ANGINAL DRUGS

Overview of Angina Pectoris

Anti-anginal drugs are a distinct class of medications used to manage angina pectoris, a condition characterized by chest pain or discomfort due to reduced blood flow to the heart muscle. While they are not classified as antiarrhythmic drugs per se, they are often included in discussions related to drugs acting on the cardiovascular system due to their role in managing ischemic heart disease. Here's an overview of anti-anginal drugs:

1. **Organic Nitrates**:

    a. Organic nitrates, such as nitroglycerin, isosorbide dinitrate, and isosorbide mononitrate, are vasodilators that work by releasing nitric oxide, which relaxes vascular smooth muscle and dilates coronary arteries.

    b. By dilating coronary arteries, organic nitrates increase blood flow to the heart muscle, relieving angina symptoms.

    c. These drugs are available in various formulations, including sublingual tablets, sprays, patches, and oral tablets.

2. **Beta-Blockers**:

    a. Beta-blockers, such as propranolol, metoprolol, atenolol, and bisoprolol, are medications that block beta-adrenergic receptors in the heart, leading to decreased heart rate, myocardial contractility, and oxygen demand.

b. By reducing myocardial oxygen demand, beta-blockers help alleviate angina symptoms and prevent ischemic events.

c. Beta-blockers are considered first-line therapy for stable angina and are also used for secondary prevention in patients with a history of myocardial infarction.

3. **Calcium Channel Blockers**:

   a. Calcium channel blockers, such as verapamil, diltiazem, and amlodipine, inhibit calcium influx into vascular smooth muscle and myocardial cells, leading to vasodilation and decreased myocardial oxygen demand.

   b. These drugs are particularly useful in patients with contraindications to beta-blockers or as adjunctive therapy in those with inadequate response to beta-blockers alone.

   c. Calcium channel blockers can be further subclassified into dihydropyridines (e.g., amlodipine) and non-dihydropyridines (e.g., verapamil, diltiazem), with differences in their effects on heart rate and conduction.

4. **Ranolazine**:

   a. Ranolazine is a relatively newer anti-anginal medication that works by inhibiting the late sodium current in myocardial cells, leading to decreased intracellular calcium overload and improved myocardial oxygen utilization.

   b. Ranolazine is indicated for the treatment of chronic angina, particularly in patients who have not responded adequately to other anti-anginal therapies.

While anti-anginal drugs primarily target the symptoms and underlying mechanisms of angina, they may also have indirect effects on cardiac arrhythmias. For example, beta-blockers and calcium channel blockers can help prevent arrhythmias by reducing myocardial oxygen demand and stabilizing cardiac electrical activity. Additionally, some anti-anginal drugs may be used in combination with antiarrhythmic medications for the management of certain arrhythmias associated with ischemic heart disease. However, the primary focus of anti-anginal drugs remains the relief of angina symptoms and improvement in quality of life for patients with ischemic heart disease.

Classes of Anti-Anginal Drugs

1. **Nitrates**
    a. **Mechanism of Action**: Nitrates are converted to nitric oxide (NO) in the vascular smooth muscle, leading to vasodilation. They primarily dilate veins, reducing venous return (preload), and thus myocardial oxygen demand. They also dilate coronary arteries, increasing oxygen supply to the heart.
    b. **Examples**:
        i. **Short-Acting Nitrates**: Nitroglycerin (sublingual tablets or spray).
        ii. **Long-Acting Nitrates**: Isosorbide mononitrate, Isosorbide dinitrate.
    c. **Indications**: Acute relief of angina symptoms (short-acting) and prevention of angina episodes (long-acting).
2. **Beta-Blockers**
    a. **Mechanism of Action**: Beta-blockers block beta-adrenergic receptors, reducing heart rate, myocardial contractility, and blood pressure, all of which decrease myocardial oxygen demand.
    b. **Examples**: Metoprolol, Atenolol, Propranolol.
    c. **Indications**: First-line therapy for chronic stable angina, particularly beneficial in patients with a history of myocardial infarction or heart failure.
3. **Calcium Channel Blockers (CCBs)**

a. **Mechanism of Action**: CCBs inhibit the influx of calcium ions into vascular smooth muscle and myocardial cells, leading to vasodilation and reduced myocardial contractility.

b. **Types**:

   i. **Dihydropyridines**: Primarily cause vasodilation. Examples: Amlodipine, Nifedipine.

   ii. **Non-Dihydropyridines**: Reduce heart rate and contractility. Examples: Verapamil, Diltiazem.

c. **Indications**: Used when beta-blockers are contraindicated or not tolerated. Also useful in variant (Prinzmetal's) angina due to their coronary vasodilatory effects.

4. **Ranolazine**

   a. **Mechanism of Action**: Ranolazine inhibits the late phase of the sodium current in myocardial cells, reducing intracellular sodium and calcium overload. This improves myocardial relaxation and reduces oxygen demand.

   b. **Example**: Ranolazine (Ranexa).

   c. **Indications**: Used as an adjunctive therapy for chronic stable angina, particularly in patients who remain symptomatic despite optimal doses of other anti-anginal agents.

5. **Antiplatelet Agents**

   a. **Mechanism of Action**: Inhibit platelet aggregation, reducing the risk of thrombus formation and improving blood flow in coronary arteries.

   b. **Examples**: Aspirin, Clopidogrel.

   c. **Indications**: Often used as part of the treatment regimen for angina to prevent myocardial infarction.

6. **Statins**

a. **Mechanism of Action**: Inhibit HMG-CoA reductase, reducing cholesterol synthesis and stabilizing atherosclerotic plaques, which can improve coronary blood flow.

b. **Examples**: Atorvastatin, Simvastatin, Rosuvastatin.

c. **Indications**: Used in patients with angina to manage dyslipidemia and reduce the risk of cardiovascular events.

Combination Therapy

Combination therapy in the context of antiarrhythmic drugs involves the use of multiple medications either from the same class or from different classes to achieve better control of cardiac arrhythmias. Here are some scenarios where combination therapy may be considered in the pharmacological management of arrhythmias:

1. **Inadequate Response to Monotherapy**:

    a. When a patient does not achieve adequate control of arrhythmias with a single antiarrhythmic drug, combining medications with complementary mechanisms of action may be necessary to improve efficacy.

    b. For example, if a patient with atrial fibrillation does not respond adequately to a single antiarrhythmic drug, combination therapy with drugs from different classes, such as a sodium channel blocker (Class I) and a potassium channel blocker (Class III), may be considered.

2. **Synergistic Effects**:

    a. Combining antiarrhythmic drugs with synergistic effects may enhance their efficacy in controlling arrhythmias.

    b. For example, combining a sodium channel blocker with a potassium channel blocker may have additive effects in prolonging the cardiac action potential duration and stabilizing cardiac rhythm.

3. **Reducing Adverse Effects**:

a. Combining lower doses of two or more antiarrhythmic drugs may reduce the risk of adverse effects associated with higher doses of a single medication.

b. For example, using a combination of a beta-blocker and a calcium channel blocker may allow for lower doses of each drug, thereby minimizing side effects such as bradycardia or hypotension.

4. **Management of Complex Arrhythmias**:

   a. Some arrhythmias, such as certain types of ventricular tachycardia or refractory atrial fibrillation, may require combination therapy with multiple antiarrhythmic drugs to achieve adequate rhythm control.

   b. In these cases, a multidisciplinary approach involving electrophysiologists and cardiologists is often necessary to develop a tailored treatment plan.

5. **Control of Underlying Conditions**:

   a. Addressing underlying conditions that contribute to arrhythmias, such as hypertension, heart failure, or electrolyte imbalances, may require combination therapy with antiarrhythmic drugs and medications targeting these comorbidities.

6. **Risk Stratification and Personalized Medicine**:

   a. Individualizing treatment based on the patient's risk factors, underlying cardiac pathology, and response to therapy may involve combination therapy with antiarrhythmic drugs selected according to the specific characteristics of the arrhythmia and the patient's clinical profile.

Clinical Considerations

When considering the clinical use of antiarrhythmic drugs in the pharmacology of drugs acting on the cardiovascular system, several important clinical considerations come into play:

1. **Arrhythmia Type and Etiology**:
   a. Accurate diagnosis of the type and underlying cause of the arrhythmia is crucial for selecting the most appropriate antiarrhythmic medication.
   b. Different drugs may be more effective for specific arrhythmias, and some medications may exacerbate certain types of arrhythmias or underlying cardiac conditions.

2. **Risk-Benefit Assessment**:
   a. The potential benefits of antiarrhythmic therapy, such as symptom control, improvement in quality of life, and prevention of adverse outcomes, must be carefully weighed against the risks of adverse effects and proarrhythmia.
   b. Patient-specific factors, including age, comorbidities, concomitant medications, and electrolyte disturbances, should be considered when assessing the risk-benefit profile.

3. **Baseline Evaluation**:
   a. Before initiating antiarrhythmic therapy, a comprehensive baseline evaluation should be conducted, including a thorough medical history, physical examination, electrocardiogram (ECG), echocardiogram, and assessment of electrolyte levels.
   b. Identifying and correcting any reversible factors contributing to arrhythmias, such as electrolyte imbalances or thyroid dysfunction, is essential.

4. **Drug Selection and Dosing**:
   a. The choice of antiarrhythmic drug should be guided by the specific characteristics of the arrhythmia, underlying cardiac pathology, and patient-specific factors.

b. Dosing should be individualized based on the patient's renal function, hepatic function, age, and other factors that may affect drug metabolism and elimination.

5. **Monitoring and Follow-Up**:
   a. Regular monitoring of the patient's response to antiarrhythmic therapy is crucial, including serial ECGs, assessment of symptoms, and evaluation of drug levels where applicable.
   b. Close follow-up appointments allow for dose adjustments, assessment of drug efficacy and tolerability, and early detection of adverse effects or proarrhythmic events.

6. **Electrolyte Monitoring**:
   a. Many antiarrhythmic drugs can affect electrolyte levels, particularly potassium and magnesium. Regular monitoring of electrolytes is essential to prevent electrolyte imbalances, which can predispose to arrhythmias.

7. **Potential Drug Interactions**:
   a. Antiarrhythmic drugs may interact with other medications, leading to alterations in drug efficacy or toxicity. Healthcare providers should be vigilant for potential drug interactions and adjust therapy as needed.

8. **Patient Education**:
   a. Patient education is vital for promoting medication adherence, recognizing signs of drug toxicity or worsening arrhythmias, and understanding the importance of regular follow-up appointments and monitoring.

9. **Shared Decision Making**:
   a. Involving patients in treatment decisions and discussing the potential risks, benefits, and alternatives of antiarrhythmic therapy

fosters shared decision making and improves treatment adherence and patient satisfaction.

ANTI-ARRHYTHMIC DRUGS

Overview of Cardiac Arrhythmias

Cardiac arrhythmias refer to abnormal heart rhythms, which can range from relatively benign to life-threatening. Antiarrhythmic drugs are medications used to manage and treat these abnormal heart rhythms by restoring normal cardiac electrical activity. Here's an overview of cardiac arrhythmias and the pharmacology of drugs used to treat them:

1. **Classification of Arrhythmias**:

    a. **Atrial Fibrillation (AF)**: This is the most common type of arrhythmia characterized by rapid, irregular electrical activity in the upper chambers (atria) of the heart.

    b. **Supraventricular Tachycardia (SVT)**: SVT includes various rapid heart rhythms originating above the ventricles.

    c. **Ventricular Arrhythmias**: These arrhythmias originate in the lower chambers (ventricles) of the heart and include ventricular tachycardia (VT) and ventricular fibrillation (VF), which can be life-threatening.

2. **Mechanism of Action of Antiarrhythmic Drugs**:

    a. Antiarrhythmic drugs work through various mechanisms to stabilize cardiac electrical activity and restore normal heart rhythm. These mechanisms may include blocking ion channels involved in cardiac conduction, altering autonomic nervous system activity, and affecting intracellular signaling pathways.

    b. The Vaughan-Williams classification system categorizes antiarrhythmic drugs into four main classes (Class I, II, III, and IV) based on their primary mechanisms of action.

3. **Classes of Antiarrhythmic Drugs**:
   a. **Class I**: Sodium channel blockers, subdivided into subclasses (IA, IB, IC) based on their effects on cardiac action potentials. Examples include quinidine, lidocaine, and flecainide.
   b. **Class II**: Beta-adrenergic blockers (beta-blockers) that reduce sympathetic stimulation of the heart. Examples include propranolol and metoprolol.
   c. **Class III**: Potassium channel blockers prolong the cardiac action potential duration, helping to stabilize cardiac rhythm. Examples include amiodarone, sotalol, and dofetilide.
   d. **Class IV**: Calcium channel blockers that inhibit calcium influx into cardiac cells, thereby slowing conduction through the AV node. Examples include verapamil and diltiazem.
4. **Drug Selection**:
   a. The choice of antiarrhythmic drug depends on the type and severity of the arrhythmia, underlying cardiac pathology, presence of comorbidities, and individual patient factors.
   b. For example, amiodarone is often used for ventricular arrhythmias and atrial fibrillation, while beta-blockers may be preferred for supraventricular arrhythmias.
5. **Considerations and Monitoring**:
   a. Antiarrhythmic drugs can have significant side effects and may worsen certain arrhythmias or exacerbate underlying cardiac conditions.
   b. Regular monitoring of cardiac rhythm, electrolytes, and drug levels (where applicable) is essential to ensure efficacy and safety.
   c. Dose adjustments and periodic reassessment are often necessary, especially in patients with renal or hepatic impairment.

6. **Other Treatment Modalities**:

    a. In addition to pharmacotherapy, other treatment options for cardiac arrhythmias include catheter ablation, implantable cardioverter-defibrillators (ICDs), and cardiac pacemakers, depending on the specific arrhythmia and patient characteristics.

Classification of Anti-Arrhythmic Drugs

The classification of antiarrhythmic drugs is based on the Vaughan-Williams classification system, which categorizes these medications into four main classes (Class I, II, III, and IV) based on their primary mechanisms of action on cardiac ion channels and cardiac electrical activity. Here's an overview of each class:

1. **Class I Antiarrhythmic Drugs**:

    a. These drugs primarily act by blocking sodium channels in cardiac cell membranes, thereby reducing the rate of depolarization and slowing conduction velocity.

    b. Class I drugs are further subdivided into three subclasses:

        i. **Class IA**: Moderate sodium channel blockade with additional effects on potassium channels, leading to prolongation of the action potential duration. Examples include quinidine, procainamide, and disopyramide.

        ii. **Class IB**: Weak sodium channel blockade, primarily effective during the depolarized state. These drugs have a fast onset of action and are often used for ventricular arrhythmias. Examples include lidocaine and mexiletine.

        iii. **Class IC**: Potent sodium channel blockade with minimal effects on action potential duration. These drugs have the most marked effects on conduction velocity and are used primarily for supraventricular arrhythmias. Examples include flecainide and propafenone.

2. **Class II Antiarrhythmic Drugs**:
   a. These drugs are beta-adrenergic blockers that primarily work by antagonizing the effects of catecholamines (such as epinephrine and norepinephrine) on the heart.
   b. By blocking beta-adrenergic receptors, these drugs decrease sympathetic stimulation of the heart, leading to a reduction in heart rate and myocardial contractility.
   c. Examples include propranolol, metoprolol, and atenolol.
3. **Class III Antiarrhythmic Drugs**:
   a. These drugs primarily target potassium channels, prolonging the action potential duration and refractory period of cardiac cells.
   b. By prolonging repolarization, Class III drugs help stabilize cardiac rhythm and prevent reentrant arrhythmias.
   c. Examples include amiodarone, sotalol, dofetilide, and ibutilide.
4. **Class IV Antiarrhythmic Drugs**:
   a. These drugs are calcium channel blockers that primarily act by inhibiting calcium influx through voltage-gated calcium channels in cardiac cells.
   b. By reducing calcium entry into cardiac cells, Class IV drugs decrease myocardial contractility and slow conduction through the atrioventricular (AV) node.
   c. These drugs are particularly useful for controlling ventricular rate in atrial fibrillation and flutter.
   d. Examples include verapamil and diltiazem.

Other Anti-Arrhythmic Agents

In addition to the four main classes of antiarrhythmic drugs classified by the Vaughan-Williams system, there are other agents with antiarrhythmic properties that may not fit neatly into these categories. Some of these agents include:

1. **Adenosine**: Adenosine is a naturally occurring nucleoside that acts as a potent vasodilator and inhibits conduction through the AV node. It is used primarily for the termination of supraventricular tachycardias, particularly paroxysmal supraventricular tachycardia (PSVT).

2. **Magnesium Sulfate**: Magnesium is an essential mineral involved in numerous physiological processes, including cardiac function. Intravenous magnesium sulfate can be used to treat certain types of arrhythmias, particularly torsades de pointes, which is associated with QT interval prolongation and magnesium deficiency.

3. **Digoxin**: Digoxin is a cardiac glycoside that primarily acts by inhibiting the sodium-potassium ATPase pump, leading to increased intracellular calcium levels and enhanced myocardial contractility. While digoxin is primarily used for heart failure, it may also have antiarrhythmic effects, particularly in atrial fibrillation with rapid ventricular response.

4. **Ivabradine**: Ivabradine is a selective inhibitor of the If current (funny current) in the sinoatrial node, leading to a reduction in heart rate without affecting myocardial contractility or conduction. It is primarily used for the treatment of stable angina pectoris and heart failure with reduced ejection fraction but may also have antiarrhythmic effects in certain contexts.

5. **Potassium and Calcium Supplements**: Potassium and calcium are essential ions involved in cardiac electrical activity and muscle contraction. Hypokalemia (low potassium levels) and hypocalcemia (low calcium levels) can predispose to cardiac arrhythmias, and supplementation may be necessary to correct these imbalances and prevent arrhythmias.

6. **Fish Oil (Omega-3 Fatty Acids)**: Omega-3 fatty acids, found in fish oil supplements, have been studied for their potential antiarrhythmic effects, particularly in reducing the risk of sudden cardiac death in patients with a

history of myocardial infarction or heart failure. However, the evidence for their efficacy in preventing arrhythmias is mixed.

7. **Vagal Maneuvers**: Vagal maneuvers, such as carotid sinus massage, Valsalva maneuver, and diving reflex, can be used to terminate certain types of supraventricular tachycardias by increasing vagal tone and slowing conduction through the AV node.

These agents may be used alone or in combination with traditional antiarrhythmic drugs depending on the specific type and severity of the arrhythmia, underlying cardiac pathology, and individual patient factors. It's important for healthcare providers to consider the unique properties and indications of each agent when managing patients with cardiac arrhythmias.

Clinical Considerations

When considering the clinical use of antiarrhythmic drugs in the pharmacology of drugs acting on the cardiovascular system, several important clinical considerations come into play:

1. **Arrhythmia Type and Etiology**:
   a. Different antiarrhythmic drugs may be more effective for specific types of arrhythmias. Therefore, accurately diagnosing the type and underlying cause of the arrhythmia is essential for selecting the most appropriate medication.

2. **Risk-Benefit Assessment**:
   a. The potential benefits of antiarrhythmic therapy, such as symptom control and prevention of adverse outcomes, must be weighed against the risks of adverse effects and proarrhythmia (the induction or worsening of arrhythmias).
   b. Patient-specific factors, including age, comorbidities, concomitant medications, and electrolyte disturbances, should be considered when assessing the risk-benefit profile.

3. **Baseline Evaluation**:

a. Before initiating antiarrhythmic therapy, a comprehensive baseline evaluation should be conducted, including a thorough medical history, physical examination, electrocardiogram (ECG), echocardiogram, and assessment of electrolyte levels.

b. Identifying and correcting any reversible factors contributing to arrhythmias, such as electrolyte imbalances or thyroid dysfunction, is essential.

4. **Monitoring and Follow-Up**:

a. Regular monitoring of the patient's response to antiarrhythmic therapy is crucial, including serial ECGs, assessment of symptoms, and evaluation of drug levels where applicable.

b. Close follow-up appointments allow for dose adjustments, assessment of drug efficacy and tolerability, and early detection of adverse effects or proarrhythmic events.

5. **Individualized Treatment Approach**:

a. Antiarrhythmic therapy should be individualized based on the patient's specific arrhythmia type, underlying cardiac pathology, comorbidities, and response to therapy.

b. Some patients may require combination therapy with multiple antiarrhythmic drugs or adjunctive treatments, such as catheter ablation or implantable devices.

6. **Electrolyte Monitoring**:

a. Many antiarrhythmic drugs can affect electrolyte levels, particularly potassium and magnesium. Regular monitoring of electrolytes is essential to prevent electrolyte imbalances, which can predispose to arrhythmias.

7. **Potential Drug Interactions**:

a. Antiarrhythmic drugs may interact with other medications, leading to alterations in drug efficacy or toxicity. Healthcare providers should be vigilant for potential drug interactions and adjust therapy as needed.

8. **Patient Education**:
   a. Patient education is vital for promoting medication adherence, recognizing signs of drug toxicity or worsening arrhythmias, and understanding the importance of regular follow-up appointments and monitoring.

9. **Shared Decision Making**:
   a. Involving patients in treatment decisions and discussing the potential risks, benefits, and alternatives of antiarrhythmic therapy fosters shared decision making and improves treatment adherence and patient satisfaction.

ANTI-HYPERLIPIDEMIC DRUGS

Anti-hyperlipidemic drugs, also known as lipid-lowering drugs, are an essential part of pharmacotherapy for managing dyslipidemia and reducing cardiovascular risk. These drugs work by lowering the levels of lipids in the blood, such as cholesterol and triglycerides, which are risk factors for atherosclerosis and cardiovascular diseases like coronary artery disease, stroke, and myocardial infarction.

Here's a detailed overview of the primary classes of anti-hyperlipidemic drugs used in the pharmacology of the cardiovascular system:

1. Statins (HMG-CoA Reductase Inhibitors)

Statins, or HMG-CoA reductase inhibitors, are a cornerstone in the pharmacological management of hyperlipidemia and cardiovascular disease prevention. Here's a detailed overview of statins, focusing on their pharmacology, mechanisms of action, clinical benefits, and considerations in cardiovascular pharmacotherapy:

Statins (HMG-CoA Reductase Inhibitors)

Examples of Statins

1. **Atorvastatin (Lipitor)**

2. **Simvastatin (Zocor)**

3. **Rosuvastatin (Crestor)**

4. **Lovastatin (Mevacor)**

5. **Pravastatin (Pravachol)**

6. **Fluvastatin (Lescol)**

7. **Pitavastatin (Livalo)**

Mechanism of Action

1. **Inhibition of HMG-CoA Reductase:** Statins competitively inhibit the enzyme HMG-CoA reductase, which is responsible for the conversion of HMG-CoA to mevalonate, a crucial early step in cholesterol synthesis.

2. **Increased LDL Receptor Expression:** By reducing hepatic cholesterol synthesis, statins cause a compensatory upregulation of LDL receptors on hepatocyte membranes. This increases the clearance of low-density lipoprotein cholesterol (LDL-C) from the bloodstream.

Pharmacokinetics

1. **Absorption:** Statins are well-absorbed orally, but their bioavailability varies among different agents due to first-pass metabolism.

2. **Distribution:** Statins are widely distributed in the body, with varying degrees of lipid solubility. Lipophilic statins (e.g., atorvastatin, simvastatin) can penetrate cell membranes more easily than hydrophilic statins (e.g., pravastatin, rosuvastatin).

3. **Metabolism:** Most statins are metabolized by the liver, primarily through the cytochrome P450 system, particularly CYP3A4 (e.g., atorvastatin, simvastatin) and CYP2C9 (e.g., fluvastatin, rosuvastatin).

4. **Excretion:** Statins are excreted via the bile and urine.

Clinical Benefits

1. **Reduction in LDL-C:** Statins can lower LDL-C levels by 20-60%, depending on the dose and specific statin used.

2. **Increase in HDL-C:** Statins typically increase high-density lipoprotein cholesterol (HDL-C) by 5-10%.

3. **Reduction in Triglycerides:** Statins can reduce triglyceride levels by 10-30%.

4. **Cardiovascular Outcomes:** Statins have been shown to reduce the risk of major cardiovascular events, including myocardial infarction, stroke, and cardiovascular mortality.

5. **Anti-inflammatory Effects:** Statins have pleiotropic effects, including anti-inflammatory properties and stabilization of atherosclerotic plaques.

Indications

1. **Primary Hyperlipidemia:** Statins are indicated for the treatment of elevated LDL-C levels.

2. **Mixed Dyslipidemia:** Used to manage patients with both elevated LDL-C and triglycerides.

3. **Prevention of Cardiovascular Disease:**
   a. **Primary Prevention:** For patients at high risk of cardiovascular events (e.g., those with diabetes, hypertension).
   b. **Secondary Prevention:** For patients with established cardiovascular disease (e.g., those with a history of myocardial infarction, stroke, or coronary artery disease).

Side Effects

1. **Myopathy:** Muscle pain and weakness; rare cases of rhabdomyolysis (severe muscle breakdown).

2. **Hepatotoxicity:** Elevations in liver enzymes (transaminases), usually transient and asymptomatic.

3. **New-Onset Diabetes:** Slightly increased risk of developing type 2 diabetes, especially in patients with predisposing factors.

4. **Gastrointestinal Symptoms:** Nausea, constipation, and abdominal pain.

5. **Cognitive Effects:** Rare reports of memory loss and confusion.

Contraindications

1. **Liver Disease:** Active liver disease or unexplained persistent elevations in hepatic transaminases.

2. **Pregnancy and Lactation:** Statins are contraindicated due to potential teratogenic effects.

3. **Drug Interactions:** Caution with drugs that inhibit or induce cytochrome P450 enzymes, particularly CYP3A4 inhibitors (e.g., certain antifungals, macrolide antibiotics, and protease inhibitors).

Monitoring and Considerations

1. **Lipid Panels:** Regular monitoring of lipid levels to assess efficacy.

2. **Liver Function Tests:** Baseline and periodic liver function tests to detect hepatotoxicity.

3. **Creatine Kinase (CK) Levels:** Monitoring CK levels in patients with symptoms of myopathy or in those at high risk for myopathy.

2. Bile Acid Sequestrants (Resins)

Bile acid sequestrants, also known as bile acid-binding resins, are a class of anti-hyperlipidemic drugs used to lower cholesterol levels, particularly low-density lipoprotein cholesterol (LDL-C). These drugs are used in the pharmacology of cardiovascular systems to manage dyslipidemia and reduce cardiovascular risk.

Bile Acid Sequestrants (Resins)

Examples

1. **Cholestyramine (Questran)**

2. **Colestipol (Colestid)**

3. **Colesevelam (Welchol)**

Mechanism of Action

1. **Binding Bile Acids in the Intestine:** Bile acid sequestrants are non-absorbable resins that bind bile acids in the intestinal lumen. This binding

prevents the reabsorption of bile acids back into the enterohepatic circulation.

2. **Increased Conversion of Cholesterol to Bile Acids:** By sequestering bile acids, these drugs deplete the hepatic bile acid pool, leading to an upregulation of hepatic cholesterol 7-alpha-hydroxylase, the enzyme responsible for converting cholesterol to bile acids. This process increases the demand for cholesterol in the liver.

3. **Upregulation of LDL Receptors:** The increased conversion of cholesterol to bile acids results in a decrease in intracellular cholesterol levels in hepatocytes. In response, the liver upregulates LDL receptors, increasing the clearance of LDL-C from the blood.

Clinical Benefits

1. **Reduction in LDL-C:** Bile acid sequestrants can lower LDL-C levels by approximately 15-30%.

2. **Modest Increase in HDL-C:** These drugs may cause a slight increase in high-density lipoprotein cholesterol (HDL-C).

3. **Potential Use in Combination Therapy:** Often used in combination with statins or other lipid-lowering agents for additive effects on LDL-C reduction.

Indications

1. **Primary Hypercholesterolemia:** Used as monotherapy or as adjunctive therapy with statins for patients with elevated LDL-C levels.

2. **Mixed Dyslipidemia:** Can be used in combination with other lipid-lowering agents to manage mixed dyslipidemia.

3. **Pruritus Associated with Biliary Obstruction:** Cholestyramine is also used to treat pruritus caused by partial biliary obstruction due to its ability to bind bile acids.

Side Effects

1. **Gastrointestinal Distress:** Common side effects include constipation, bloating, abdominal pain, and flatulence. These effects can limit the tolerability of these drugs.

2. **Malabsorption of Fat-Soluble Vitamins:** Bile acid sequestrants can interfere with the absorption of fat-soluble vitamins (A, D, E, K) and other medications, leading to potential deficiencies and drug interactions.

3. **Hypertriglyceridemia:** These drugs can increase triglyceride levels and should be used cautiously in patients with hypertriglyceridemia.

Contraindications

1. **Complete Biliary Obstruction:** These drugs are contraindicated in patients with complete biliary obstruction where bile cannot reach the intestine.

2. **Severe Hypertriglyceridemia:** Bile acid sequestrants can exacerbate hypertriglyceridemia, so they should not be used in patients with triglyceride levels >300 mg/dL.

Drug Interactions

1. **Reduced Absorption of Other Drugs:** Bile acid sequestrants can bind to other drugs and reduce their absorption. It is recommended to administer other medications either 1 hour before or 4-6 hours after taking bile acid sequestrants.

2. **Fat-Soluble Vitamins:** Supplementation with fat-soluble vitamins may be necessary to prevent deficiencies.

Monitoring and Considerations

1. **Lipid Panels:** Regular monitoring of lipid levels to assess efficacy and ensure that triglyceride levels do not become elevated.

2. **Gastrointestinal Symptoms:** Monitoring for and managing gastrointestinal side effects to improve tolerability.

3. **Vitamin Levels:** Monitoring for potential deficiencies in fat-soluble vitamins and providing supplementation if necessary.

3. Fibrates

Fibrates are a class of medications used to lower elevated levels of triglycerides and to raise levels of high-density lipoprotein (HDL) cholesterol in the blood. They are primarily used in the management of dyslipidemia, particularly in patients with high triglyceride levels or low HDL cholesterol levels. Here's a comprehensive overview of fibrates in the context of anti-hyperlipidemic drugs in the pharmacology of the cardiovascular system:

Fibrates

Examples

1. **Gemfibrozil**
2. **Fenofibrate**
3. **Bezafibrate**

Mechanism of Action

1. **Activation of PPAR-α:** Fibrates primarily exert their effects by activating peroxisome proliferator-activated receptor alpha (PPAR-α) nuclear receptors.
2. **Regulation of Lipid Metabolism:** Activation of PPAR-α leads to increased transcription of genes involved in lipid metabolism, resulting in:
   a. Increased lipolysis of triglyceride-rich lipoproteins.
   b. Increased clearance of triglycerides by enhancing lipoprotein lipase activity.
   c. Reduced hepatic production of triglycerides.
   d. Increased synthesis of apolipoproteins involved in HDL metabolism.
3. **Modulation of HDL and LDL:** Fibrates typically lead to a decrease in triglycerides and an increase in HDL cholesterol levels. They may also

cause a modest reduction in LDL cholesterol levels, primarily in patients with elevated triglycerides.

4. **Anti-inflammatory Effects:** Fibrates have been shown to have anti-inflammatory properties, which may contribute to their cardiovascular benefits beyond lipid modification.

Clinical Benefits

1. **Reduction in Triglycerides:** Fibrates are particularly effective in lowering elevated triglyceride levels, often by 20-50% or more.

2. **Increase in HDL Cholesterol:** Fibrates can raise HDL cholesterol levels by approximately 10-20%.

3. **Modest Reduction in LDL Cholesterol:** Fibrates may lead to a slight reduction in LDL cholesterol levels, especially in patients with elevated triglycerides.

4. **Cardiovascular Risk Reduction:** Clinical trials have demonstrated that fibrates can reduce the risk of cardiovascular events, especially in patients with high triglyceride levels or low HDL cholesterol levels.

5. **Treatment of Dyslipidemia:** Fibrates are indicated for the treatment of mixed dyslipidemia, characterized by elevated triglycerides and low HDL cholesterol.

Indications

1. **Hypertriglyceridemia:** Fibrates are particularly useful in the management of severe hypertriglyceridemia (triglyceride levels >500 mg/dL).

2. **Mixed Dyslipidemia:** Used in patients with a combination of elevated triglycerides and low HDL cholesterol levels.

3. **Prevention of Cardiovascular Events:** Fibrates may be considered as adjunctive therapy for cardiovascular risk reduction, especially in patients with residual risk despite statin therapy.

Side Effects

1. **Gastrointestinal Symptoms:** Common side effects include dyspepsia, abdominal pain, and diarrhea.
2. **Myopathy:** Fibrates, particularly gemfibrozil, can increase the risk of myopathy and rhabdomyolysis, especially when used in combination with statins.
3. **Cholelithiasis:** Fibrates may increase the risk of gallstones.
4. **Liver Dysfunction:** Elevated liver enzymes (transaminases) may occur, but severe hepatotoxicity is rare.

Contraindications

1. **Severe Renal Dysfunction:** Fibrates are contraindicated in patients with severe renal impairment due to the risk of severe myopathy and rhabdomyolysis.
2. **Gallbladder Disease:** Fibrates should be used with caution in patients with a history of gallbladder disease or cholelithiasis.

Drug Interactions

1. **Statins:** Caution is advised when combining fibrates with statins due to an increased risk of myopathy and rhabdomyolysis. Gemfibrozil, in particular, is associated with a higher risk of this interaction.
2. **Warfarin:** Fibrates may potentiate the effects of warfarin, leading to an increased risk of bleeding.

Monitoring and Considerations

1. **Lipid Panels:** Regular monitoring of lipid levels, liver function tests, and creatine kinase levels (especially when used with statins).
2. **Renal Function:** Monitoring renal function, particularly in patients with pre-existing renal impairment.
3. **Muscle Symptoms:** Monitoring for signs and symptoms of myopathy, especially in patients receiving combination therapy with statins.

4. Niacin (Nicotinic Acid)

Niacin, also known as nicotinic acid or vitamin B3, is a medication used in the management of dyslipidemia and cardiovascular disease prevention. It is classified as an anti-hyperlipidemic drug and is particularly effective in modifying lipid profiles. Here's an overview of niacin in the context of anti-hyperlipidemic drugs in the pharmacology of the cardiovascular system:

Niacin (Nicotinic Acid)

Mechanism of Action

1. **Inhibition of Lipolysis:** Niacin inhibits lipolysis in adipose tissue, reducing the release of free fatty acids into the bloodstream.

2. **Decreased Hepatic VLDL Production:** By reducing the availability of free fatty acids, niacin decreases the hepatic production of very-low-density lipoproteins (VLDL), which are precursors to low-density lipoprotein cholesterol (LDL-C).

3. **Increase in HDL-C:** Niacin stimulates the activity of lipoprotein lipase, an enzyme involved in the catabolism of triglyceride-rich lipoproteins. This leads to an increase in high-density lipoprotein cholesterol (HDL-C) levels.

4. **Reduction in LDL-C:** Niacin may also directly reduce LDL-C levels, although its effects on LDL-C are generally less pronounced compared to its effects on HDL-C and triglycerides.

Clinical Benefits

1. **Increase in HDL-C:** Niacin is one of the most effective medications for increasing HDL-C levels, with increases of 15-35% commonly observed.

2. **Reduction in Triglycerides:** Niacin can reduce triglyceride levels by approximately 20-50%, depending on the dose and patient characteristics.

3. **Modest Reduction in LDL-C:** Niacin typically leads to a 5-25% reduction in LDL-C levels, with higher doses associated with greater reductions.

4. **Improvement in Lipid Profiles:** Niacin therapy results in a favorable shift in lipid profiles, characterized by increased HDL-C levels and decreased triglycerides and LDL-C levels.

5. **Potential Cardiovascular Benefits:** Clinical trials have demonstrated that niacin therapy can reduce cardiovascular events, particularly in patients with dyslipidemia and established cardiovascular disease.

Indications

1. **Dyslipidemia:** Niacin is indicated for the treatment of dyslipidemia, particularly in patients with low HDL-C levels and/or high triglyceride levels.

2. **Mixed Dyslipidemia:** Used as monotherapy or in combination with other lipid-lowering agents for the management of mixed dyslipidemia.

3. **Secondary Prevention of Cardiovascular Disease:** Niacin may be considered as adjunctive therapy for secondary prevention of cardiovascular events in patients with established cardiovascular disease.

Side Effects

1. **Cutaneous Flushing:** Niacin commonly causes cutaneous flushing, characterized by redness, warmth, and itching of the skin, particularly in the face and upper body. Extended-release formulations may reduce flushing.

2. **Gastrointestinal Symptoms:** Niacin can cause gastrointestinal side effects such as nausea, vomiting, diarrhea, and abdominal discomfort.

3. **Hepatotoxicity:** Rare cases of hepatotoxicity, including elevated liver enzymes and hepatocellular injury, have been reported with niacin therapy.

4. **Hyperglycemia:** Niacin may worsen glycemic control in patients with diabetes or prediabetes.

Contraindications

1. **Active Liver Disease:** Niacin is contraindicated in patients with active liver disease or unexplained elevations in liver enzymes.
2. **Peptic Ulcer Disease:** Niacin should be used with caution in patients with active peptic ulcer disease due to the potential for exacerbating gastrointestinal symptoms.

Drug Interactions

1. **Statins:** Niacin can be used concomitantly with statins to achieve complementary effects on lipid profiles. However, combination therapy may increase the risk of myopathy and hepatotoxicity.
2. **Aspirin:** Aspirin can attenuate niacin-induced flushing when taken 30 minutes before niacin administration.

Monitoring and Considerations

1. **Flushing:** Counseling patients about the potential for flushing and strategies to minimize its impact, such as taking aspirin or using extended-release formulations.
2. **Liver Function Tests:** Monitoring liver function tests before initiating niacin therapy and periodically thereafter, especially in patients at risk for hepatotoxicity.
3. **Glycemic Control:** Monitoring glycemic control in patients with diabetes or prediabetes receiving niacin therapy.

5. Cholesterol Absorption Inhibitors

Cholesterol absorption inhibitors are a class of medications used to lower cholesterol levels, particularly low-density lipoprotein cholesterol (LDL-C). They work by inhibiting the absorption of dietary and biliary cholesterol from the small intestine. Here's an overview of cholesterol absorption inhibitors in the context of anti-hyperlipidemic drugs in the pharmacology of the cardiovascular system:

Cholesterol Absorption Inhibitors

Example

Ezetimibe

Mechanism of Action

1. **Inhibition of NPC1L1:** Cholesterol absorption inhibitors primarily target the Niemann-Pick C1-Like 1 (NPC1L1) protein, which is located in the brush border membrane of enterocytes in the small intestine.

2. **Reduced Intestinal Cholesterol Absorption:** By inhibiting NPC1L1, these drugs reduce the uptake of cholesterol from the intestinal lumen into enterocytes, thereby decreasing the amount of cholesterol available for incorporation into chylomicrons and subsequent absorption into the circulation.

3. **Increased Clearance of LDL-C:** The reduction in intestinal cholesterol absorption leads to upregulation of hepatic LDL receptors, resulting in increased clearance of LDL-C from the bloodstream.

Clinical Benefits

1. **Reduction in LDL-C:** Cholesterol absorption inhibitors can lower LDL-C levels by approximately 15-20% when used as monotherapy. When used in combination with statins, they provide additional LDL-C lowering, resulting in a total reduction of up to 25-30%.

2. **Modest Increase in HDL-C:** Ezetimibe may lead to a slight increase in high-density lipoprotein cholesterol (HDL-C) levels.

3. **Reduction in Total Cholesterol and Triglycerides:** Cholesterol absorption inhibitors can also decrease total cholesterol and triglyceride levels to a lesser extent.

Indications

1. **Primary Hypercholesterolemia:** Cholesterol absorption inhibitors are indicated for the treatment of primary hypercholesterolemia (elevated LDL-C) as monotherapy or in combination with other lipid-lowering agents.

2. **Mixed Dyslipidemia:** Used in patients with mixed dyslipidemia (elevated LDL-C and triglycerides) in combination with other lipid-lowering therapies.

Side Effects

1. **Gastrointestinal Symptoms:** Common side effects include diarrhea, abdominal pain, and flatulence. These symptoms are generally mild and transient.
2. **Elevated Liver Enzymes:** Rare cases of elevated liver enzymes (transaminases) have been reported with ezetimibe therapy, although the clinical significance is unclear.
3. **Myopathy and Rhabdomyolysis:** Cholesterol absorption inhibitors are generally well-tolerated, but cases of myopathy and rhabdomyolysis have been reported, particularly when used in combination with statins.

Contraindications

1. **Hypersensitivity:** Cholesterol absorption inhibitors are contraindicated in patients with a known hypersensitivity to ezetimibe or any component of the formulation.

Drug Interactions

1. **Statins:** Cholesterol absorption inhibitors are commonly used in combination with statins to achieve additional LDL-C lowering. However, this combination may increase the risk of myopathy and rhabdomyolysis, especially at higher doses.
2. **Fibrates:** Caution is advised when combining cholesterol absorption inhibitors with fibrates due to the potential for increased risk of myopathy.

Monitoring and Considerations

1. **Lipid Panels:** Regular monitoring of lipid levels to assess efficacy and safety.

2. **Liver Function Tests:** Periodic monitoring of liver function tests, especially during the first few months of therapy.

3. **Muscle Symptoms:** Monitoring for signs and symptoms of myopathy, particularly when cholesterol absorption inhibitors are used in combination with statins.

6. Omega-3 Fatty Acids

Omega-3 fatty acids, also known as polyunsaturated fatty acids (PUFAs), are essential nutrients with various health benefits, including cardiovascular protection. In the context of pharmacology and the cardiovascular system, omega-3 fatty acids are utilized as anti-hyperlipidemic drugs to help manage dyslipidemia and reduce the risk of cardiovascular events. Here's an overview of omega-3 fatty acids in this context:

Omega-3 Fatty Acids

Types of Omega-3 Fatty Acids

The main omega-3 fatty acids include:

1. **Eicosapentaenoic acid (EPA)**

2. **Docosahexaenoic acid (DHA)**

3. **Alpha-linolenic acid (ALA):** This omega-3 fatty acid is found in plant sources such as flaxseeds, chia seeds, and walnuts. EPA and DHA are derived primarily from marine sources such as fatty fish and fish oil supplements.

Mechanism of Action

1. **Reduction of Triglycerides:** Omega-3 fatty acids, particularly EPA and DHA, can reduce triglyceride levels in the bloodstream by inhibiting hepatic triglyceride synthesis and secretion.

2. **Modulation of Lipoprotein Metabolism:** Omega-3 fatty acids may also affect lipoprotein metabolism by increasing the clearance of triglyceride-rich lipoproteins and altering the composition of lipoproteins.

3. **Anti-inflammatory Effects:** Omega-3 fatty acids possess anti-inflammatory properties, which may contribute to their cardiovascular benefits by reducing inflammation within the arterial wall and improving endothelial function.

Clinical Benefits

1. **Reduction in Triglycerides:** Omega-3 fatty acids are particularly effective in lowering elevated triglyceride levels, with reductions of 20-50% commonly observed, especially at higher doses.

2. **Modest Increase in HDL Cholesterol:** EPA and DHA supplementation may lead to a slight increase in high-density lipoprotein cholesterol (HDL-C) levels.

3. **Potential Cardiovascular Benefits:** Clinical trials and epidemiological studies suggest that omega-3 fatty acids may reduce the risk of cardiovascular events, including coronary artery disease, myocardial infarction, stroke, and sudden cardiac death.

4. **Other Health Benefits:** Omega-3 fatty acids have also been associated with numerous other health benefits, including improved cognitive function, mood regulation, and joint health.

Indications

1. **Hypertriglyceridemia:** Omega-3 fatty acids, particularly EPA and DHA, are indicated for the treatment of severe hypertriglyceridemia (triglyceride levels >500 mg/dL).

2. **Mixed Dyslipidemia:** Used as adjunctive therapy in patients with mixed dyslipidemia (elevated triglycerides and low HDL-C) along with other lipid-lowering agents.

3. **Secondary Prevention of Cardiovascular Disease:** Omega-3 fatty acids may be considered as adjunctive therapy for secondary prevention of cardiovascular events in patients with established cardiovascular disease.

Side Effects

1. **Gastrointestinal Symptoms:** Common side effects include fishy aftertaste, belching, and gastrointestinal discomfort, particularly with higher doses.

2. **Bleeding Risk:** Omega-3 fatty acids may increase the risk of bleeding, especially in patients taking anticoagulant medications or with a history of bleeding disorders.

3. **Potential Interactions:** Omega-3 fatty acid supplements may interact with certain medications, including anticoagulants, antiplatelet drugs, and some psychiatric medications.

Monitoring and Considerations

1. **Lipid Panels:** Regular monitoring of lipid levels to assess efficacy, particularly triglyceride levels.

2. **Bleeding Risk:** Caution is advised in patients at increased risk of bleeding, and monitoring for signs of bleeding should be performed, especially when omega-3 fatty acids are used in combination with anticoagulant medications.

3. **Quality of Supplements:** When recommending omega-3 fatty acid supplements, it's important to ensure the quality and purity of the product, as well as adherence to recommended dosages.

7. PCSK9 Inhibitors

PCSK9 inhibitors are a relatively new class of anti-hyperlipidemic drugs that have revolutionized the treatment of dyslipidemia, particularly in patients with familial hypercholesterolemia (FH) or atherosclerotic cardiovascular disease (ASCVD). Here's an overview of PCSK9 inhibitors in the context of pharmacology and drugs acting on the cardiovascular system:

PCSK9 Inhibitors

Examples

1. **Alirocumab (Praluent)**

2. **Evolocumab (Repatha)**

Mechanism of Action

1. **Inhibition of PCSK9:** PCSK9 (proprotein convertase subtilisin/kexin type 9) is a protein produced in the liver that plays a key role in regulating levels of low-density lipoprotein cholesterol (LDL-C) in the bloodstream.

2. **Enhancement of LDL Receptor Recycling:** PCSK9 inhibitors bind to PCSK9 and prevent it from binding to LDL receptors on the surface of hepatocytes. This allows LDL receptors to remain active on the cell surface for a longer period, leading to increased clearance of LDL-C from the bloodstream.

3. **Reduction in LDL-C Levels:** By enhancing LDL receptor recycling and increasing LDL clearance, PCSK9 inhibitors significantly reduce LDL-C levels, often by 50% or more.

Clinical Benefits

1. **Potent LDL-C Lowering:** PCSK9 inhibitors are highly effective in lowering LDL-C levels, even in patients with heterozygous or homozygous FH, who typically have very high LDL-C levels that are difficult to control with traditional lipid-lowering therapies.

2. **Reduction in Cardiovascular Events:** Clinical trials have demonstrated that PCSK9 inhibitors can significantly reduce the risk of cardiovascular events, including myocardial infarction, stroke, and cardiovascular mortality, especially in patients with established ASCVD or FH.

3. **Improvement in Lipid Profiles:** PCSK9 inhibitors may also lead to modest increases in high-density lipoprotein cholesterol (HDL-C) and reductions in triglyceride levels.

Indications

1. **Heterozygous Familial Hypercholesterolemia (HeFH):** PCSK9 inhibitors are indicated as adjunctive therapy to diet and maximally

tolerated statin therapy in patients with HeFH or clinical ASCVD who require additional LDL-C lowering.

2. **Homozygous Familial Hypercholesterolemia (HoFH):** Used in combination with other lipid-lowering treatments in patients with HoFH who require additional LDL-C lowering.

3. **Secondary Prevention of Cardiovascular Events:** PCSK9 inhibitors may be considered for secondary prevention in patients with clinical ASCVD who require further LDL-C reduction despite maximally tolerated statin therapy and other lipid-lowering therapies.

Side Effects

1. **Injection Site Reactions:** Common side effects include mild reactions at the injection site, such as pain, redness, or itching.

2. **Allergic Reactions:** Rare cases of hypersensitivity reactions, including rash, urticaria, and angioedema, have been reported.

3. **Neurocognitive Effects:** Some studies have suggested a potential association between PCSK9 inhibitors and neurocognitive adverse events, such as memory impairment or confusion, although the clinical significance of these findings is uncertain.

Contraindications

1. **Hypersensitivity:** PCSK9 inhibitors are contraindicated in patients with a known hypersensitivity to the active substance or any component of the formulation.

Monitoring and Considerations

1. **Lipid Panels:** Regular monitoring of lipid levels to assess efficacy and safety, particularly LDL-C levels.

2. **Injection Technique:** Proper training in subcutaneous injection technique to minimize injection site reactions.

3. **Adherence:** Ensuring patient adherence to the prescribed dosing schedule, as PCSK9 inhibitors are typically administered via subcutaneous injection every 2 to 4 weeks.

8. CETP Inhibitors (Investigational)

CETP (cholesteryl ester transfer protein) inhibitors are a class of investigational drugs used in the treatment of hyperlipidemia, a condition characterized by high levels of lipids (fats) in the blood. Hyperlipidemia, particularly high levels of low-density lipoprotein (LDL) cholesterol, is a major risk factor for cardiovascular diseases such as atherosclerosis, heart attack, and stroke.

CETP inhibitors work by inhibiting the activity of the cholesteryl ester transfer protein, which plays a role in transferring cholesterol esters from high-density lipoproteins (HDL) to other lipoproteins like LDL and very-low-density lipoprotein (VLDL). By inhibiting CETP, these drugs promote an increase in HDL cholesterol levels and a decrease in LDL cholesterol levels, thus potentially reducing the risk of cardiovascular events.

Some investigational CETP inhibitors include:

1. Anacetrapib
2. Evacetrapib
3. Dalcetrapib

However, it's worth noting that the development of CETP inhibitors has faced challenges. Several drugs in this class have shown promising effects on lipid profiles but have also encountered safety concerns, such as off-target effects leading to adverse cardiovascular outcomes. As a result, while CETP inhibitors remain an area of active research, their clinical utility and future availability depend on further study and regulatory approval.

Clinical Considerations

When considering the clinical use of anti-hyperlipidemic drugs in the pharmacology of drugs acting on the cardiovascular system, several important considerations come into play:

1. **Risk Assessment**: Before initiating pharmacotherapy, assessing the patient's overall cardiovascular risk profile is essential. This includes evaluating factors such as age, gender, smoking status, blood pressure, lipid profile (including LDL cholesterol levels), presence of diabetes mellitus, and family history of cardiovascular disease.

2. **Treatment Goals**: Treatment goals should be individualized based on the patient's risk factors and cardiovascular risk profile. The primary objective is to reduce the risk of cardiovascular events such as heart attack and stroke. This often involves targeting specific lipid parameters, such as LDL cholesterol levels, triglycerides, and HDL cholesterol levels.

3. **Drug Selection**: The choice of anti-hyperlipidemic drugs depends on various factors, including the patient's lipid profile, comorbidities, drug interactions, tolerability, and cost. Commonly used drugs include statins, ezetimibe, fibrates, PCSK9 inhibitors, and, as previously mentioned, investigational agents like CETP inhibitors.

4. **Statins as First-Line Therapy**: Statins are typically considered first-line therapy for the treatment of hyperlipidemia due to their proven efficacy in reducing LDL cholesterol levels and improving cardiovascular outcomes. They are generally well-tolerated and have a robust evidence base supporting their use in primary and secondary prevention of cardiovascular events.

5. **Combination Therapy**: In some cases, combination therapy with multiple anti-hyperlipidemic agents may be necessary to achieve lipid targets, especially in patients with very high cardiovascular risk or those who do not adequately respond to monotherapy. However, the benefits of combination therapy should be weighed against the potential for increased side effects and drug interactions.

6. **Monitoring and Follow-Up**: Regular monitoring of lipid levels and clinical parameters is essential to assess the effectiveness of therapy and

make necessary adjustments. Patients should also be monitored for adherence to medication regimens and educated about lifestyle modifications, including diet, exercise, and smoking cessation.

7. **Safety Considerations**: While anti-hyperlipidemic drugs are generally safe and well-tolerated, they may be associated with certain adverse effects, including myopathy, hepatotoxicity, and new-onset diabetes mellitus. Clinicians should be aware of these potential risks and monitor patients accordingly.

8. **Patient Education**: Patient education is crucial for promoting adherence to medication regimens, lifestyle modifications, and understanding the importance of lipid management in reducing cardiovascular risk. This includes providing information about the benefits and potential side effects of anti-hyperlipidemic drugs.

Multiple-Choice Questions (MCQs) Based on the Text

1. What is the primary mechanism of action of statins?

    A) Increasing HDL cholesterol

    B) Inhibiting HMG-CoA reductase

    C) Blocking beta-adrenergic receptors

    D) Inhibiting calcium channels

2. Which of the following is a side effect common to bile acid sequestrants?

    A) Cutaneous flushing

    B) Constipation

    C) Myopathy

    D) Hepatotoxicity

3. PCSK9 inhibitors are primarily used to treat:

    A) Hypertriglyceridemia

    B) Familial hypercholesterolemia

C) Hypertension

D) Heart failure

4. Which class of drugs is particularly effective at increasing HDL cholesterol levels?

   A) Statins

   B) Niacin

   C) Fibrates

   D) ACE inhibitors

5. What is the main effect of omega-3 fatty acids on lipids?

   A) Reduction of LDL cholesterol

   B) Increase of HDL cholesterol

   C) Reduction of triglycerides

   D) Increase of total cholesterol

6. Which medication is used primarily for the acute relief of angina symptoms?

   A) Amlodipine

   B) Ranolazine

   C) Nitroglycerin

   D) Lisinopril

7. What is the primary benefit of using SGLT2 inhibitors in heart failure?

   A) Lowering LDL cholesterol

   B) Reducing systolic blood pressure

   C) Reducing hospitalizations for heart failure

   D) Increasing HDL cholesterol

8. Which drug class inhibits the reabsorption of sodium and water to reduce blood volume?

   A) Beta-blockers

   B) Diuretics

   C) ACE inhibitors

   D) Calcium channel blockers

9. Which antiarrhythmic drug class works by blocking potassium channels?

   A) Class I

   B) Class II

   C) Class III

   D) Class IV

10. Ranolazine works by:

   A) Dilating blood vessels

   B) Blocking calcium channels

   C) Inhibiting the late sodium current in myocardial cells

   D) Increasing potassium flow

11. What is the primary action of angiotensin-converting enzyme (ACE) inhibitors?

   A) Block the formation of angiotensin II

   B) Block the effects of angiotensin II on blood vessels

   C) Increase sodium and water retention

   D) Decrease the breakdown of bradykinin

12. What does the PCSK9 protein do in the body?

   A) Promotes lipid storage

   B) Promotes the degradation of LDL receptors

   C) Reduces inflammation

   D) Activates renin

13. Ezetimibe reduces cholesterol absorption by inhibiting which intestinal protein?

   A) Apolipoprotein B

   B) NPC1L1

   C) PPAR-α

   D) CETP

14. What is the effect of digoxin on the heart?

   A) Reduces heart rate and increases contractility

B) Increases heart rate and reduces contractility

C) Reduces heart rate and reduces contractility

D) Increases heart rate and increases contractility

15. Which drug is known for its severe side effect of rhabdomyolysis when combined with statins?

A) Gemfibrozil

B) Ezetimibe

C) Sevelamer

D) Clopidogrel

16. What is the primary use of calcium channel blockers in cardiovascular therapy?

A) Reducing triglycerides

B) Controlling arrhythmias

C) Treating hypertension

D) Treating hyperlipidemia

17. How do beta-blockers aid in the treatment of hypertension?

A) By increasing the heart rate

B) By dilating blood vessels

C) By reducing heart rate and cardiac output

D) By blocking angiotensin-converting enzyme

18. Which of the following is a correct effect of dihydropyridine calcium channel blockers?

A) Increase heart rate

B) Primarily affect vascular smooth muscle leading to vasodilation

C) Reduce heart rate and contractility

D) Primarily inhibit the influx of calcium in the heart

19. In what way do thiazide diuretics primarily reduce blood pressure?

A) Enhancing calcium retention

B) Increasing blood volume

C) Inhibiting sodium reabsorption in the kidneys

D) Increasing potassium excretion

20.Fibrates are primarily indicated for:

A) Lowering LDL cholesterol

B) Lowering blood pressure

C) Increasing HDL cholesterol and lowering triglycerides

D) Blocking calcium channels

Short Answer Type Questions

1. Describe the main function of the cardiovascular system.
2. What role do diuretics play in managing hypertension?
3. How do beta-blockers help in the treatment of heart failure?
4. Explain the mechanism of action of calcium channel blockers.
5. What is the significance of ACE inhibitors in treating heart disease?
6. Differentiate between ARBs and ACE inhibitors in their action on the renin-angiotensin system.
7. What are the clinical uses of cardiac glycosides?
8. How do class I antiarrhythmic drugs affect the cardiac action potential?
9. Describe the electrophysiological effects of potassium channel blockers.
10. Why are anticoagulants used in cardiovascular therapy?
11. Explain how statins lower cholesterol levels.
12. What is the function of fibrates in managing hyperlipidemia?
13. How does niacin affect plasma lipid levels?
14. Describe the mechanism of action of cholesterol absorption inhibitors.
15. Explain the role of omega-3 fatty acids in cardiovascular health.
16. What are PCSK9 inhibitors and how do they lower cholesterol?
17. Discuss the impact of antiarrhythmic drugs on the cardiac conduction system.
18. How do vasodilators work to relieve angina?

19. What is the primary mechanism by which SGLT2 inhibitors benefit heart failure patients?

20. Describe the interaction between lipid-lowering drugs and the risk of cardiovascular disease.

Long Answer Type Questions

1. Discuss the pharmacological management strategies for chronic heart failure, including the roles of different classes of drugs.
2. Explain the pathophysiology of hypertension and the various pharmacological treatments used to manage this condition.
3. Describe the different classes of antiarrhythmic drugs and their specific uses in treating various types of cardiac arrhythmias.
4. Outline the steps involved in the cardiac action potential and the effects of modifying ion channel activity.
5. Discuss the role of lipid-lowering drugs in preventing atherosclerosis and reducing cardiovascular risk.
6. Explain the use of antianginal drugs in the management of ischemic heart disease and how they alleviate symptoms.
7. Detail the mechanisms by which diuretics, ACE inhibitors, and beta-blockers work together to treat hypertension.
8. Describe the development and function of the cardiac conduction system and the implications of its dysfunction.
9. Discuss the role and mechanisms of anticoagulant and antiplatelet therapy in the management of cardiovascular diseases.
10. Explain the benefits and risks associated with the use of PCSK9 inhibitors in the treatment of hypercholesterolemia.

Answer Key

1. B) Inhibiting HMG-CoA reductase

2. B) Constipation

3. B) Familial hypercholesterolemia

4. B) Niacin

5. C) Reduction of triglycerides

6. C) Nitroglycerin

7. C) Reducing hospitalizations for heart failure

8. B) Diuretics

9. C) Class III

10. C) Inhibiting the late sodium current in myocardial cells

11. A) Block the formation of angiotensin II

12. B) Promotes the degradation of LDL receptors

13. B) NPC1L1

14. A) Reduces heart rate and increases contractility

15. A) Gemfibrozil

16. C) Treating hypertension

17. C) By reducing heart rate and cardiac output

18. B) Primarily affect vascular smooth muscle leading to vasodilation

19. C) Inhibiting sodium reabsorption in the kidneys

20. C) Increasing HDL cholesterol and lowering triglycerides

CHAPTER – 2

CELL SIGNALLINGCELL SIGNALLING

INTRODUCTION:

Cell signaling is a complex system of communication that governs basic cellular activities and coordinates cell actions. Understanding cell signaling is crucial for comprehending how cells function, respond to their environment, and maintain homeostasis. Here's an in-depth look at cell signaling:

1. Overview of Cell Signaling

Cell signaling involves the transmission of signals from a cell's exterior to its interior, allowing cells to respond to changes in their environment. These signals can be in the form of chemical molecules, mechanical stimuli, or electromagnetic waves. The process involves several key steps:

a. **Signal reception**: A signaling molecule binds to a receptor on the cell surface or inside the cell.

b. **Signal transduction**: The signal is relayed inside the cell through a series of molecular events.

c. **Signal response**: The cell executes a specific response, such as altering gene expression or changing cell behavior.

2. Types of Cell Signaling

Cell signaling can be categorized based on the distance the signal travels:

a. **Autocrine signaling**: Cells respond to signals they produce themselves.

b. **Paracrine signaling**: Signals are released by one cell and affect nearby cells.

c. **Endocrine signaling**: Signals (hormones) are released into the bloodstream and affect distant cells.

d. **Juxtacrine signaling**: Direct contact between neighboring cells is required for signal transmission.

3. Key Components of Cell Signaling

  a. **Signaling molecules (ligands):** These are the molecules that initiate the signaling process, such as hormones, neurotransmitters, and growth factors.

  b. **Receptors:** These are proteins on the cell surface or within cells that bind to signaling molecules. They include:

     i. **G-protein-coupled receptors (GPCRs):** Transmembrane receptors that activate G-proteins.

     ii. **Receptor tyrosine kinases (RTKs):** Transmembrane receptors with enzymatic activity.

     iii. **Ion channel receptors**: Receptors that allow ions to pass through the cell membrane.

     iv. **Intracellular receptors**: Receptors located inside the cell that bind to hydrophobic signaling molecules like steroid hormones.

4. Signal Transduction Pathways

These pathways amplify the signal and lead to a cellular response. Key pathways include:

  a. **Second Messengers**: Small molecules like cAMP, IP3, and Ca2+ that propagate the signal inside the cell.

  b. **Protein Kinase Cascades**: Sequential activation of protein kinases that amplify and transmit the signal.

  c. **MAPK/ERK Pathway**: Involved in cell growth and differentiation.

  d. **PI3K/AKT Pathway**: Involved in cell survival and metabolism.

  e. **JAK/STAT Pathway**: Involved in immune responses and cell growth.

5. Mechanisms of Signal Termination

To maintain homeostasis and prevent overstimulation, signals must be terminated. This can occur through:

  a. **Degradation of signaling molecules**: Enzymatic breakdown of the ligand.

b. **Receptor desensitization**: Receptors become less responsive to the signaling molecule.

c. **Endocytosis of receptors**: Receptors are internalized and degraded.

d. **Deactivation of signal transduction proteins**: Phosphatases remove phosphate groups from proteins, deactivating them.

6. Examples of Cell Signaling Pathways

a. **Insulin signaling**: Regulates glucose uptake and metabolism.

b. **Notch signaling:** Involved in cell differentiation.

c. **Wnt signaling**: Regulates cell fate and proliferation.

d. **TGF-beta signaling**: Controls cell growth and differentiation.

7. Clinical Relevance

Dysregulation of cell signaling pathways can lead to diseases such as cancer, diabetes, and autoimmune disorders. Targeted therapies, such as tyrosine kinase inhibitors and monoclonal antibodies, have been developed to modulate these pathways in disease treatment.

INTERCELLULAR AND INTRACELLULAR SIGNALLING PATHWAYS

Cell signaling encompasses both intercellular (between cells) and intracellular (within a cell) pathways. Each type plays a critical role in ensuring proper communication and function within the body. Here's a detailed examination of these pathways:

Intercellular signalling pathways

Intercellular signaling involves the transmission of signals from one cell to another. This can occur through various mechanisms:

1. Autocrine Signaling

a. **Definition**: A cell secretes signaling molecules that bind to receptors on its own surface, affecting its own activity.

b. **Example:** Growth factors like TGF-β (transforming growth factor-beta) that regulate cell proliferation.

2. Paracrine Signaling

a. **Definition**: Signaling molecules released by a cell affect nearby target cells.

b. **Example:** Neurotransmitters such as acetylcholine released at synaptic junctions between neurons.

3. Endocrine Signaling

a. **Definition**: Hormones are released into the bloodstream by endocrine cells and travel to distant target cells.

b. **Example:** Insulin released by pancreatic beta cells regulates glucose uptake in distant tissues.

4. Juxtacrine Signaling

a. **Definition:** Direct cell-to-cell contact through membrane-bound signaling molecules.

b. **Example**: Notch signaling where the Notch receptor on one cell interacts with its ligand on an adjacent cell, playing a crucial role in cell differentiation.

5. Synaptic Signaling

a. **Definition:** Specialized form of paracrine signaling used by neurons, where neurotransmitters are released into the synaptic cleft.

b. **Example:** Dopamine signaling in the brain influencing mood and behavior.

Intracellular Signaling Pathways

Intracellular signaling refers to the cascades of molecular events within a cell that lead to a specific response following the reception of an extracellular signal. These pathways typically involve a series of steps that amplify and propagate the signal:

1. Second Messenger Systems

a. **Definition**: Small molecules generated inside the cell in response to an extracellular signal that amplify and transmit the signal.

b. **Key Second Messengers**:

    i.   **cAMP (Cyclic Adenosine Monophosphate)**: Activates protein kinase A (PKA), influencing metabolism and gene expression.

    ii.   **IP3 (Inositol Triphosphate)**: Triggers release of $Ca2+$ from the endoplasmic reticulum.

    iii. **DAG (Diacylglycerol)**: Activates protein kinase C (PKC), involved in various cellular responses.

    iv. **Ca2+ (Calcium Ions):** Act as a versatile second messenger regulating processes like muscle contraction and neurotransmitter release.

2. Protein Kinase Cascades

a. **Definition:** Sequential activation of protein kinases that phosphorylate target proteins, altering their activity.

b. **Key Pathways:**

    i.   **MAPK/ERK Pathway**: Mediates cell growth and differentiation signals. Involves Ras, Raf, MEK, and ERK proteins.

    ii.   **PI3K/AKT Pathway**: Regulates cell survival and metabolism. Involves PI3K activation leading to PIP3 production and subsequent activation of AKT.

    iii. **JAK/STAT Pathway**: Transduces signals from cytokines and growth factors leading to transcriptional regulation. Involves JAK kinases and STAT transcription factors.

3. Receptor Tyrosine Kinases (RTKs)

a. **Mechanism**: Binding of ligands such as growth factors leads to dimerization and autophosphorylation of RTKs, activating downstream signaling pathways.

b. **Example:** Epidermal growth factor receptor (EGFR) activation leading to cellular proliferation.

4. G-Protein-Coupled Receptors (GPCRs)

a. **Mechanism**: Ligand binding to GPCRs causes activation of heterotrimeric G-proteins, which then activate or inhibit downstream effectors such as adenylyl cyclase or phospholipase C.

b. **Example**: β-adrenergic receptors regulating cardiac function through cAMP.

5. Nuclear Receptors

a. **Mechanism**: Lipophilic ligands like steroid hormones diffuse into the cell, bind to intracellular receptors, and directly regulate gene transcription.

b. **Example:** Glucocorticoid receptor regulating genes involved in metabolism and immune response.

Integration and Crosstalk

Intracellular signaling pathways often interact, leading to complex networks of signaling cascades. This crosstalk allows for fine-tuned regulation and integration of multiple signals:

a. **Positive and Negative Feedback**: Pathways often include feedback mechanisms to regulate the intensity and duration of the signal.

b. **Pathway Crosstalk**: Signals from different pathways can converge, diverge, or cross-regulate each other, ensuring coordinated cellular responses.

Clinical Relevance

Aberrations in cell signaling pathways can lead to various diseases:

a. **Cancer:** Mutations in RTKs or downstream signaling molecules (e.g., Ras, PI3K) can lead to uncontrolled cell growth.

b. **Diabetes**: Insulin signaling pathway defects result in impaired glucose metabolism.

c. **Autoimmune Diseases**: Dysregulated JAK/STAT signaling can lead to improper immune responses.

Therapeutic interventions often target specific components of these pathways to restore normal signaling and function. For example, kinase inhibitors are used in cancer treatment to block overactive signaling pathways.

CLASSIFICATION OF RECEPTOR FAMILY AND MOLECULAR STRUCTURE LIGAND GATED ION CHANNELS

Receptors play a crucial role in cell signaling by recognizing and binding specific signaling molecules (ligands), leading to cellular responses. Receptor families can be classified based on their molecular structure and mechanism of action. Among these, ligand-gated ion channels are a unique class of receptors that mediate rapid responses to extracellular signals. Here is a detailed examination of the classification of receptor families and the molecular structure of ligand-gated ion channels.

Classification of Receptor Families

Receptor families can be broadly classified into four main categories based on their structure and signaling mechanisms:

1. G-Protein-Coupled Receptors (GPCRs)

  a. **Structure:** Seven transmembrane alpha helices.
  b. **Mechanism**: Ligand binding activates an associated G-protein, which then modulates the activity of downstream effectors (e.g., adenylyl cyclase, phospholipase C).
  c. **Examples**: β-adrenergic receptors, muscarinic acetylcholine receptors.

2. Receptor Tyrosine Kinases (RTKs)

  a. **Structure:** Single transmembrane domain with an extracellular ligand-binding domain and an intracellular kinase domain.
  b. **Mechanism:** Ligand binding induces receptor dimerization and autophosphorylation, activating downstream signaling pathways.
  c. **Examples:** Epidermal growth factor receptor (EGFR), insulin receptor.

3. Ionotropic Receptors (Ligand-Gated Ion Channels)

a. **Structure**: Typically composed of multiple subunits forming a pore through the cell membrane.

b. **Mechanism**: Ligand binding causes a conformational change that opens the ion channel, allowing specific ions to flow across the membrane, altering the cell's electrical potential.

c. **Examples**: Nicotinic acetylcholine receptor (nAChR), GABA_A receptor.

4. Nuclear Receptors

a. **Structure:** Intracellular receptors with a DNA-binding domain and a ligand-binding domain.

b. **Mechanism:** Ligand binding allows the receptor to regulate gene transcription by directly interacting with DNA.

c. **Examples**: Estrogen receptor, glucocorticoid receptor.

Molecular Structure of Ligand-Gated Ion Channels

Ligand-gated ion channels (LGICs) are a subset of ionotropic receptors that are critical for rapid synaptic transmission. They respond to specific neurotransmitters and are essential for processes such as muscle contraction, neural communication, and sensory perception.

General Structure

1. **Subunit Composition:**

   a. LGICs are typically pentameric (composed of five subunits) or tetrameric (composed of four subunits).

   b. Each subunit is a polypeptide chain with multiple transmembrane domains (usually 4 or more).

2. **Transmembrane Domains:**

   a. Each subunit has multiple (often four) transmembrane alpha-helices (M1-M4).

   b. The M2 domain usually lines the ion pore and plays a crucial role in ion selectivity and gating.

3. **Extracellular Domain:**

   a. The extracellular domain contains the ligand-binding site.

   b. Ligand binding induces a conformational change that opens the ion channel.

4. **Pore and Ion Selectivity:**

   a. The ion channel pore allows specific ions (e.g., Na+, K+, Ca2+, Cl-) to flow across the cell membrane.

   b. Ion selectivity is determined by the size and charge of the pore and specific amino acid residues within the pore region.

Examples of Ligand-Gated Ion Channels

1. **Nicotinic Acetylcholine Receptor (nAChR)**

   a. **Structure:** Pentameric receptor typically composed of α, β, γ (or ε), and δ subunits.

   b. **Function**: Mediates excitatory synaptic transmission in neuromuscular junctions by allowing Na+ and K+ ions to pass, leading to muscle contraction.

   c. **Ligand:** Acetylcholine (ACh).

2. **Gamma-Aminobutyric Acid Type A (GABA_A) Receptor**

   a. **Structure:** Pentameric receptor typically composed of α, β, and γ subunits.

   b. **Function**: Mediates inhibitory synaptic transmission in the central nervous system by allowing Cl- ions to pass, leading to hyperpolarization and inhibition of neuronal activity.

   c. **Ligand**: GABA (Gamma-Aminobutyric Acid).

3. **Glutamate Receptors (e.g., NMDA, AMPA, and Kainate Receptors)**

   a. **Structure**: Tetrameric receptors composed of various subunits (e.g., GluN1, GluN2 for NMDA receptors).

b. **Function**: Mediate excitatory synaptic transmission by allowing Na+ and Ca2+ ions to pass, playing crucial roles in synaptic plasticity and memory formation.

c. **Ligand:** Glutamate.

4. **P2X Receptors**

a. **Structure:** Trimeric receptors composed of three subunits.

b. **Function:** Respond to extracellular ATP by allowing Na+ and Ca2+ ions to pass, involved in processes like pain sensation and inflammation.

c. **Ligand**: ATP (Adenosine Triphosphate).

Mechanism of Action

1. **Resting State**: In the absence of a ligand, the ion channel is typically closed.

2. **Ligand Binding**: The ligand binds to the extracellular domain, causing a conformational change.

3. **Channel Opening**: This conformational change opens the ion channel pore, allowing ions to flow down their electrochemical gradient.

4. **Desensitization/Inactivation**: Prolonged exposure to the ligand can lead to desensitization, where the receptor becomes less responsive to the ligand despite its presence.

Clinical Relevance

LGICs are targets for various drugs and toxins:

1. **Anesthetics and Sedatives**: Many act on GABA_A receptors to enhance inhibitory neurotransmission.

2. **Nicotine:** Binds to nAChRs, affecting the central nervous system and leading to addiction.

3. **Antiepileptic Drugs**: Some target GABA_A receptors to increase inhibitory signaling and prevent seizures.

G-PROTEIN COUPLED RECEPTORS

G-protein coupled receptors (GPCRs) represent one of the largest and most diverse families of membrane receptors in eukaryotes. They play a crucial role in cell signaling, mediating responses to a wide variety of extracellular signals. Here is a detailed examination of GPCRs, including their structure, function, signaling mechanisms, and clinical relevance.

Structure of GPCRs

GPCRs share a common structural framework:

1. **Seven Transmembrane Helices:**
   a. GPCRs have seven alpha-helical transmembrane domains (TM1 to TM7).
   b. These helices span the cell membrane, creating an extracellular N-terminus and an intracellular C-terminus.

2. **Extracellular and Intracellular Loops:**
   a. Three extracellular loops (ECL1, ECL2, ECL3) connect the transmembrane helices and are involved in ligand binding.
   b. Three intracellular loops (ICL1, ICL2, ICL3) interact with G-proteins and other intracellular signaling molecules.

3. **Ligand-Binding Domain:**
   a. The binding site for ligands can be located within the transmembrane region, on the extracellular loops, or the N-terminal domain, depending on the receptor.

4. **Intracellular C-Terminal Tail:**
   a. The C-terminal tail interacts with intracellular proteins, including G-proteins and regulatory molecules such as kinases and arrestins.

Function of GPCRs

GPCRs mediate a wide array of physiological responses by detecting extracellular signals and activating intracellular signaling pathways. These signals include hormones, neurotransmitters, and environmental stimuli like light and odorants.

Mechanism of GPCR Signaling

The GPCR signaling mechanism involves several key steps:

1. **Ligand Binding:**
   a. A ligand (e.g., hormone, neurotransmitter) binds to the extracellular domain of the GPCR.
   b. This induces a conformational change in the receptor.

2. **G-Protein Activation:**
   a. The conformational change in the GPCR allows it to interact with a heterotrimeric G-protein (composed of α, β, and γ subunits) on the intracellular side.
   b. The G-protein binds to the receptor, causing GDP bound to the Gα subunit to be exchanged for GTP, activating the G-protein.

3. **Dissociation of G-Protein Subunits:**
   a. The binding of GTP causes the Gα subunit to dissociate from the Gβγ dimer.
   b. Both the Gα-GTP and Gβγ subunits can then interact with and regulate various downstream effectors.

4. **Signal Propagation:**
   a. The activated G-protein subunits interact with target proteins, such as adenylyl cyclase, phospholipase C, and ion channels, to propagate the signal.
   b. This leads to the production of second messengers like cAMP, IP3, DAG, and Ca2+.

5. **Termination of Signal:**
   a. The intrinsic GTPase activity of the Gα subunit hydrolyzes GTP to GDP, inactivating the G-protein.

b. The Gα subunit re-associates with the Gβγ dimer, returning to the inactive state.

6. **Receptor Desensitization:**

   a. Prolonged stimulation of GPCRs can lead to receptor desensitization, often mediated by phosphorylation of the receptor by G-protein-coupled receptor kinases (GRKs) and binding of arrestins.

   b. Arrestins prevent further G-protein activation and can also mediate receptor internalization.

Types of G-Proteins and Their Effects

G-proteins are classified based on their Gα subunits, each triggering distinct signaling pathways:

1. **Gαs (Stimulatory G-protein):**

   a. Activates adenylyl cyclase, increasing the production of cAMP.

   b. **Example:** β-adrenergic receptors.

2. **Gαi/o (Inhibitory G-protein):**

   a. Inhibits adenylyl cyclase, decreasing cAMP levels.

   b. **Example:** α2-adrenergic receptors.

3. **Gαq/11:**

   a. Activates phospholipase C (PLC), leading to the production of IP3 and DAG.

   b. IP3 induces Ca2+ release from the endoplasmic reticulum, while DAG activates protein kinase C (PKC).

   c. **Example:** α1-adrenergic receptors.

4. **Gα12/13:**

   a. Regulates the Rho family of GTPases, affecting cytoskeletal dynamics and cell migration.

   b. **Example:** Thrombin receptors.

Examples of GPCR Signaling Pathways

1. **Adrenergic Receptors:**
    a. **β-Adrenergic Receptors**: Respond to adrenaline/noradrenaline, activating Gαs, leading to increased cAMP and protein kinase A (PKA) activity, which enhances heart rate and muscle contraction.
    b. **α1-Adrenergic Receptors**: Activate Gαq, leading to increased IP3 and DAG, which causes smooth muscle contraction.
2. **Muscarinic Acetylcholine Receptors (mAChRs):**
    a. **M2 and M4 Receptors**: Inhibit adenylyl cyclase via Gαi, decreasing cAMP levels, involved in slowing heart rate.
    b. **M1, M3, and M5 Receptors**: Activate Gαq, increasing IP3 and DAG, involved in smooth muscle contraction and glandular secretion.
3. **Rhodopsin:**
    a. Light-activated GPCR in the retina.
    b. Activates Gαt (transducin), leading to a decrease in cGMP and hyperpolarization of photoreceptor cells, which is crucial for vision.

Clinical Relevance

GPCRs are targets for a significant portion of therapeutic drugs due to their involvement in various physiological processes and diseases:

1. **Beta-Blockers:**
    a. Target β-adrenergic receptors to treat hypertension and heart disease.
2. **Antihistamines:**
    a. Block histamine H1 receptors to alleviate allergy symptoms.
3. **Antipsychotics:**
    a. Target dopamine receptors to manage schizophrenia and other psychiatric disorders.

4. **Opioids:**

   a. Bind to opioid receptors (GPCRs) to relieve pain.

5. **Antidepressants:**

   a. Many influence GPCR-mediated neurotransmitter pathways to alleviate depression.

TYROSINE KINASE RECEPTORS AND NUCLEAR RECEPTORS

Receptor Tyrosine Kinases (RTKs) are a prominent class of receptors that play vital roles in various cellular processes, including growth, differentiation, metabolism, and apoptosis. They are particularly significant in the context of cancer biology and therapy.

Structure of RTKs

1. **Extracellular Domain:**

   a. **Ligand-Binding Domain**: Responsible for binding to specific ligands such as growth factors (e.g., EGF, insulin). This domain varies greatly among different RTKs, allowing for specificity in ligand binding.

2. **Transmembrane Domain:**

   a. A single alpha-helix that anchors the receptor in the cell membrane.

3. **Intracellular Domain:**

   a. **Tyrosine Kinase Domain**: Contains enzymatic activity that phosphorylates tyrosine residues on target proteins, including the receptor itself (autophosphorylation).

   b. **Regulatory Regions**: Contain sites for autophosphorylation and interaction with downstream signaling molecules.

Mechanism of RTK Signaling

1. **Ligand Binding:**

a. Ligand binding induces dimerization (or oligomerization) of the receptor, bringing the intracellular kinase domains into close proximity.

2. **Autophosphorylation:**

   a. The kinase domains phosphorylate each other on specific tyrosine residues, activating the receptor.

3. **Recruitment of Adaptor Proteins:**

   a. Phosphorylated tyrosine residues serve as docking sites for adaptor proteins and other signaling molecules containing SH2 (Src Homology 2) or PTB (Phosphotyrosine Binding) domains.

4. **Signal Propagation:**

   a. Downstream signaling pathways are activated, including the MAPK/ERK, PI3K/AKT, and PLCγ pathways, leading to diverse cellular responses such as proliferation, survival, and differentiation.

Examples of RTK Signaling Pathways

1. **EGF Receptor (EGFR):**

   a. **Ligand:** Epidermal Growth Factor (EGF).

   b. **Pathway Activation**: EGFR activation leads to the recruitment of Grb2 and SOS, which activate the Ras/MAPK pathway, promoting cell proliferation and survival.

   c. **Clinical Relevance**: Overexpression or mutation of EGFR is associated with various cancers, and EGFR inhibitors (e.g., erlotinib) are used in cancer therapy.

2. **Insulin Receptor (IR):**

   a. **Ligand:** Insulin.

   b. **Pathway Activation**: Insulin binding activates the PI3K/AKT pathway, promoting glucose uptake and metabolism.

c. **Clinical Relevance**: Defects in insulin receptor signaling are implicated in diabetes mellitus.

3. **VEGF Receptor (VEGFR):**
   a. **Ligand**: Vascular Endothelial Growth Factor (VEGF).
   b. **Pathway Activation**: VEGFR activation stimulates angiogenesis through the PLCγ and PI3K/AKT pathways.
   c. **Clinical Relevance**: VEGF inhibitors (e.g., bevacizumab) are used to treat cancers by inhibiting tumor angiogenesis.

Nuclear Receptors in Cell Signaling

Nuclear receptors are a class of intracellular receptors that function as transcription factors. They are involved in regulating gene expression in response to lipophilic ligands such as steroid hormones, thyroid hormones, and other small molecules.

Structure of Nuclear Receptors

1. **Ligand-Binding Domain (LBD):**
   a. Located at the C-terminal end of the receptor, this domain binds to specific ligands, inducing conformational changes necessary for receptor activation.

2. **DNA-Binding Domain (DBD):**
   a. Located centrally, this highly conserved domain contains zinc finger motifs that allow the receptor to bind to specific DNA sequences known as hormone response elements (HREs).

3. **Activation Function Domains (AF-1 and AF-2):**
   a. Located in the N-terminal (AF-1) and C-terminal (AF-2) regions, these domains are involved in the recruitment of coactivators and corepressors that modulate transcriptional activity.

Mechanism of Nuclear Receptor Signaling

1. **Ligand Binding:**

a. The ligand diffuses across the cell membrane and binds to the nuclear receptor's LBD, inducing a conformational change that activates the receptor.

2. **Receptor Dimerization:**

   a. Ligand binding often promotes the dimerization (homo- or heterodimerization) of nuclear receptors.

3. **DNA Binding:**

   a. The activated receptor dimer translocates to the nucleus (if it is not already there) and binds to specific HREs in the promoter region of target genes.

4. **Transcriptional Regulation:**

   a. The receptor complex recruits coactivators or corepressors and other components of the transcriptional machinery, modulating the transcription of target genes.

Examples of Nuclear Receptor Signaling Pathways

1. **Glucocorticoid Receptor (GR):**

   a. **Ligand:** Glucocorticoids (e.g., cortisol).

   b. **Function:** Regulates genes involved in glucose metabolism, immune response, and inflammation.

   c. **Clinical Relevance**: Glucocorticoids are used as anti-inflammatory and immunosuppressive agents in conditions such as asthma and autoimmune diseases.

2. **Estrogen Receptor (ER):**

   a. **Ligand:** Estrogens (e.g., estradiol).

   b. **Function:** Regulates genes involved in reproductive function, bone density, and cardiovascular health.

   c. **Clinical Relevance**: ER modulators (e.g., tamoxifen) are used in the treatment of estrogen receptor-positive breast cancer.

3. Thyroid Hormone Receptor (TR):

   a. **Ligand:** Thyroid hormones (e.g., T3, T4).

   b. **Function**: Regulates genes involved in metabolism, development, and growth.

   c. **Clinical Relevance**: Dysregulation of thyroid hormone signaling can lead to conditions such as hypothyroidism and hyperthyroidism.

SECONDARY MESSENGERS: CYCLIC AMP, CYCLIC GMP, CALCIUM ION, INOSITOL 1,4,5-TRISPHOSPHATE, (IP3), NO, AND DIACYLGLYCEROL

Secondary messengers are intracellular signaling molecules released by cells in response to exposure to extracellular signaling molecules (the primary messengers). These molecules help amplify the signal and elicit a physiological response within the cell. Here, we will detail the key secondary messengers: cyclic AMP (cAMP), cyclic GMP (cGMP), calcium ions ($Ca2+$), inositol 1,4,5-trisphosphate (IP3), nitric oxide (NO), and diacylglycerol (DAG).

Cyclic AMP (cAMP)

Cyclic adenosine monophosphate (cAMP) is a critical secondary messenger molecule involved in cell signaling. It is synthesized from ATP by the enzyme adenylate cyclase and functions to transduce extracellular signals into intracellular responses. Here's a detailed exploration of the role of cAMP in cell signaling:

1. Synthesis and Regulation of cAMP:

   a. **Adenylate Cyclase Activation**: Extracellular stimuli, such as hormones or neurotransmitters, bind to their respective receptors (e.g., G protein-coupled receptors), leading to the activation of adenylate cyclase.

   b. **cAMP Production**: Activated adenylate cyclase catalyzes the conversion of ATP to cAMP, which serves as a second messenger in the signaling cascade.

c. **cAMP Degradation**: cAMP levels are tightly regulated by phosphodiesterases (PDEs), enzymes that hydrolyze cAMP to AMP, terminating the signaling cascade.

2. Signaling Pathways Mediated by cAMP:

a. **Protein Kinase A (PKA) Activation:**

    i. cAMP binds to the regulatory subunits of PKA, causing their dissociation from the catalytic subunits.

    ii. Released catalytic subunits of PKA phosphorylate serine and threonine residues on target proteins, modulating their activity and cellular functions.

    iii. PKA phosphorylates various substrates, including enzymes, ion channels, and transcription factors, to regulate processes such as metabolism, gene expression, and cell proliferation.

b. **cAMP-Regulated Ion Channels:**

    i. cAMP can directly bind to and modulate the activity of ion channels, such as cyclic nucleotide-gated (CNG) channels and hyperpolarization-activated cyclic nucleotide-gated (HCN) channels.

    ii. Activation of cAMP-regulated ion channels alters ion flux across the plasma membrane, leading to changes in membrane potential and cellular excitability.

c. **cAMP-Responsive Element-Binding Protein (CREB) Activation:**

    i. PKA-mediated phosphorylation of CREB promotes its binding to cAMP response elements (CREs) in the promoter regions of target genes.

    ii. CREB activation induces the transcription of genes involved in neuronal plasticity, cell survival, and long-term memory formation.

3. Physiological Roles of cAMP:

a. **Hormone Signaling**: cAMP mediates the effects of various hormones, including adrenaline, glucagon, and thyroid-stimulating hormone (TSH), in processes such as glycogen metabolism, lipolysis, and hormone secretion.

b. **Neuronal Signaling**: cAMP regulates synaptic transmission, neuronal excitability, and synaptic plasticity in the central nervous system, influencing learning, memory, and behavior.

c. **Cardiac Function**: cAMP signaling modulates cardiac contractility, heart rate, and ion channel activity in cardiomyocytes, regulating cardiovascular function and blood pressure.

d. **Immune Responses**: cAMP regulates immune cell activation, cytokine production, and inflammatory responses, influencing immune cell function and inflammation.

4. Pathological Implications of Dysregulated cAMP Signaling:

a. **Endocrine Disorders**: Dysregulated cAMP signaling is implicated in endocrine disorders such as hyperthyroidism, where excessive cAMP production leads to increased thyroid hormone secretion.

b. **Neurological Disorders**: Altered cAMP signaling contributes to neurological disorders such as depression, anxiety disorders, and schizophrenia, affecting neuronal function and synaptic plasticity.

c. **Cardiovascular Diseases**: Dysregulated cAMP signaling is associated with cardiovascular diseases such as heart failure and arrhythmias, affecting cardiac contractility and ion channel function.

d. **Immune Disorders**: Aberrant cAMP signaling is linked to immune disorders such as autoimmune diseases and inflammatory disorders, influencing immune cell activation and cytokine production.

Cyclic GMP (cGMP)

Cyclic guanosine monophosphate (cGMP), similar to cyclic adenosine monophosphate (cAMP), is a critical secondary messenger molecule involved in cell signaling. It is synthesized from guanosine triphosphate (GTP) by the enzyme guanylate cyclase and regulates various physiological processes within cells. Here's a detailed exploration of the role of cGMP in cell signaling, along with comparisons to cAMP:

1. Synthesis and Regulation of cGMP:

a. **Guanylate Cyclase Activation**: Guanylate cyclase can be activated by different stimuli, leading to the conversion of GTP to cGMP.

b. **cGMP Production**: Activated guanylate cyclase synthesizes cGMP, which serves as a second messenger in the signaling cascade.

c. **cGMP Degradation**: cGMP levels are regulated by phosphodiesterases (PDEs), which hydrolyze cGMP to GMP, thereby terminating the signaling cascade.

2. Signaling Pathways Mediated by cGMP:

a. Protein Kinase G (PKG) Activation:

    i. cGMP binds to the regulatory domains of PKG, leading to its activation.

    ii. Activated PKG phosphorylates specific serine and threonine residues on target proteins, modulating their activity and cellular functions.

    iii. PKG regulates processes such as smooth muscle relaxation, platelet aggregation, and gene expression.

b. cGMP-Regulated Ion Channels:

    i. cGMP can modulate the activity of ion channels, such as cyclic nucleotide-gated (CNG) channels and voltage-gated calcium channels (VGCCs).

    ii. Activation of cGMP-regulated ion channels alters ion flux across the plasma membrane, affecting cellular excitability and neurotransmitter release.

c. **cGMP-Dependent Protein Kinases (cGKs):**

    i. In some cells, cGMP activates cGKs, which regulate cellular processes similar to PKGs, including smooth muscle relaxation and platelet aggregation.

3. Physiological Roles of cGMP:

a. **Vasodilation:** cGMP signaling mediates vasodilation by relaxing vascular smooth muscle cells, leading to decreased peripheral resistance and improved blood flow.

b. **Platelet Aggregation: cGMP inhibits platelet aggregation and thrombus formation by activating PKG**, which phosphorylates proteins involved in platelet activation and aggregation.

c. **Neuronal Signaling**: cGMP regulates synaptic transmission, neuronal excitability, and synaptic plasticity in the central nervous system, influencing learning, memory, and behavior.

d. **Vision**: cGMP plays a crucial role in phototransduction in the retina, where it regulates the opening and closing of cyclic nucleotide-gated channels in response to light stimuli.

4. Pathological Implications of Dysregulated cGMP Signaling:

a. **Cardiovascular Disorders**: Dysregulated cGMP signaling is associated with cardiovascular disorders such as hypertension, heart failure, and atherosclerosis, affecting vascular tone and blood pressure regulation.

b. **Platelet Dysfunction**: Altered cGMP signaling contributes to platelet dysfunction and thrombotic disorders, increasing the risk of myocardial infarction, stroke, and other cardiovascular events.

c. **Neurological Disorders**: Aberrant cGMP signaling is implicated in neurological disorders such as migraine, epilepsy, and neurodegenerative diseases, affecting neuronal function and synaptic transmission.

Comparison with cAMP:

a. **Similarities:**

i. Both cAMP and cGMP are cyclic nucleotide second messengers synthesized by adenylate cyclase and guanylate cyclase, respectively.

ii. They regulate cellular processes by activating protein kinases, modulating ion channels, and influencing gene expression.

b. Differences:

i. cAMP primarily activates protein kinase A (PKA), while cGMP activates protein kinase G (PKG).

ii. cAMP is more commonly associated with hormone signaling, while cGMP is often involved in nitric oxide (NO)-mediated signaling and ion channel regulation.

iii. cAMP and cGMP have distinct physiological roles and signaling pathways, although there is some overlap in their functions.

Calcium Ions (Ca2+)

Calcium ions (Ca2+) are ubiquitous secondary messengers involved in numerous cellular signaling processes. Their dynamic concentration within cells is tightly regulated by various mechanisms, including influx through plasma membrane channels, release from intracellular stores, and extrusion by pumps. Here's a detailed exploration of the role of calcium ions in cell signaling:

1. Calcium Signaling Mechanisms:

a. Calcium Influx:

i. Calcium ions enter the cell through various plasma membrane channels in response to extracellular stimuli, such as ligand binding to receptors or changes in membrane potential.

ii. Voltage-gated calcium channels (VGCCs), ligand-gated calcium channels (e.g., NMDA receptors), and receptor-operated calcium channels (ROCCs) are examples of calcium influx pathways.

b. Calcium Release from Intracellular Stores:

i. Calcium ions are released from intracellular stores, such as the endoplasmic reticulum (ER) or sarcoplasmic reticulum (SR), in response to signals such as IP3 or cyclic ADP-ribose (cADPR).

ii. Inositol 1,4,5-trisphosphate (IP3) binds to IP3 receptors (IP3Rs) on the ER membrane, leading to calcium release into the cytoplasm.

c. Calcium Extrusion and Sequestration:

i. Calcium ions are actively pumped out of the cell or sequestered into intracellular organelles (e.g., mitochondria) by calcium ATPases and calcium-binding proteins, respectively, to maintain cytosolic calcium homeostasis.

2. Calcium-Dependent Signaling Pathways:

a. Calcium-Calmodulin-Dependent Protein Kinase (CaMK) Pathway:

i. Calcium binds to calmodulin, forming a calcium-calmodulin complex.

ii. Calcium-calmodulin complex activates CaMK, which phosphorylates target proteins involved in various cellular processes, including gene expression, metabolism, and synaptic plasticity.

b. Calcineurin-Nuclear Factor of Activated T Cells (NFAT) Pathway:

i. Calcium activates the phosphatase calcineurin, which dephosphorylates NFAT transcription factors.

ii. Dephosphorylated NFAT translocates to the nucleus, where it regulates the expression of genes involved in immune responses, development, and cell proliferation.

c. Calcium-Dependent Ion Channels and Transporters:

i. Calcium ions directly modulate the activity of ion channels and transporters, such as voltage-gated potassium channels (Kv channels), sodium-calcium exchangers (NCX), and calcium-activated potassium channels (KCa channels), regulating membrane excitability and ion flux.

3. Physiological Roles of Calcium Signaling:

a. **Muscle Contraction**: Calcium signaling plays a crucial role in regulating muscle contraction by triggering the release of calcium ions from the sarcoplasmic reticulum (SR) in response to action potentials.

b. **Neuronal Signaling**: Calcium signaling regulates synaptic transmission, neurotransmitter release, and neuronal excitability, influencing processes such as learning, memory, and synaptic plasticity.

c. **Cell Proliferation and Differentiation**: Calcium signaling contributes to the regulation of cell proliferation, differentiation, and apoptosis by modulating the activity of signaling pathways involved in cell cycle progression and gene expression.

d. **Secretion and Exocytosis**: Calcium signaling mediates the exocytosis of neurotransmitters, hormones, and other signaling molecules from secretory cells, such as neurons, endocrine cells, and immune cells.

4. Pathological Implications of Dysregulated Calcium Signaling:

a. **Neurological Disorders**: Dysregulated calcium signaling is implicated in neurological disorders such as Alzheimer's disease, Parkinson's disease, and epilepsy, contributing to neuronal dysfunction and cell death.

b. **Cardiovascular Diseases**: Altered calcium signaling is associated with cardiovascular diseases such as arrhythmias, heart failure, and hypertension, affecting cardiac muscle contraction and vascular tone.

c. **Musculoskeletal Disorders**: Dysregulated calcium signaling contributes to musculoskeletal disorders such as osteoporosis, muscle weakness, and dystrophies, affecting bone remodeling and muscle function.

Inositol 1,4,5-Trisphosphate (IP3)

Inositol 1,4,5-trisphosphate (IP3) is a crucial secondary messenger molecule involved in cell signaling. It is generated through the hydrolysis of phosphatidylinositol 4,5-bisphosphate (PIP2) by phospholipase C (PLC) in response to various extracellular stimuli. IP3 acts to mobilize calcium ions (Ca2+) from intracellular stores, primarily the endoplasmic reticulum (ER), thereby regulating a multitude of cellular processes. Here's a detailed exploration of the role of IP3 in cell signaling:

1. Generation of IP3:

a. Activation of Phospholipase C (PLC):

    i. Extracellular stimuli, such as hormones or neurotransmitters, bind to their respective receptors, including G protein-coupled receptors (GPCRs) or receptor tyrosine kinases (RTKs).

    ii. Receptor activation triggers the activation of PLC, which cleaves PIP2 into two secondary messengers: diacylglycerol (DAG) and IP3.

2. Signaling Pathways Mediated by IP3:

a. Release of Calcium Ions (Ca2+):

    i. IP3 binds to IP3 receptors (IP3Rs) on the ER membrane, inducing conformational changes that lead to the release of calcium ions stored within the ER lumen into the cytoplasm.

    ii. Increased cytosolic calcium concentration triggers downstream signaling events and modulates various cellular processes.

3. Physiological Roles of IP3:

a. Neuronal Signaling:

    i. IP3-mediated calcium release regulates synaptic transmission, neuronal excitability, and synaptic plasticity in the central nervous system, influencing learning, memory, and behavior.

b. Muscle Contraction:

    i. In smooth muscle cells, IP3-induced calcium release plays a crucial role in regulating muscle contraction, particularly in response to neurotransmitters or hormones.

c. **Cell Proliferation and Differentiation:**
   i. IP3 signaling contributes to the regulation of cell proliferation, differentiation, and apoptosis by modulating calcium-dependent signaling pathways involved in cell cycle progression and gene expression.

d. **Secretion and Exocytosis:**
   i. IP3-mediated calcium release triggers the exocytosis of neurotransmitters, hormones, and other signaling molecules from secretory cells, such as neurons, endocrine cells, and immune cells.

4. Pathological Implications of Dysregulated IP3 Signaling:

a. **Neurological Disorders:**
   i. Dysregulated IP3 signaling is implicated in neurological disorders such as Alzheimer's disease, Huntington's disease, and ischemic stroke, contributing to neuronal dysfunction and cell death.

b. **Cardiovascular Diseases:**
   i. Altered IP3 signaling is associated with cardiovascular diseases such as arrhythmias, heart failure, and hypertension, affecting cardiac muscle contraction and vascular tone.

c. **Immune Disorders:**
   i. Dysregulated IP3 signaling contributes to immune disorders such as autoimmune diseases and inflammatory disorders, influencing immune cell activation and cytokine production.

Nitric Oxide (NO)

Nitric oxide (NO) is a critical signaling molecule that functions as a secondary messenger in various cellular processes. It is synthesized from the amino acid L-arginine by nitric oxide synthase (NOS) enzymes and plays diverse roles in cell signaling, particularly in the cardiovascular, nervous, and immune systems. Here's a detailed exploration of the role of NO as a secondary messenger in cell signaling:

1. Generation of NO:

    a. Nitric Oxide Synthase (NOS) Activation:

        i.   NOS enzymes catalyze the conversion of L-arginine into NO and L-citrulline in a calcium and calmodulin-dependent manner.

        ii.   NOS enzymes exist in three isoforms: neuronal NOS (nNOS or NOS1), inducible NOS (iNOS or NOS2), and endothelial NOS (eNOS or NOS3), each with distinct regulatory mechanisms and tissue distributions.

2. Signaling Pathways Mediated by NO:

    a. Activation of Soluble Guanylate Cyclase (sGC):

        i.   NO diffuses across cell membranes and binds to the heme group of sGC, converting it from its inactive to its active form.

        ii.   Activated sGC catalyzes the conversion of guanosine triphosphate (GTP) to cyclic guanosine monophosphate (cGMP), which serves as a secondary messenger in downstream signaling pathways.

    b. cGMP-Dependent Signaling Pathways:

        i.   cGMP activates protein kinase G (PKG), which phosphorylates target proteins involved in various cellular processes, including smooth muscle relaxation, platelet aggregation, and gene expression.

        ii.   Activation of cGMP-dependent pathways mediates many of the physiological effects of NO, particularly in the cardiovascular and nervous systems.

    c. Regulation of Ion Channels and Transporters:

        i.   NO can directly modulate the activity of ion channels and transporters, including calcium channels, potassium channels, and sodium channels, influencing membrane potential and cellular excitability.

3. Physiological Roles of NO:

a. Vasodilation:

i. NO plays a key role in regulating vascular tone by promoting vasodilation through the activation of sGC-cGMP signaling pathways in vascular smooth muscle cells.

ii. NO-mediated vasodilation helps to maintain blood pressure, improve blood flow, and prevent vascular diseases such as hypertension.

b. Neuronal Signaling:

i. NO serves as a neurotransmitter in the central and peripheral nervous systems, where it modulates synaptic transmission, neuronal excitability, and synaptic plasticity.

ii. NO signaling is involved in processes such as learning, memory, and pain perception.

c. Immune Responses:

i. NO produced by immune cells, particularly macrophages and neutrophils, acts as a cytotoxic agent against pathogens by inducing oxidative stress and DNA damage in target cells.

ii. NO also regulates immune cell function, cytokine production, and inflammation in the context of innate and adaptive immunity.

4. Pathological Implications of Dysregulated NO Signaling:

a. Cardiovascular Diseases:

i. Dysregulated NO signaling is associated with cardiovascular diseases such as hypertension, atherosclerosis, and heart failure, leading to impaired vasodilation, endothelial dysfunction, and vascular inflammation.

b. Neurological Disorders:

    i.   Altered NO signaling is implicated in neurological disorders such as Alzheimer's disease, Parkinson's disease, and stroke, contributing to neuronal dysfunction, neuroinflammation, and neurodegeneration.

c. Inflammatory Diseases:

    i.   Dysregulated NO signaling is involved in inflammatory diseases such as rheumatoid arthritis, inflammatory bowel disease, and sepsis, contributing to excessive inflammation, tissue damage, and organ dysfunction.

Diacylglycerol (DAG)

Diacylglycerol (DAG) is another critical secondary messenger involved in cell signaling, particularly in the activation of protein kinase C (PKC) and the regulation of various cellular processes. DAG is generated through the hydrolysis of phosphatidylinositol 4,5-bisphosphate (PIP2) by phospholipase C (PLC), alongside inositol 1,4,5-trisphosphate (IP3). Here's a detailed exploration of the role of DAG in cell signaling:

1. Generation of DAG:

a. Activation of Phospholipase C (PLC):

    i.   PLC cleaves PIP2 into two secondary messengers: DAG and IP3.

    ii.   This hydrolysis occurs in response to extracellular stimuli such as hormones, neurotransmitters, or growth factors binding to their receptors.

2. Signaling Pathways Mediated by DAG:

a. Activation of Protein Kinase C (PKC):

    i.   DAG acts as a crucial activator of PKC by binding to its C1 regulatory domain.

    ii.   Binding of DAG to PKC, in conjunction with calcium ions (Ca2+) and phosphatidylserine, leads to the translocation of PKC from the cytosol to the plasma membrane, where it becomes activated.

b. Phosphorylation of Target Proteins:

  i. Activated PKC phosphorylates specific serine and threonine residues on target proteins, modulating their activity and cellular functions.

  ii. PKC regulates various cellular processes, including cell growth, differentiation, apoptosis, gene expression, and neurotransmitter release.

3. Physiological Roles of DAG:

a. Cell Growth and Proliferation:

  i. DAG-mediated activation of PKC contributes to the regulation of cell growth, proliferation, and survival by modulating signaling pathways involved in cell cycle progression and apoptosis.

b. Neuronal Signaling:

  i. DAG/PKC signaling regulates synaptic transmission, neuronal excitability, and synaptic plasticity in the central nervous system, influencing learning, memory, and behavior.

c. Immune Responses:

  i. DAG/PKC signaling plays a role in immune cell activation, cytokine production, and inflammatory responses, influencing immune cell function and inflammation.

d. Metabolic Regulation:

  i. DAG/PKC signaling is involved in the regulation of metabolic processes such as glucose metabolism, lipid metabolism, and insulin signaling, affecting energy homeostasis and nutrient utilization.

4. Pathological Implications of Dysregulated DAG Signaling:

a. Cancer:

i. Dysregulated DAG/PKC signaling is implicated in cancer development and progression, contributing to abnormal cell proliferation, survival, angiogenesis, and metastasis.

b. Neurological Disorders:

i. Altered DAG/PKC signaling is associated with neurological disorders such as Alzheimer's disease, epilepsy, and schizophrenia, affecting neuronal function and synaptic plasticity.

c. Cardiovascular Diseases:

i. Dysregulated DAG/PKC signaling is linked to cardiovascular diseases such as heart failure, arrhythmias, and hypertrophy, affecting cardiac function and vascular tone.

d. Immune Disorders:

i. Aberrant DAG/PKC signaling contributes to immune disorders such as autoimmune diseases and inflammatory disorders, influencing immune cell activation and cytokine production.

DETAILED STUDY OF FOLLOWING INTRACELLULAR SIGNALLING PATHWAYS: CYCLIC AMP SIGNALING PATHWAY

The cyclic AMP (cAMP) signaling pathway is one of the most well-characterized and essential pathways in cell signaling. It plays a pivotal role in regulating numerous physiological processes, including metabolism, gene transcription, and cell growth.

Key Components of the cAMP Signaling Pathway

1. **G-Protein-Coupled Receptors (GPCRs)**

   a. GPCRs are membrane-bound receptors that activate intracellular G-proteins in response to ligand binding. Examples include β-adrenergic receptors, which bind adrenaline.

2. **Heterotrimeric G-Proteins**

   a. G-proteins consist of three subunits: α, β, and γ. The Gα subunit binds GDP in its inactive state and GTP when activated. The G$\beta\gamma$

dimer is involved in signaling but remains associated with the membrane.

3. **Adenylyl Cyclase (AC)**

   a. An enzyme that converts ATP to cAMP upon activation by the Gαs subunit of the G-protein.

4. **Cyclic AMP (cAMP)**

   a. A secondary messenger that activates downstream targets, primarily protein kinase A (PKA).

5. **Protein Kinase A (PKA)**

   a. A cAMP-dependent enzyme that phosphorylates various target proteins, leading to changes in their activity.

6. **Phosphodiesterases (PDEs)**

   a. Enzymes that degrade cAMP to AMP, thus terminating the signaling.

7. **CREB (cAMP Response Element-Binding Protein)**

   a. A transcription factor activated by PKA, which binds to cAMP response elements (CRE) in DNA to regulate gene expression.

Mechanism of the cAMP Signaling Pathway

1. **Ligand Binding and GPCR Activation**

   a. An extracellular ligand (e.g., adrenaline) binds to a GPCR on the cell surface, inducing a conformational change in the receptor.

2. **G-Protein Activation**

   a. The activated GPCR acts as a guanine nucleotide exchange factor (GEF) for the associated G-protein, facilitating the exchange of GDP for GTP on the Gαs subunit.

   b. Gαs-GTP dissociates from the Gβγ dimer and interacts with adenylyl cyclase.

3. **Adenylyl Cyclase Activation**

a. The Gαs-GTP complex activates adenylyl cyclase, which catalyzes the conversion of ATP to cAMP.

4. cAMP Production

a. cAMP levels increase in the cytoplasm, acting as a secondary messenger.

5. PKA Activation

a. cAMP binds to the regulatory subunits of PKA, causing the release and activation of the catalytic subunits.

b. Activated PKA then phosphorylates target proteins, leading to various cellular responses.

6. Cellular Responses

a. Immediate Responses: Phosphorylation of proteins involved in metabolic pathways, ion channels, and other signaling cascades.

b. Long-Term Responses: PKA phosphorylates CREB, which binds to CREs in the promoter regions of target genes, regulating their transcription.

7. Signal Termination

a. Phosphodiesterases (PDEs) degrade cAMP to AMP, reducing its levels and thereby inactivating PKA.

b. The Gαs subunit hydrolyzes GTP to GDP, reassociating with the Gβγ dimer and returning to its inactive state.

Physiological Roles of the cAMP Signaling Pathway

1. Metabolism

a. Glycogen Breakdown: In liver and muscle cells, adrenaline activates β-adrenergic receptors, leading to increased cAMP and PKA activation. PKA phosphorylates and activates glycogen phosphorylase kinase, which then activates glycogen phosphorylase, promoting glycogen breakdown to glucose.

2. **Cardiac Function**
   a. Heart Rate and Contractility: Adrenaline binding to β-adrenergic receptors in heart cells increases cAMP levels, activating PKA. PKA phosphorylates voltage-gated calcium channels, enhancing calcium influx and increasing heart rate and contractility.

3. **Gene Expression**
   a. CREB Activation: In neurons and other cells, cAMP activates PKA, which phosphorylates CREB. Activated CREB binds to CREs in DNA, regulating the transcription of genes involved in neuronal plasticity, memory formation, and survival.

4. **Hormone Regulation**
   a. Thyroid-Stimulating Hormone (TSH): TSH binding to its receptor on thyroid cells increases cAMP levels, leading to the activation of PKA and subsequent thyroid hormone production.

5. **Sensory Perception**
   a. Olfactory Receptors: Binding of odorants to olfactory receptors (a type of GPCR) increases cAMP, opening cAMP-gated ion channels and leading to depolarization and the generation of a nerve impulse.

Clinical Relevance

1. **Pharmacological Agents**
   a. **β-Blockers:** Used to treat hypertension and cardiac arrhythmias by blocking β-adrenergic receptors, thereby reducing cAMP levels and heart rate.
   b. **Phosphodiesterase Inhibitors**: Such as sildenafil (Viagra), used to treat erectile dysfunction by inhibiting PDE5, increasing cGMP levels, and promoting vasodilation.

2. **Disease States**

a. **Heart Failure:** Altered cAMP signaling can lead to heart failure. β-adrenergic agonists and PDE inhibitors are used therapeutically to modulate this pathway.

b. **Asthma**: β2-adrenergic agonists are used to relax bronchial smooth muscle by increasing cAMP levels.

MITOGEN-ACTIVATED PROTEIN KINASE (MAPK) SIGNALLING

The Mitogen-Activated Protein Kinase (MAPK) signaling pathway is a critical intracellular pathway that transmits extracellular signals into a variety of cellular responses, including growth, differentiation, proliferation, survival, and apoptosis. The pathway is highly conserved across eukaryotes and involves a series of protein kinases that activate each other through phosphorylation.

Key Components of the MAPK Signaling Pathway

The mitogen-activated protein kinase (MAPK) signaling pathway is a highly conserved intracellular signaling cascade involved in various cellular processes, including cell proliferation, differentiation, apoptosis, and response to extracellular stimuli. Here are the key components of the MAPK signaling pathway in detail:

1. **Receptor Tyrosine Kinases (RTKs) or G Protein-Coupled Receptors (GPCRs):**

   a. The MAPK pathway can be activated by diverse extracellular stimuli, such as growth factors, cytokines, hormones, and stress signals.

   b. RTKs and GPCRs serve as cell surface receptors that sense these extracellular signals and initiate signaling cascades.

2. **Ras Proteins:**

   a. Ras proteins (H-Ras, K-Ras, N-Ras) are small GTPases that function as molecular switches in the MAPK pathway.

   b. They are located at the inner leaflet of the plasma membrane and become activated upon stimulation of RTKs or GPCRs.

c. Activated Ras proteins exchange GDP for GTP, leading to a conformational change that enables them to interact with downstream effector proteins.

3. **Raf Kinases (Raf-1, B-Raf, A-Raf):**
   a. Raf kinases are serine/threonine protein kinases that serve as immediate downstream effectors of activated Ras.
   b. Upon binding to GTP-bound Ras, Raf kinases undergo conformational changes and become activated.
   c. Activated Raf kinases phosphorylate and activate downstream kinases in the MAPK pathway.

4. **MAP Kinase Kinases (MAPKKs or MEKs):**
   a. MAPKKs are dual-specificity protein kinases that phosphorylate and activate MAP kinases (MAPKs) in the MAPK pathway.
   b. The primary MAPKKs involved in the canonical MAPK pathway are MEK1 and MEK2.
   c. MEKs are activated by phosphorylation at specific serine and threonine residues by Raf kinases.

5. **MAP Kinases (MAPKs):**
   a. MAPKs are serine/threonine protein kinases that are phosphorylated and activated by MAPKKs.
   b. The major MAPKs in the MAPK pathway include extracellular signal-regulated kinases (ERKs), c-Jun N-terminal kinases (JNKs), and p38 MAP kinases.
   c. ERKs are primarily activated by growth factors and mitogens, while JNKs and p38 MAP kinases are activated by stress stimuli.

6. **Substrates and Transcription Factors:**
   a. Activated MAPKs phosphorylate a wide range of substrates, including cytoplasmic and nuclear proteins.

b. MAPK-mediated phosphorylation of transcription factors, such as c-Fos, c-Jun, Elk-1 (targeted by ERKs), ATF2 (targeted by JNKs), and ATF2/CREB (targeted by p38), regulates gene expression and cellular responses.

Regulation and Feedback Mechanisms:

a. Negative Feedback Regulation:

i. Phosphatases, such as MAPK phosphatases (MKPs), dephosphorylate and inactivate MAPKs, providing negative feedback to attenuate signaling.

ii. Inhibition of upstream signaling components, such as Raf and Ras, by negative regulators, including kinases and scaffolding proteins, also contributes to negative feedback regulation.

b. Cross-talk with Other Signaling Pathways:

i. The MAPK pathway can crosstalk with other signaling pathways, such as the PI3K/Akt pathway and the JAK/STAT pathway, leading to integrated cellular responses.

ii. Cross-talk provides additional layers of regulation and enables cells to integrate multiple signals to generate specific responses.

c. Spatial and Temporal Regulation:

i. The localization of signaling components, such as receptors, Ras, and MAPKs, in specific cellular compartments contributes to the spatial regulation of MAPK signaling.

ii. Temporal regulation of MAPK signaling is achieved through the dynamic modulation of protein expression, post-translational modifications, and feedback mechanisms.

Mechanism of the MAPK Signaling Pathway

The mitogen-activated protein kinase (MAPK) signaling pathway is a highly conserved intracellular signaling cascade involved in transducing extracellular stimuli into a wide range of cellular responses, including cell proliferation, differentiation, survival, and apoptosis. Here's a detailed overview of the mechanism of the MAPK signaling pathway:

1. **Extracellular Stimulation:**
   a. The MAPK pathway is activated in response to various extracellular stimuli, including growth factors (e.g., epidermal growth factor, insulin), cytokines, hormones, and environmental stressors (e.g., UV radiation, heat shock).
   b. These stimuli bind to their respective cell surface receptors, which can be receptor tyrosine kinases (RTKs) or G protein-coupled receptors (GPCRs).

2. **Activation of Ras Proteins:**
   a. Upon ligand binding, RTKs or GPCRs undergo conformational changes that lead to the activation of intracellular signaling proteins.
   b. One key mediator of MAPK pathway activation is Ras, a small GTPase protein located at the inner leaflet of the plasma membrane.
   c. Ras exists in an inactive GDP-bound form and an active GTP-bound form. Binding of the extracellular ligand to the receptor induces the exchange of GDP for GTP on Ras, resulting in Ras activation.

3. **Activation of Raf Kinases:**
   a. Activated Ras recruits and activates Raf kinases (Raf-1, B-Raf, A-Raf) to the plasma membrane.
   b. Raf kinases are serine/threonine protein kinases that serve as immediate downstream effectors of Ras.
   c. Binding of Ras-GTP induces conformational changes in Raf, leading to its activation and subsequent phosphorylation.

4. **Phosphorylation of MAP Kinase Kinases (MAPKKs or MEKs):**

a. Activated Raf kinases phosphorylate and activate MAP kinase kinases (MAPKKs or MEKs), including MEK1 and MEK2.

b. MEKs are dual-specificity protein kinases that phosphorylate and activate MAP kinases (MAPKs) on specific threonine and tyrosine residues within the conserved Thr-Xaa-Tyr motif (where Xaa represents any amino acid).

5. **Activation of MAP Kinases (MAPKs):**

a. Once phosphorylated and activated by MEKs, MAPKs are released from MEKs and translocate to the nucleus or other cellular compartments.

b. The major MAPKs involved in the canonical MAPK pathway include extracellular signal-regulated kinases (ERKs), c-Jun N-terminal kinases (JNKs), and p38 MAP kinases.

c. Each MAPK subtype phosphorylates and activates a distinct set of downstream substrates, including transcription factors and cytoplasmic proteins.

6. **Gene Transcription and Cellular Responses:**

a. Activated MAPKs phosphorylate a wide range of substrates, including transcription factors (e.g., c-Fos, c-Jun, Elk-1), cytoplasmic proteins, and other kinases.

b. Phosphorylation of transcription factors regulates gene expression by modulating their activity, stability, or subcellular localization.

c. The transcriptional changes induced by MAPK signaling lead to various cellular responses, such as cell proliferation, differentiation, survival, and apoptosis.

Termination of Signaling:

1. The duration and amplitude of MAPK signaling are tightly regulated to ensure proper cellular responses and prevent aberrant activation.

2. Negative feedback mechanisms, such as the action of MAPK phosphatases (MKPs), attenuate signaling by dephosphorylating and inactivating MAPKs.

3. Downregulation of upstream signaling components, including Raf and Ras, by negative regulators further contributes to the termination of MAPK signaling.

Specific MAPK Pathways

The mitogen-activated protein kinase (MAPK) signaling pathway encompasses several distinct cascades that mediate cellular responses to extracellular stimuli. Each MAPK pathway is activated by specific upstream signaling events and regulates unique cellular processes. Here's an overview of specific MAPK pathways in detail:

1. Extracellular Signal-Regulated Kinase (ERK) Pathway:

a. **Activation:** The ERK pathway is primarily activated by growth factors, mitogens, and receptor tyrosine kinases (RTKs).

b. **Key Components:**

    i. **Upstream**: RTKs, Ras, Raf (Raf-1, B-Raf), MEK1/2

    ii. **Downstream:** ERK1/2, various substrates including transcription factors (Elk-1, c-Fos, c-Jun), cytoplasmic proteins (kinases, phosphatases)

c. **Mechanism:**

    i. Extracellular stimuli activate RTKs or GPCRs, leading to Ras activation.

    ii. Activated Ras recruits and activates Raf kinases, which phosphorylate and activate MEK1/2.

    iii. MEK1/2 phosphorylates and activates ERK1/2.

    iv. Activated ERK1/2 translocates to the nucleus and phosphorylates transcription factors, leading to changes in gene expression.

v. ERK1/2 also phosphorylates cytoplasmic proteins involved in cell proliferation, survival, and differentiation.

d. **Physiological Roles**: Regulation of cell proliferation, differentiation, survival, migration, and gene expression.

2. c-Jun N-terminal Kinase (JNK) Pathway:

a. **Activation**: The JNK pathway is activated by various stress stimuli, including UV radiation, inflammatory cytokines, and osmotic stress.

b. **Key Components**:

  i. **Upstream**: MAP3Ks (e.g., MEKK1-4), MKK4/7

  ii. **Downstream**: JNK1/2/3, transcription factors (c-Jun, ATF2), cytoplasmic proteins (Bcl-2, p53)

c. **Mechanism**:

  i. Stress stimuli activate MAP3Ks, such as MEKK1-4.

  ii. Activated MAP3Ks phosphorylate and activate MKK4/7.

  iii. MKK4/7 phosphorylate and activate JNK1/2/3.

  iv. Activated JNKs translocate to the nucleus and phosphorylate transcription factors, such as c-Jun and ATF2.

  v. Phosphorylated c-Jun forms homo- or heterodimers and regulates gene expression involved in apoptosis, inflammation, and stress responses.

d. **Physiological Roles**: Regulation of apoptosis, inflammation, cell survival, and stress responses.

3. p38 MAP Kinase Pathway:

a. **Activation**: The p38 pathway is activated by various stress stimuli, including inflammatory cytokines, UV radiation, osmotic stress, and heat shock.

b. **Key Components**:

  i. **Upstream**: MAP3Ks (e.g., ASK1, MEKK3-4), MKK3/6

ii. **Downstream**: p38α/β/γ/δ, transcription factors (ATF2, p53, NF-κB), cytoplasmic proteins (MAPKAPK2/3)

c. **Mechanism:**

  i. Stress stimuli activate MAP3Ks, such as ASK1 and MEKK3-4.

  ii. Activated MAP3Ks phosphorylate and activate MKK3/6.

  iii. MKK3/6 phosphorylate and activate p38α/β/γ/δ.

  iv. Activated p38 MAPKs phosphorylate transcription factors, such as ATF2 and p53, and cytoplasmic proteins, such as MAPKAPK2/3.

  v. Phosphorylation of downstream targets regulates gene expression, apoptosis, inflammation, and cellular responses to stress.

d. **Physiological Roles**: Regulation of inflammation, apoptosis, cell differentiation, immune responses, and stress responses.

Regulation of MAPK Signaling

The regulation of MAPK signaling is essential for maintaining cellular homeostasis and ensuring appropriate responses to extracellular stimuli. The pathway is subject to tight control at multiple levels to prevent aberrant activation and to fine-tune the amplitude and duration of signaling. Here's a detailed overview of the regulation of MAPK signaling:

1. Regulation of MAPK Activation:

1. Receptor-Level Regulation:

a. **Desensitization**: Receptors undergo desensitization through mechanisms like receptor internalization and degradation, mediated by arrestins or ubiquitin ligases, to attenuate signaling in response to prolonged stimulation.

b. **Feedback Inhibition**: Activated MAPKs can phosphorylate and inhibit upstream signaling components, such as receptors or adaptor proteins, to dampen signaling.

2. Ras Activation:

a. **Ras GTPase Activity**: Ras activity is regulated by guanine nucleotide exchange factors (GEFs) that promote GDP-GTP exchange and GTPase-activating proteins (GAPs) that accelerate GTP hydrolysis, leading to Ras inactivation.

b. **Scaffold Proteins**: Scaffold proteins, such as KSR (kinase suppressor of Ras), facilitate the assembly of signaling complexes and enhance Ras-mediated MAPK activation.

3. **Raf Activation:**

a. **Phosphorylation:** Raf kinases are activated by phosphorylation at specific sites, typically within their regulatory domains, by upstream activators like Ras or other signaling proteins.

b. **Dimerization:** Raf activation often involves the formation of homo- or heterodimers, which stabilize the active conformation of Raf and promote kinase activity.

4. **MAPKK Activation:**

a. **Phosphorylation:** MAPKKs are activated by dual-specificity MAP kinase kinases (MAPKK kinases or MAP3Ks), which phosphorylate specific serine/threonine residues within the activation loop of MAPKKs.

b. **Scaffold Proteins**: Scaffold proteins facilitate the recruitment and activation of MAPKKs by promoting their interaction with upstream kinases and substrates.

2. Regulation of MAPK Activity:

1. Phosphorylation and Dephosphorylation:

a. **MAPK Phosphorylation**: MAPKKs phosphorylate specific threonine and tyrosine residues within the activation loop of MAPKs, leading to their activation.

b. **MAPK Dephosphorylation**: MAPK phosphatases (MKPs) dephosphorylate and inactivate MAPKs by removing phosphate groups from their activation loop, terminating signaling.

2. **Feedback Regulation:**

   a. **Negative Feedback**: Active MAPKs can phosphorylate and inhibit upstream components of the pathway, such as RTKs, Ras, Raf, or MAPKKs, to attenuate signaling.

   b. **Positive Feedback**: MAPK signaling can induce the expression of feedback regulators, such as scaffold proteins or phosphatases, to modulate pathway activity.

3. **Spatial and Temporal Regulation:**

   1. **Subcellular Localization:**

      a. **Scaffold Proteins**: Scaffold proteins localize signaling components to specific subcellular compartments, ensuring efficient signal propagation and substrate specificity.

      b. **Nuclear Translocation**: Activated MAPKs can translocate to the nucleus, where they phosphorylate transcription factors and regulate gene expression.

   2. **Temporal Dynamics:**

      a. **Transient Activation**: MAPK signaling is often transient, with rapid activation followed by attenuation due to negative feedback and phosphatase activity.

      b. **Oscillatory Behavior**: MAPK signaling can exhibit oscillatory dynamics, characterized by repeated cycles of activation and inactivation, which may contribute to cell fate decisions and developmental processes.

Physiological and Pathological Roles of MAPK Signaling

The mitogen-activated protein kinase (MAPK) signaling pathway plays crucial roles in both physiological and pathological processes by regulating diverse cellular responses to extracellular stimuli. Here's a detailed exploration of the physiological and pathological roles of MAPK signaling:

Physiological Roles:

1. **Cell Proliferation and Survival:**
   a. MAPK signaling promotes cell proliferation and survival in response to growth factors and mitogens.
   b. Physiological processes such as tissue growth, development, and wound healing rely on the regulation of cell proliferation by MAPK signaling.

2. **Cell Differentiation and Development:**
   a. MAPK signaling controls cell fate decisions and differentiation processes during embryonic development and tissue morphogenesis.
   b. Differentiation of stem cells into specialized cell types, such as neurons, muscle cells, and epithelial cells, is regulated by MAPK signaling.

3. **Immune Responses:**
   a. MAPK signaling regulates immune cell activation, cytokine production, and inflammatory responses.
   b. Physiological immune responses, including host defense against pathogens and tissue repair, depend on the precise regulation of MAPK signaling in immune cells.

4. **Neuronal Plasticity:**
   a. MAPK signaling is involved in synaptic plasticity, neuronal development, and synaptic transmission in the central nervous system.
   b. Physiological processes such as learning, memory formation, and neuronal survival are modulated by MAPK signaling pathways in neurons.

5. **Metabolic Regulation:**
   a. MAPK signaling regulates metabolic processes such as glucose metabolism, lipid metabolism, and energy homeostasis.
   b. Physiological responses to nutrient availability, hormonal signals, and stress conditions are mediated by MAPK signaling in metabolic tissues.

Pathological Roles:

1. **Cancer:**
   a. Dysregulated MAPK signaling is implicated in the pathogenesis of various cancers, including melanoma, colorectal cancer, lung cancer, and pancreatic cancer.
   b. Aberrant activation of MAPK signaling promotes uncontrolled cell proliferation, survival, angiogenesis, and metastasis in cancer cells.

2. **Inflammatory Diseases:**
   a. Dysregulated MAPK signaling contributes to the pathogenesis of inflammatory diseases, such as rheumatoid arthritis, inflammatory bowel disease, and psoriasis.
   b. Excessive MAPK activation leads to increased production of pro-inflammatory cytokines, chemokines, and inflammatory mediators.

3. **Neurological Disorders:**
   a. Altered MAPK signaling is associated with neurodegenerative diseases, including Alzheimer's disease, Parkinson's disease, and Huntington's disease.
   b. Aberrant MAPK activation contributes to neuronal dysfunction, oxidative stress, neuroinflammation, and neuronal cell death in neurodegenerative disorders.

4. **Cardiovascular Diseases:**

a. Dysregulated MAPK signaling is implicated in the pathogenesis of cardiovascular diseases, such as hypertension, atherosclerosis, and myocardial infarction.

b. MAPK signaling regulates vascular smooth muscle cell proliferation, endothelial cell function, and cardiac hypertrophy in cardiovascular diseases.

5. Metabolic Disorders:

a. Altered MAPK signaling is associated with metabolic disorders, including obesity, type 2 diabetes, and non-alcoholic fatty liver disease.

b. Dysregulated MAPK signaling contributes to insulin resistance, inflammation, dyslipidemia, and aberrant lipid metabolism in metabolic disorders.

JANUS KINASE (JAK)/SIGNAL TRANSDUCER AND ACTIVATOR OF TRANSCRIPTION (STAT) SIGNALING PATHWAY

The Janus kinase (JAK)/signal transducer and activator of transcription (STAT) signaling pathway is a critical mechanism for transmitting signals from extracellular cytokines and growth factors to the cell nucleus, resulting in gene expression changes. This pathway is fundamental for various cellular processes, including immune function, cell growth, differentiation, and apoptosis.

Key Components of the JAK/STAT Pathway

Here's a detailed overview of the key components involved in the Janus kinase (JAK)/signal transducer and activator of transcription (STAT) signaling pathway:

1. Cytokine Receptors:

a. These are cell surface receptors that bind to cytokines, growth factors, and hormones. They typically consist of multiple subunits and lack intrinsic kinase activity. Upon ligand binding, they undergo conformational changes that lead to receptor dimerization or oligomerization.

2. **Janus Kinases (JAKs):**

   a. JAKs are cytoplasmic tyrosine kinases associated with the intracellular domains of cytokine receptors. They are activated when cytokine binding induces receptor dimerization, bringing JAKs into close proximity, allowing them to trans-phosphorylate each other and become catalytically active.

3. **Signal Transducers and Activators of Transcription (STATs):**

   a. STATs are a family of transcription factors that become activated in response to phosphorylation by JAKs. Once phosphorylated, they form homo- or heterodimers via their SH2 (Src homology 2) domains. These dimers then translocate to the nucleus, where they regulate gene expression by binding to specific DNA sequences in the promoters of target genes.

4. **Negative Regulators:**

   a. **Suppressor of Cytokine Signaling (SOCS):** SOCS proteins are negative regulators of the JAK/STAT pathway. They are induced by cytokine signaling and act as feedback inhibitors by binding to JAKs or cytokine receptors, thereby inhibiting their activity and promoting their degradation.

   b. **Protein Inhibitors of Activated STATs (PIAS):** PIAS proteins also act as negative regulators by inhibiting STAT activity. They can block the DNA binding ability of STATs or promote their sumoylation, which prevents their function.

5. **Cytokines and Growth Factors:**

   a. These extracellular signaling molecules bind to their respective receptors, leading to receptor activation and initiation of downstream signaling through the JAK/STAT pathway. Examples of cytokines and growth factors include interferons (IFNs), interleukins (ILs), growth hormone (GH), erythropoietin (EPO), and prolactin.

6. **Interferon-Stimulated Response Elements (ISREs) and Gamma-Activated Sites** (GAS):

    a. These are specific DNA sequences found in the promoters of genes regulated by the JAK/STAT pathway. STAT dimers bind to ISREs or GAS elements to initiate or enhance the transcription of target genes.

Mechanism of the JAK/STAT Signaling Pathway

The Janus kinase (JAK)/signal transducer and activator of transcription (STAT) signaling pathway is a critical mechanism for transmitting extracellular signals from cytokines, growth factors, and hormones to the nucleus, resulting in changes in gene expression. This pathway plays crucial roles in various cellular processes, including immune responses, cell growth, differentiation, and apoptosis. Here's a detailed overview of the mechanism of the JAK/STAT signaling pathway:

1. **Cytokine Binding and Receptor Activation:**

    a. The pathway is initiated by the binding of cytokines, growth factors, or hormones to their respective receptors on the cell surface. These receptors typically exist as monomers or inactive dimers in the absence of ligand binding.

2. **Receptor Dimerization and JAK Activation:**

    a. Ligand binding induces conformational changes in the receptor, leading to receptor dimerization or oligomerization. This dimerization brings the associated Janus kinases (JAKs) into close proximity, facilitating their trans-phosphorylation and activation.

3. **Phosphorylation of Receptor Tyrosine Residues:**

a. Activated JAKs phosphorylate specific tyrosine residues on the intracellular domains of the receptor. These phosphotyrosine residues serve as docking sites for downstream signaling molecules, particularly members of the STAT family.

4. **STAT Recruitment and Phosphorylation:**

   a. Phosphorylated receptor tyrosine residues recruit and activate cytoplasmic STAT proteins via their SH2 (Src homology 2) domains. The STAT proteins are then phosphorylated by the activated JAKs on specific tyrosine residues.

5. **STAT Dimerization and Nuclear Translocation:**

   a. Phosphorylated STAT proteins undergo conformational changes that promote their dimerization through reciprocal SH2 domain interactions. These STAT dimers can be homodimers or heterodimers depending on the specific STAT proteins involved.

   b. Once dimerized, the phosphorylated STAT proteins translocate from the cytoplasm to the nucleus, facilitated by nuclear localization signals (NLS) within the proteins.

6. **Gene Transcription and Regulation:**

   a. Within the nucleus, STAT dimers bind to specific DNA sequences known as gamma-activated sites (GAS) or interferon-stimulated response elements (ISREs) located in the promoters of target genes.

   b. The binding of STAT dimers to these regulatory elements initiates or enhances the transcription of target genes, leading to changes in gene expression.

   c. STAT proteins can directly activate gene transcription by recruiting co-activators or indirectly regulate gene expression by interacting with other transcription factors.

7. **Termination of Signaling:**

a. The duration and intensity of JAK/STAT signaling are tightly regulated to prevent excessive cellular responses. Negative regulators, such as suppressor of cytokine signaling (SOCS) proteins and protein inhibitors of activated STATs (PIAS), play crucial roles in terminating signaling by inhibiting JAK activity, dephosphorylating STATs, or promoting their degradation.

Specific JAK/STAT Pathways

The Janus kinase (JAK)/signal transducer and activator of transcription (STAT) signaling pathway encompasses various specific pathways that are activated by different cytokines, growth factors, and hormones. Each pathway regulates distinct cellular processes and involves specific JAKs, STATs, and target genes. Here, we'll delve into some specific JAK/STAT pathways in detail:

1. JAK1/JAK2 and STAT1/STAT2 Pathway:

a. **Activation:** This pathway is typically activated by interferons (IFNs), including IFN-α and IFN-γ.

b. **JAKs Involved**: JAK1 and JAK2 are the primary Janus kinases involved in this pathway.

c. **STATs Involved**: STAT1 and STAT2 are the primary STAT proteins activated in response to IFNs.

d. **Mechanism**:

   i. Binding of IFNs to their receptors induces receptor dimerization and activation of associated JAK1 and JAK2.

   ii. Activated JAKs phosphorylate tyrosine residues on the receptor cytoplasmic domains, creating docking sites for STAT proteins.

   iii. Phosphorylated STAT1 and STAT2 proteins bind to the receptor complex.

   iv. Upon binding, STAT1 and STAT2 are phosphorylated by JAKs.

v. Phosphorylated STAT1 and STAT2 form heterodimers, which associate with interferon regulatory factor 9 (IRF9) to form the ISGF3 complex.

vi. ISGF3 translocates to the nucleus and binds to interferon-stimulated response elements (ISREs) in the promoters of interferon-stimulated genes (ISGs).

vii. ISGF3 binding to ISREs activates the transcription of ISGs, including antiviral proteins and immunomodulatory factors.

2. JAK2 and STAT5 Pathway:

a. **Activation: This** pathway is activated by cytokines such as growth hormone (GH), erythropoietin (EPO), and prolactin.

b. **JAKs Involved**: JAK2 is the primary Janus kinase involved in this pathway.

c. **STATs Involved**: STAT5A and STAT5B are the primary STAT proteins activated in response to cytokine stimulation.

d. **Mechanism:**

i. Binding of cytokines such as GH or EPO to their respective receptors leads to receptor dimerization and activation of associated JAK2.

ii. Activated JAK2 phosphorylates tyrosine residues on the receptor cytoplasmic domains.

iii. Phosphorylated tyrosine residues serve as docking sites for STAT5 proteins.

iv. Phosphorylated STAT5 proteins bind to the receptor complex.

v. Upon binding, STAT5 proteins are phosphorylated by JAK2.

vi. Phosphorylated STAT5 proteins form homodimers or heterodimers.

vii. STAT5 dimers translocate to the nucleus and bind to specific DNA sequences in the promoters of target genes, regulating their transcription.

viii. Target genes include those involved in cell proliferation, survival, and differentiation, as well as lactation and erythropoiesis.

3. JAK1 and STAT6 Pathway:

a. **Activation:** This pathway is activated by interleukin-4 (IL-4) and interleukin-13 (IL-13).

b. **JAKs Involved**: JAK1 is the primary Janus kinase involved in this pathway.

c. **STATs Involved**: STAT6 is the primary STAT protein activated in response to IL-4 and IL-13.

d. **Mechanism:**

i. IL-4 or IL-13 binding to their respective receptors induces receptor dimerization and activation of associated JAK1.

ii. Activated JAK1 phosphorylates tyrosine residues on the receptor cytoplasmic domains.

iii. Phosphorylated tyrosine residues serve as docking sites for STAT6 proteins.

iv. Phosphorylated STAT6 proteins bind to the receptor complex.

v. Upon binding, STAT6 proteins are phosphorylated by JAK1.

vi. Phosphorylated STAT6 proteins form homodimers.

vii. STAT6 dimers translocate to the nucleus and bind to specific DNA sequences in the promoters of target genes, regulating their transcription.

viii. Target genes include those involved in Th2 cell differentiation, allergic responses, and immunomodulation.

Regulation of the JAK/STAT Pathway

The Janus kinase (JAK)/signal transducer and activator of transcription (STAT) signaling pathway is tightly regulated to ensure appropriate cellular responses to extracellular stimuli while preventing excessive activation or inappropriate signaling. Regulation of this pathway occurs at multiple levels and involves various negative and positive feedback mechanisms. Here's a detailed overview of the regulation of the JAK/STAT pathway:

Regulation of the JAK/STAT Pathway:

1. **Suppressor of Cytokine Signaling (SOCS) Proteins:**
   a. SOCS proteins are negative regulators of the JAK/STAT pathway. They are induced by cytokine signaling and act as feedback inhibitors.
   b. **Mechanism:**
      i. SOCS proteins inhibit JAK activity by binding to JAKs or to the activation loop of cytokine receptors, preventing further signaling.
      ii. They also compete with STATs for binding to phosphorylated tyrosine residues on receptors, blocking STAT recruitment and activation.
      iii. SOCS proteins can recruit E3 ubiquitin ligases to target JAKs or cytokine receptors for ubiquitination and degradation, further attenuating signaling.

2. **Protein Inhibitors of Activated STATs (PIAS):**
   a. PIAS proteins are negative regulators of STAT activity. They inhibit STAT function by various mechanisms.
   b. Mechanism:
      i. PIAS proteins can block the DNA binding ability of STATs by binding to their DNA-binding domains, preventing transcriptional activation.

ii. They can promote the sumoylation of STATs, which inhibits their function by altering their activity or subcellular localization.

iii. PIAS proteins can also recruit histone deacetylases (HDACs) to STAT-bound promoters, leading to transcriptional repression.

3. Protein Tyrosine Phosphatases (PTPs):

a. PTPs are enzymes that dephosphorylate tyrosine residues on JAKs and STATs, terminating signaling.

b. **Mechanism:**

i. PTPs dephosphorylate activated JAKs, leading to their inactivation and dissociation from receptors.

ii. They also dephosphorylate STAT proteins, promoting their nuclear export and inactivation.

iii. PTPs help to terminate signaling by counteracting the action of protein tyrosine kinases (PTKs) that activate the pathway.

4. Cytokine-Inducible SH2-Containing Protein (CIS):

a. CIS is a family member of the SOCS proteins and acts similarly to regulate JAK/STAT signaling.

b. **Mechanism:**

i. CIS competes with STATs for binding to phosphorylated tyrosine residues on receptors, inhibiting STAT recruitment and activation.

ii. It can also target receptors for degradation, attenuating signaling.

5. Feedback Loops:

a. Negative feedback loops are essential for fine-tuning the duration and intensity of JAK/STAT signaling.

b. **Mechanism:**

i. Negative regulators like SOCS proteins and PTPs are themselves target genes of STAT-mediated transcription, creating feedback loops that help to turn off signaling.

ii. Increased expression of SOCS proteins and PTPs dampens JAK/STAT activity, preventing prolonged or excessive signaling.

6. **Crosstalk with Other Signaling Pathways:**

a. The JAK/STAT pathway can crosstalk with other signaling pathways, including the MAPK and PI3K/Akt pathways, providing additional layers of regulation.

b. **Mechanism:**

i. Cross-regulation between pathways can involve direct protein-protein interactions, phosphorylation events, or transcriptional regulation of pathway components.

ii. Crosstalk allows for integration of signals from multiple pathways and fine-tuning of cellular responses.

Physiological and Pathological Roles of the JAK/STAT Pathway

The Janus kinase (JAK)/signal transducer and activator of transcription (STAT) signaling pathway plays critical roles in various physiological processes, including immune responses, hematopoiesis, cell proliferation, differentiation, and apoptosis. Dysregulation of this pathway can contribute to the pathogenesis of numerous diseases. Here's a detailed exploration of the physiological and pathological roles of the JAK/STAT pathway:

Physiological Roles:

1. **Immune Responses:**

a. The JAK/STAT pathway is essential for mediating immune responses by regulating the development, differentiation, and function of immune cells.

b. It plays a crucial role in cytokine signaling, allowing immune cells to communicate and coordinate their activities.

c. STAT proteins regulate the expression of genes involved in immune cell proliferation, differentiation, and cytokine production.

2. Hematopoiesis:

a. JAK/STAT signaling is involved in the regulation of hematopoietic stem cell maintenance, proliferation, and differentiation.

b. Cytokines such as erythropoietin (EPO), thrombopoietin (TPO), and granulocyte colony-stimulating factor (G-CSF) signal through the JAK/STAT pathway to regulate erythropoiesis, thrombopoiesis, and myelopoiesis, respectively.

3. Cell Proliferation and Survival:

a. The pathway regulates cell proliferation and survival in various cell types, including immune cells, epithelial cells, and fibroblasts.

b. Growth factors such as growth hormone (GH) and insulin-like growth factor 1 (IGF-1) activate JAK/STAT signaling to promote cell growth and survival.

4. Development and Differentiation:

a. JAK/STAT signaling is crucial for embryonic development and tissue homeostasis.

b. It regulates the differentiation of various cell types during development, including immune cells, neurons, and muscle cells.

c. STAT proteins control the expression of genes involved in cell fate determination, tissue patterning, and organogenesis.

5. Inflammatory Responses:

a. The pathway plays a central role in mediating inflammatory responses by regulating the expression of pro-inflammatory cytokines and chemokines.

b. It controls the activation and function of immune cells, such as macrophages, dendritic cells, and T cells, in response to inflammatory stimuli.

Pathological Roles:

1. **Cancer:**
   a. Dysregulation of the JAK/STAT pathway is implicated in the pathogenesis of various cancers.
   b. Constitutive activation of JAK/STAT signaling can promote uncontrolled cell proliferation, survival, and metastasis.
   c. Mutations or aberrant expression of JAKs, STATs, or upstream regulators contribute to oncogenesis in hematological malignancies and solid tumors.

2. **Autoimmune Diseases:**
   a. Aberrant activation of the JAK/STAT pathway is associated with autoimmune diseases, such as rheumatoid arthritis, systemic lupus erythematosus, and multiple sclerosis.
   b. Dysregulated cytokine signaling and aberrant immune cell activation contribute to chronic inflammation and tissue damage in autoimmune disorders.

3. **Inflammatory Diseases:**
   a. Chronic activation of the JAK/STAT pathway contributes to the pathogenesis of inflammatory diseases, including inflammatory bowel disease, psoriasis, and asthma.
   b. Excessive production of pro-inflammatory cytokines leads to sustained inflammation and tissue injury in affected organs.

4. **Hematological Disorders:**
   a. Mutations in JAK2 and other components of the JAK/STAT pathway are associated with hematological disorders, including myeloproliferative neoplasms and lymphoproliferative disorders.

b. Dysregulated JAK/STAT signaling disrupts hematopoietic cell homeostasis, leading to abnormal proliferation and differentiation of blood cells.

5. **Neurological Disorders:**

   a. Abnormal JAK/STAT signaling has been implicated in the pathogenesis of neurological disorders, such as Alzheimer's disease, Parkinson's disease, and multiple sclerosis.

   b. Dysregulated cytokine signaling and neuroinflammation contribute to neuronal dysfunction and neurodegeneration in these disorders.

Therapeutic Targeting of the JAK/STAT Pathway

Therapeutic targeting of the Janus kinase (JAK)/signal transducer and activator of transcription (STAT) pathway has emerged as a promising strategy for the treatment of various diseases, including cancer, autoimmune disorders, and inflammatory diseases. Here's a detailed exploration of the therapeutic approaches targeting the JAK/STAT pathway:

Therapeutic Targeting Strategies:

1. **JAK Inhibitors:**

   a. Small molecule inhibitors that selectively target JAKs have been developed as therapeutic agents.

   b. These inhibitors competitively bind to the ATP-binding pocket of JAKs, preventing their phosphorylation and activation.

   c. By inhibiting JAK activity, these inhibitors block downstream STAT activation and cytokine signaling.

   d. **Examples of JAK inhibitors approved for clinical use include:**

      i. **Ruxolitinib**: Approved for the treatment of myeloproliferative neoplasms, such as polycythemia vera and myelofibrosis.

      ii. **Tofacitinib:** Approved for the treatment of rheumatoid arthritis, psoriatic arthritis, and ulcerative colitis.

    iii. **Baricitinib:** Approved for the treatment of rheumatoid arthritis and atopic dermatitis.

    iv. **Upadacitinib:** Approved for the treatment of rheumatoid arthritis.

2. **STAT Inhibitors:**

   a. Direct inhibition of STAT proteins is challenging due to their lack of enzymatic activity and the absence of well-defined binding pockets.

   b. However, strategies to disrupt STAT-DNA interactions or interfere with protein-protein interactions involved in STAT signaling are being explored.

   c. Peptide inhibitors and small molecules that target STAT dimerization or DNA binding have shown potential in preclinical studies but have yet to reach clinical application.

3. **Cytokine Inhibitors:**

   a. Since cytokines are upstream regulators of the JAK/STAT pathway, blocking their activity can indirectly inhibit JAK/STAT signaling.

   b. Monoclonal antibodies or soluble receptors that neutralize cytokines have been developed as therapeutic agents.

   c. **Examples include:**

    i. Anti-TNF antibodies (e.g., adalimumab, infliximab) for the treatment of autoimmune diseases such as rheumatoid arthritis and inflammatory bowel disease.

    ii. Anti-IL-6 antibodies (e.g., tocilizumab) for the treatment of rheumatoid arthritis and cytokine release syndrome.

    iii. Anti-IL-23 antibodies (e.g., ustekinumab) for the treatment of psoriasis and inflammatory bowel disease.

4. **Combination Therapies:**

a. Combining JAK inhibitors with other targeted therapies or immunomodulatory agents has shown promise for enhancing therapeutic efficacy and overcoming resistance.

b. Combination therapies may target multiple nodes within the JAK/STAT pathway or synergistically inhibit complementary signaling pathways.

c. Clinical trials evaluating the efficacy of combination therapies in various diseases, including cancer and autoimmune disorders, are ongoing.

5. Biosimilars and Next-Generation Inhibitors:

a. Development of biosimilars of existing JAK inhibitors aims to increase treatment accessibility and reduce costs.

b. Next-generation JAK inhibitors with improved selectivity, pharmacokinetics, and safety profiles are also under development to address limitations of current therapies, such as off-target effects and adverse events.

MCQ Questions Based on the Context

1. What type of signaling involves cells responding to their own secreted molecules?

   A) Juxtacrine

   B) Endocrine

   C) Autocrine

   D) Paracrine

2. Which receptor type involves ligand binding that typically causes ion channels to open or close?

   A) G-Protein-Coupled Receptors (GPCRs)

   B) Nuclear Receptors

   C) Receptor Tyrosine Kinases (RTKs)

D) Ionotropic Receptors

3. Which pathway is involved in cell survival and metabolism and includes PI3K activation?

   A) JAK/STAT Pathway

   B) MAPK/ERK Pathway

   C) PI3K/AKT Pathway

   D) Calcium signaling pathway

4. Which molecule acts as a second messenger in Calcium signaling?

   A) cAMP

   B) DAG

   C) IP3

   D) ATP

5. How does the MAPK/ERK pathway primarily get activated?

   A) Through G-protein coupled receptors

   B) By cytokine receptors

   C) Via receptor tyrosine kinases

   D) Through nuclear receptors

6. What is the role of phosphodiesterases in cell signaling?

   A) Amplify the signal

   B) Bind to receptors

   C) Degrade cAMP

   D) Phosphorylate proteins

7. Which of the following is NOT a component of the JAK/STAT signaling pathway? A) JAK kinases

   B) SOCS proteins

   C) Adenylyl cyclase

   D) STAT transcription factors

8. In which signaling does Notch participate by direct cell-to-cell contact?

   A) Endocrine

B) Paracrine

C) Autocrine

D) Juxtacrine

9. What type of receptors are involved in the detection of light and odors?

   A) Ionotropic receptors

   B) GPCRs

   C) RTKs

   D) Nuclear receptors

10. Which pathway uses cyclic AMP as a second messenger?

    A) PI3K/AKT

    B) Calcium signaling

    C) cAMP signaling pathway

    D) IP3 signaling pathway

11. What is the primary mechanism of action for receptor tyrosine kinases?

    A) G-protein activation

    B) Dimerization and autophosphorylation

    C) Ligand-gated ion channel opening

    D) DNA binding

12. Which signaling molecule is involved in neurotransmission and muscle contraction, primarily by allowing Na+ and K+ ions to pass?

    A) Glutamate

    B) GABA

    C) Acetylcholine

    D) Dopamine

13. Which pathway involves the transcription factor CREB?

    A) MAPK/ERK

    B) cAMP

    C) Calcium signaling

    D) JAK/STAT

14. What is the typical composition of ligand-gated ion channels?

A) Single polypeptide

B) Two subunits

C) Four subunits

D) Five subunits

15. Which kinase is directly activated by cyclic AMP?

A) Protein kinase C

B) Protein kinase A

C) Protein kinase G

D) MAP Kinase

16. Which of the following is not a characteristic function of G-protein coupled receptors (GPCRs)?

A) Activating ion channels

B) Direct phosphorylation of proteins

C) Influencing cell metabolism

D) Detecting extracellular molecules

17. What role do nuclear receptors play in the cell?

A) Phosphorylate other proteins

B) Act as transcription factors

C) Act as second messengers

D) Open ion channels

18. What is primarily responsible for the inactivation of G-proteins?

A) Hydrolysis of GTP to GDP

B) Phosphorylation by kinases

C) Binding of secondary messengers

D) Ligand dissociation from the receptor

19. What is a key feature of autocrine signaling?

A) It involves signals from distant cells.

B) It involves signals that affect the secreting cell itself.

C) It requires hormonal signaling.

D) It relies solely on nuclear receptors.

20. Which type of cell signaling is characterized by the release of hormones into the bloodstream to affect distant cells?

A) Juxtacrine signaling

B) Autocrine signaling

C) Paracrine signaling

D) Endocrine signaling

Short Answer Type Questions

1. What are G-protein-coupled receptors (GPCRs) and how do they function?
2. Describe the role of second messengers in cell signaling.
3. What is the significance of the PI3K/AKT pathway in cell survival and metabolism?
4. Explain the function of receptor tyrosine kinases (RTKs) in cell signaling.
5. How do ionotropic receptors function and what role do they play in neurotransmission?
6. What is autocrine signaling and give an example?
7. Discuss the role of calcium ions as secondary messengers.
8. How is the JAK/STAT pathway activated?
9. Describe the role of MAPK/ERK pathway in cell differentiation.
10. What is receptor desensitization and how does it occur?
11. Explain the clinical relevance of targeting cell signaling pathways in disease treatment.
12. What are the physiological roles of cyclic AMP (cAMP) in cell signaling?
13. Describe the process of signal transduction in cell signaling.

14. How do nuclear receptors function differently from membrane-bound receptors?

15. What are protein kinase cascades and their significance in signaling pathways?

16. Explain how synaptic signaling works in neurons.

17. What mechanisms are involved in the termination of cell signaling?

18. Describe the role of phosphodiesterases in the regulation of signal pathways.

19. How do ligand-gated ion channels facilitate cellular responses to external signals?

20. What is the significance of the TGF-beta signaling pathway in cell regulation?

Long Answer Type Questions

1. Discuss the molecular mechanisms involved in the activation and regulation of the G-protein-coupled receptor (GPCR) signaling pathway and its impact on human health.

2. Explain the role and regulation of calcium signaling in cardiac function and how dysregulation can lead to disease states.

3. Describe the detailed mechanism of action of receptor tyrosine kinases and their role in cancer development.

4. Analyze the JAK/STAT signaling pathway, including its activation, function, and importance in immune system regulation.

5. Discuss the role of cyclic AMP (cAMP) in neuronal signaling and its implications for learning and memory.

6. Provide a detailed description of the MAPK/ERK signaling pathway, its components, and its role in cell growth and differentiation.

7. Elaborate on the physiological and pathological roles of the PI3K/AKT pathway, with particular emphasis on its implications in cancer therapy.

8. Explain how ionotropic receptors are structured and function in the nervous system, and discuss their role in neurological diseases.

9. Describe the mechanism by which nuclear receptors influence gene expression and their impact on metabolism and reproductive health.

10. Discuss the therapeutic targeting of cell signaling pathways, focusing on the use of kinase inhibitors in treating diseases such as cancer and rheumatoid arthritis.

Answer Key

1. C) Autocrine
2. D) Ionotropic Receptors
3. C) PI3K/AKT Pathway
4. C) IP3
5. C) Via receptor tyrosine kinases
6. C) Degrade cAMP
7. C) Adenylyl cyclase
8. D) Juxtacrine
9. B) GPCRs
10. C) cAMP signaling pathway
11. B) Dimerization and autophosphorylation
12. C) Acetylcholine
13. B) cAMP
14. D) Five subunits
15. B) Protein kinase A
16. B) Direct phosphorylation of proteins
17. B) Act as transcription factors
18. A) Hydrolysis of GTP to GDP
19. B) It involves signals that affect the secreting cell itself.
20. D) Endocrine signaling

CHAPTER – 3

PHARMACOLOGY OF DRUGS ACTING ON URINARY SYSTEM

INTRODUCTION

Pharmacology of drugs acting on the urinary system encompasses the study of medications that influence renal function, bladder control, and other aspects of the urinary tract. These drugs can be categorized based on their primary therapeutic actions, such as diuretics, anticholinergics, and medications for benign prostatic hyperplasia (BPH), among others. Here, we will discuss these categories in detail, including their mechanisms of action, indications, adverse effects, and examples of drugs in each class.

1. Diuretics

Diuretics are drugs that promote the excretion of urine. They are used primarily to treat conditions such as hypertension, heart failure, and certain kidney disorders.

a. Thiazide Diuretics

i. **Mechanism of Action**: Inhibit the sodium-chloride symporter in the distal convoluted tubule, leading to increased excretion of sodium and water.

ii. **Examples**: Hydrochlorothiazide, chlorthalidone.

iii. **Indications**: Hypertension, heart failure, edema.

iv. **Adverse Effects**: Hypokalemia, hyperglycemia, hyperlipidemia, hyperuricemia.

b. Loop Diuretics

i. **Mechanism of Action**: Inhibit the sodium-potassium-chloride cotransporter in the thick ascending limb of the loop of Henle.

ii. **Examples**: Furosemide, bumetanide, torsemide.

iii. **Indications**: Acute pulmonary edema, chronic heart failure, hypercalcemia.

iv. **Adverse Effects**: Hypokalemia, ototoxicity, dehydration, metabolic alkalosis.

c. Potassium-Sparing Diuretics

a. **Mechanism of Action**: Inhibit sodium reabsorption in the distal convoluted tubule and collecting duct while conserving potassium.

b. **Examples**: Spironolactone, eplerenone, amiloride, triamterene.

c. **Indications**: Heart failure, hypertension, edema.

d. **Adverse Effects**: Hyperkalemia, gynecomastia (spironolactone).

2. Anticholinergics

Anticholinergic drugs are used to treat overactive bladder and urinary incontinence by reducing bladder spasms and urinary urgency.

a. **Mechanism of Action**: Block muscarinic receptors in the bladder, reducing involuntary contractions.

b. **Examples**: Oxybutynin, tolterodine, solifenacin, darifenacin.

c. **Indications**: Overactive bladder, urinary incontinence.

d. **Adverse Effects**: Dry mouth, constipation, blurred vision, cognitive dysfunction.

3. Alpha-Blockers

Alpha-blockers are used primarily to treat symptoms of benign prostatic hyperplasia (BPH).

a. **Mechanism of Action**: Block alpha-1 adrenergic receptors in the smooth muscle of the prostate and bladder neck, reducing urinary obstruction.

b. **Examples**: Tamsulosin, alfuzosin, doxazosin, terazosin.

c. **Indications**: BPH, hypertension (some agents).

d. **Adverse Effects**: Orthostatic hypotension, dizziness, headache, ejaculation disorders.

4. 5-Alpha Reductase Inhibitors

These drugs are used to treat BPH by reducing the size of the prostate gland.

a. **Mechanism of Action**: Inhibit the enzyme 5-alpha reductase, which converts testosterone to dihydrotestosterone (DHT), a potent androgen involved in prostate growth.

b. **Examples**: Finasteride, dutasteride.

c. **Indications**: BPH.

d. **Adverse Effects**: Sexual dysfunction, decreased libido, gynecomastia.

5. Phosphodiesterase-5 Inhibitors

Originally developed for erectile dysfunction, these drugs are also used in the treatment of BPH.

a. **Mechanism of Action**: Inhibit phosphodiesterase-5 (PDE-5), leading to relaxation of smooth muscle in the bladder and prostate.

b. **Examples**: Tadalafil.

c. **Indications**: BPH, erectile dysfunction.

d. **Adverse Effects**: Headache, flushing, dyspepsia, nasal congestion.

6. Desmopressin

Desmopressin is a synthetic analog of the hormone vasopressin, used to treat conditions like nocturnal enuresis (bedwetting).

a. **Mechanism of Action**: Increases water reabsorption in the kidneys by acting on V2 receptors in the collecting ducts.

b. **Examples**: Desmopressin acetate.

c. **Indications**: Nocturnal enuresis, diabetes insipidus.

d. **Adverse Effects**: Hyponatremia, headache, nausea.

7. Antimicrobial Agents

Antimicrobials are used to treat urinary tract infections (UTIs).

a. **Mechanism of Action**: Varies by drug; includes inhibition of bacterial cell wall synthesis, protein synthesis, or DNA replication.

b. **Examples**: Trimethoprim/sulfamethoxazole, ciprofloxacin, nitrofurantoin, fosfomycin.

c. **Indications**: UTIs.

d. **Adverse Effects**: Varies by drug; includes gastrointestinal upset, allergic reactions, antibiotic resistance.

DIURETICS

Definition:

Diuretics are a class of drugs that promote the excretion of water and electrolytes (primarily sodium) from the body through the urine. They achieve this by inhibiting the reabsorption of sodium and other ions in the kidneys, which in turn increases urine production and decreases fluid retention. Diuretics are commonly used to treat conditions associated with fluid overload, such as hypertension, heart failure, liver cirrhosis, and certain kidney disorders. Here is a detailed definition and description of diuretics, including their mechanisms of action, types, therapeutic uses, and potential side effects.

Types of Diuretics

A. Thiazide Diuretics:

Thiazide diuretics are a class of medications primarily used to manage hypertension and edema. They work by inhibiting sodium and chloride reabsorption in the distal convoluted tubule of the nephron. This inhibition leads to increased excretion of sodium and water, reducing blood volume and blood pressure.

Mechanism of Action

1. **Site of Action**: Distal convoluted tubule of the nephron.

2. **Target**: Sodium-chloride symporter (NCC).

3. **Process**:

   a. Thiazide diuretics bind to and inhibit the sodium-chloride symporter on the luminal surface of the distal convoluted tubule cells.

   b. This inhibition prevents sodium ($Na+$) and chloride ($Cl-$) ions from being reabsorbed back into the bloodstream.

c. The retention of sodium and chloride in the tubule creates an osmotic gradient that favors water retention in the tubule, increasing urine volume.

Pharmacokinetics

1. **Absorption**: Thiazide diuretics are well absorbed orally.
2. **Distribution**: They distribute widely throughout the body, often binding to plasma proteins.
3. **Metabolism**: Some thiazide diuretics are metabolized in the liver, while others are excreted unchanged.
4. **Excretion**: Primarily excreted by the kidneys.

Common Thiazide Diuretics

1. **Hydrochlorothiazide (HCTZ)**: One of the most commonly prescribed thiazides.
2. **Chlorthalidone**: Longer half-life than hydrochlorothiazide, often used for hypertension.
3. **Indapamide**: Has additional vasodilatory effects.
4. **Metolazone**: Can be used in combination with loop diuretics for synergistic effects.

Indications

1. **Hypertension**: First-line treatment for managing high blood pressure.
2. **Heart Failure**: Used to manage fluid overload and reduce symptoms.
3. **Edema**: Associated with conditions such as liver cirrhosis, kidney disorders, and chronic heart failure.
4. **Nephrogenic Diabetes Insipidus**: Helps reduce urine volume by inducing mild hypovolemia, which increases proximal tubular reabsorption of sodium and water.
5. **Calcium Nephrolithiasis**: Can reduce hypercalciuria (excessive calcium in the urine), decreasing the risk of kidney stones.

Adverse Effects

1. **Electrolyte Imbalances**:
   a. **Hypokalemia**: Low potassium levels, leading to muscle weakness, cramps, and arrhythmias.
   b. **Hyponatremia**: Low sodium levels, which can cause confusion, seizures, and coma.
   c. **Hypomagnesemia**: Low magnesium levels, contributing to muscle weakness and cramps.
   d. **Hypercalcemia**: High calcium levels, which is beneficial in some cases but can be problematic if excessive.
2. **Metabolic Effects**:
   a. **Hyperglycemia**: Increase in blood glucose levels, potentially problematic for diabetics.
   b. **Hyperlipidemia**: Increase in cholesterol and triglyceride levels.
   c. **Hyperuricemia**: Elevated uric acid levels, increasing the risk of gout.
3. **Others**:
   a. **Photosensitivity**: Increased sensitivity to sunlight.
   b. **Orthostatic Hypotension**: A drop in blood pressure upon standing, leading to dizziness and fainting.

Mechanisms of Side Effects

1. **Hypokalemia**: Caused by increased delivery of sodium to the distal tubule, where it is reabsorbed in exchange for potassium, leading to increased potassium excretion.
2. **Hyperglycemia**: Thiazides can impair insulin release and decrease tissue sensitivity to insulin.
3. **Hyperuricemia**: Thiazides compete with uric acid for secretion in the proximal tubule, leading to reduced uric acid excretion.
4. **Hyponatremia**: Resulting from the diuretic effect causing dilution of sodium in the body.

Monitoring and Management

1. **Electrolytes**: Regular monitoring of blood electrolytes (sodium, potassium, calcium, and magnesium) is essential to avoid severe imbalances.
2. **Renal Function**: Kidney function tests (serum creatinine and blood urea nitrogen) should be monitored, especially in patients with pre-existing renal impairment.
3. **Blood Pressure**: Regular monitoring to ensure the desired antihypertensive effect.
4. **Blood Glucose and Lipid Levels**: Monitoring in patients with diabetes or dyslipidemia.

Drug Interactions

1. **Lithium**: Thiazides can reduce lithium clearance, increasing the risk of lithium toxicity.
2. **NSAIDs**: Nonsteroidal anti-inflammatory drugs can reduce the diuretic and antihypertensive effects of thiazides.
3. **Antidiabetic Medications**: Thiazides may diminish the effects of antidiabetic drugs, requiring adjustments in therapy.
4. **ACE Inhibitors and ARBs**: Combined use can enhance antihypertensive effects but increases the risk of hyperkalemia.

B. Loop Diuretics

Loop diuretics are potent diuretics used primarily to treat conditions associated with fluid overload, such as heart failure, edema, and hypertension. They exert their effects by inhibiting the sodium-potassium-chloride cotransporter in the thick ascending limb of the loop of Henle, leading to significant increases in the excretion of sodium, chloride, and water.

Mechanism of Action

1. **Site of Action**: Thick ascending limb of the loop of Henle.
2. **Target**: Sodium-potassium-chloride cotransporter (NKCC2).
3. **Process**:

a. Loop diuretics bind to and inhibit the NKCC2 transporter on the luminal membrane of the cells in the thick ascending limb.

b. This inhibition prevents the reabsorption of sodium (Na+), potassium (K+), and chloride (Cl-) ions from the tubular fluid into the bloodstream.

c. The increase in tubular sodium concentration leads to an osmotic retention of water within the tubule, resulting in increased urine volume.

d. The inhibition of sodium reabsorption disrupts the countercurrent multiplier system, reducing the kidney's ability to concentrate urine and leading to the excretion of large volumes of dilute urine.

Pharmacokinetics

1. **Absorption**: Loop diuretics are well absorbed orally but can also be administered intravenously for rapid action.

2. **Distribution**: Widely distributed in the body, often binding to plasma proteins.

3. **Metabolism**: Variable metabolism; some loop diuretics are minimally metabolized while others undergo significant hepatic metabolism.

4. **Excretion**: Primarily excreted by the kidneys.

Common Loop Diuretics

1. **Furosemide (Lasix)**: Widely used for acute and chronic management of fluid overload.

2. **Bumetanide**: More potent than furosemide on a per-milligram basis.

3. **Torsemide**: Longer half-life and duration of action compared to furosemide.

4. **Ethacrynic Acid**: Used in patients who are allergic to sulfonamide-based diuretics.

Indications

1. **Heart Failure**: To manage pulmonary and systemic edema by reducing fluid overload.

2. **Edema**: Associated with liver cirrhosis, nephrotic syndrome, and chronic kidney disease.

3. **Hypertension**: Particularly in patients with renal impairment or resistant hypertension.

4. **Acute Pulmonary Edema**: Rapid reduction of fluid accumulation in the lungs.

5. **Hypercalcemia**: To promote calcium excretion.

6. **Acute Renal Failure**: To stimulate urine production in oliguric states.

Adverse Effects

1. **Electrolyte Imbalances**:
    a. **Hypokalemia**: Low potassium levels, leading to muscle weakness, cramps, and cardiac arrhythmias.
    b. **Hyponatremia**: Low sodium levels, causing confusion, seizures, and coma.
    c. **Hypocalcemia**: Low calcium levels, which can cause muscle spasms and cardiac issues.
    d. **Hypomagnesemia**: Low magnesium levels, contributing to muscle cramps and arrhythmias.

2. **Dehydration**: Excessive fluid loss can lead to dehydration and hypotension.

3. **Ototoxicity**: Hearing loss or tinnitus, particularly with high doses or rapid IV administration.

4. **Hyperuricemia**: Elevated uric acid levels, increasing the risk of gout.

5. **Metabolic Effects**:
    a. **Hyperglycemia**: Increase in blood glucose levels.
    b. **Hyperlipidemia**: Increase in cholesterol and triglyceride levels.

6. **Other Effects**:
    a. **Allergic Reactions**: Particularly with sulfonamide-based diuretics.
    b. **Photosensitivity**: Increased sensitivity to sunlight.

Mechanisms of Side Effects

1. **Hypokalemia**: Increased sodium delivery to the distal nephron enhances sodium reabsorption in exchange for potassium excretion.
2. **Ototoxicity**: Direct toxic effects on the inner ear structures, especially at high doses.
3. **Hyperuricemia**: Competition between loop diuretics and uric acid for secretion in the proximal tubule.
4. **Hyperglycemia and Hyperlipidemia**: Potential interference with insulin secretion and lipid metabolism.

Monitoring and Management

1. **Electrolytes**: Regular monitoring of blood electrolytes (sodium, potassium, calcium, magnesium) is crucial to prevent severe imbalances.
2. **Renal Function**: Assess kidney function tests (serum creatinine and blood urea nitrogen) to detect any impairment.
3. **Hearing**: Monitor for signs of ototoxicity, especially in patients receiving high doses or rapid IV infusions.
4. **Fluid Balance**: Ensure adequate hydration and monitor for signs of dehydration.

Drug Interactions

1. **NSAIDs**: Can reduce the efficacy of loop diuretics by decreasing renal blood flow and inhibiting prostaglandin synthesis.
2. **Aminoglycosides**: Combined use increases the risk of ototoxicity.
3. **Digoxin**: Increased risk of digoxin toxicity in the presence of hypokalemia.
4. **Corticosteroids**: Can exacerbate hypokalemia.
5. **Lithium**: Reduced clearance of lithium, leading to potential toxicity.

C. Potassium-Sparing Diuretics

Potassium-sparing diuretics are a class of medications used to promote diuresis (increased urine production) without causing significant potassium loss, a common issue with other diuretic classes. They are often used in combination with other diuretics to counteract hypokalemia (low potassium levels).

Mechanism of Action

Potassium-sparing diuretics work by either antagonizing the action of aldosterone or directly blocking sodium channels in the distal convoluted tubule and collecting duct of the nephron.

1. **Aldosterone Antagonists**:
    a. **Examples**: Spironolactone, Eplerenone.
    b. **Mechanism**: These drugs bind to and inhibit the mineralocorticoid receptor, which is normally activated by aldosterone. Aldosterone promotes sodium reabsorption and potassium excretion. By blocking its action, these drugs decrease sodium reabsorption and increase potassium retention.
2. **Sodium Channel Blockers**:
    a. **Examples**: Amiloride, Triamterene.
    b. **Mechanism**: These drugs directly block epithelial sodium channels (ENaC) in the distal convoluted tubule and collecting duct. This action prevents sodium reabsorption and reduces the electrochemical gradient that drives potassium excretion, thus sparing potassium.

Pharmacokinetics

1. **Absorption**: Well absorbed orally.
2. **Distribution**: Widely distributed in body tissues.
3. **Metabolism**:
    a. **Spironolactone** is metabolized in the liver to active metabolites.
    b. **Eplerenone** undergoes hepatic metabolism.
    c. **Amiloride** and **Triamterene** have minimal hepatic metabolism.
4. **Excretion**: Primarily renal, with variable excretion rates depending on the specific drug.

Common Potassium-Sparing Diuretics

1. **Spironolactone**:
   a. **Uses**: Heart failure, hypertension, primary hyperaldosteronism, polycystic ovary syndrome (PCOS).
   b. **Side Effects**: Hyperkalemia, gynecomastia, menstrual irregularities, impotence.
2. **Eplerenone**:
   a. **Uses**: Heart failure post-myocardial infarction, hypertension.
   b. **Side Effects**: Hyperkalemia, fewer endocrine side effects compared to spironolactone.
3. **Amiloride**:
   a. **Uses**: Edema, hypertension (often in combination with thiazide or loop diuretics).
   b. **Side Effects**: Hyperkalemia, gastrointestinal disturbances.
4. **Triamterene**:
   a. **Uses**: Edema, hypertension (often in combination with thiazide or loop diuretics).
   b. **Side Effects**: Hyperkalemia, nephrotoxicity (rare), kidney stones.

Indications

1. **Heart Failure**: To manage fluid retention and reduce the risk of hypokalemia.
2. **Hypertension**: Often used in combination with thiazide or loop diuretics to prevent potassium loss.
3. **Edema**: Associated with conditions like liver cirrhosis and nephrotic syndrome.
4. **Primary Hyperaldosteronism**: To counteract the effects of excessive aldosterone.
5. **Polycystic Ovary Syndrome (PCOS)**: Spironolactone is used for its anti-androgen effects.

Adverse Effects

1. **Hyperkalemia**: Elevated potassium levels, which can cause muscle weakness, cardiac arrhythmias, and even cardiac arrest.
2. **Endocrine Effects** (specific to spironolactone):
    a. **Gynecomastia**: Development of breast tissue in men.
    b. **Menstrual Irregularities**: In women, due to anti-androgenic effects.
    c. **Impotence**: Sexual dysfunction in men.
3. **Gastrointestinal Disturbances**: Nausea, vomiting, diarrhea.
4. **Nephrotoxicity** (rare): Specifically with triamterene, leading to kidney stones.

Mechanisms of Side Effects

1. **Hyperkalemia**: Due to reduced potassium excretion.
2. **Endocrine Effects**: Spironolactone's structure is similar to steroid hormones, allowing it to bind to androgen and progesterone receptors, leading to hormonal side effects.
3. **Nephrotoxicity**: Triamterene can precipitate in the urine, potentially causing kidney stones.

Monitoring and Management

1. **Electrolytes**: Regular monitoring of potassium levels to detect hyperkalemia.
2. **Renal Function**: Monitoring of serum creatinine and blood urea nitrogen (BUN) to assess kidney function.
3. **Blood Pressure**: Regular monitoring to ensure therapeutic effectiveness.
4. **Endocrine Symptoms**: Observing for signs of gynecomastia, menstrual irregularities, or impotence.

Drug Interactions

1. **ACE Inhibitors and ARBs**: Concurrent use increases the risk of hyperkalemia.
2. **NSAIDs**: Can reduce the effectiveness of diuretics and increase the risk of hyperkalemia.

3. **Potassium Supplements**: Increase the risk of hyperkalemia when used with potassium-sparing diuretics.

4. **Lithium**: Potassium-sparing diuretics can increase lithium levels and the risk of toxicity.

D. Carbonic Anhydrase Inhibitors

Carbonic anhydrase inhibitors (CAIs) are a class of diuretics that act on the proximal convoluted tubule of the nephron to inhibit the enzyme carbonic anhydrase. This inhibition reduces the reabsorption of bicarbonate, leading to increased excretion of sodium, bicarbonate, and water. These diuretics are less potent compared to others like loop diuretics or thiazides and are primarily used for specific medical conditions.

Mechanism of Action

1. **Site of Action**: Proximal convoluted tubule of the nephron.

2. **Target**: Carbonic anhydrase enzyme.

3. **Process**:

    a. Carbonic anhydrase facilitates the conversion of carbon dioxide (CO_2) and water (H_2O) to carbonic acid (H_2CO_3), which dissociates into bicarbonate (HCO_3^-) and hydrogen ions (H^+).

    b. CAIs inhibit this enzyme, reducing the formation of bicarbonate and hydrogen ions.

    c. Reduced availability of hydrogen ions limits the sodium-hydrogen exchange (NHE3), decreasing sodium reabsorption.

    d. Bicarbonate, sodium, and water are retained in the tubular fluid and excreted as urine.

    e. This results in alkaline urine and mild diuresis.

Pharmacokinetics

1. **Absorption**: Well absorbed orally.

2. **Distribution**: Distributed throughout the body, including to the eye (useful for glaucoma treatment).

3. **Metabolism**: Minimal hepatic metabolism.

4. **Excretion**: Primarily excreted unchanged by the kidneys.

Common Carbonic Anhydrase Inhibitors

1. **Acetazolamide**: The most commonly used CAI.

2. **Methazolamide**: Similar to acetazolamide but with a longer duration of action.

3. **Dorzolamide**: Used topically in the form of eye drops for glaucoma.

Indications

1. **Glaucoma**: Reduces intraocular pressure by decreasing aqueous humor production.

2. **Mountain Sickness**: Prevents and treats altitude sickness by inducing metabolic acidosis, which stimulates ventilation.

3. **Epilepsy**: Adjunctive therapy for certain types of seizures.

4. **Edema**: Rarely used for edema due to its weak diuretic effect but can be used in combination with other diuretics.

5. **Metabolic Alkalosis**: Used to correct alkalosis by increasing bicarbonate excretion.

Adverse Effects

1. **Metabolic Acidosis**: Due to increased bicarbonate excretion and decreased reabsorption, leading to systemic acidosis.

2. **Electrolyte Imbalances**:

   a. **Hypokalemia**: Increased sodium delivery to the distal nephron enhances potassium excretion.

   b. **Hyponatremia**: Reduced sodium reabsorption can lead to low sodium levels.

3. **Renal Effects**:

a. **Kidney Stones**: Increased excretion of calcium and phosphate can lead to the formation of renal calculi.

4. **Gastrointestinal Disturbances**: Nausea, vomiting, diarrhea.

5. **CNS Effects**: Paresthesia, drowsiness, confusion.

6. **Allergic Reactions**: Rash, fever, interstitial nephritis, particularly in patients allergic to sulfonamides.

Mechanisms of Side Effects

1. **Metabolic Acidosis**: Inhibition of carbonic anhydrase reduces bicarbonate reabsorption, leading to a decrease in blood bicarbonate levels.

2. **Hypokalemia**: Increased delivery of sodium to the distal nephron promotes potassium excretion.

3. **Kidney Stones**: Increased urinary pH and excretion of calcium and phosphate can promote stone formation.

Monitoring and Management

1. **Electrolytes**: Regular monitoring of blood electrolytes (sodium, potassium, bicarbonate) to detect imbalances.

2. **Renal Function**: Monitoring serum creatinine and blood urea nitrogen (BUN) to assess kidney function.

3. **Blood Gas Analysis**: To monitor acid-base status, particularly in patients at risk of metabolic acidosis.

4. **Eye Examination**: Regular intraocular pressure checks for patients using CAIs for glaucoma.

Drug Interactions

1. **Salicylates**: Can increase the risk of metabolic acidosis when used with CAIs.

2. **Amphetamines**: Reduced excretion of amphetamines, leading to increased effects.

3. **Quinidine**: Increased risk of toxicity due to decreased renal excretion.

4. **Lithium**: Decreased renal clearance of lithium, increasing the risk of toxicity.

E. Osmotic Diuretics

Osmotic diuretics are a unique class of diuretics that work by increasing the osmolarity of the glomerular filtrate, which inhibits the reabsorption of water and electrolytes in the renal tubules. They are primarily used in medical situations requiring rapid diuresis, such as reducing intracranial pressure or treating acute renal failure.

Mechanism of Action

1. **Site of Action**: Primarily the proximal convoluted tubule and the descending limb of the loop of Henle.
2. **Mechanism**:
   a. Osmotic diuretics are freely filtered by the glomerulus but are not reabsorbed by the renal tubules.
   b. They increase the osmolarity of the filtrate, which reduces water reabsorption by creating an osmotic gradient.
   c. The increased osmolarity also hinders the reabsorption of sodium and other electrolytes.
   d. This results in an increased volume of urine that contains a higher concentration of electrolytes and water.

Pharmacokinetics

1. **Absorption**: Poorly absorbed from the gastrointestinal tract; thus, they are typically administered intravenously.
2. **Distribution**: Distribute throughout the extracellular fluid compartment but do not cross cell membranes easily.
3. **Metabolism**: They are not metabolized to a significant extent.
4. **Excretion**: Excreted unchanged by the kidneys.

Common Osmotic Diuretics

1. **Mannitol**: The most commonly used osmotic diuretic.

2. **Glycerin**: Used orally for its osmotic effects.

3. **Isosorbide**: Another osmotic diuretic used for similar indications.

4. **Urea**: Less commonly used due to its side effects and availability of better options.

Indications

1. **Cerebral Edema**: To reduce intracranial pressure in conditions like traumatic brain injury or brain surgery.

2. **Glaucoma**: To reduce intraocular pressure during acute glaucoma attacks.

3. **Acute Renal Failure**: To initiate and maintain urine flow in oliguric states.

4. **Toxic Ingestions**: To promote the excretion of toxic substances in certain poisonings.

5. **Prevention of Renal Failure**: In patients undergoing major surgeries or receiving nephrotoxic drugs.

Adverse Effects

1. **Electrolyte Imbalances**:
   a. **Hyponatremia**: Initially, due to dilutional effects as water is drawn into the intravascular space.
   b. **Hypernatremia**: With prolonged use, due to excessive water loss.

2. **Volume Overload**: Can lead to pulmonary edema and heart failure, particularly in patients with compromised cardiac function.

3. **Dehydration**: Excessive diuresis can lead to dehydration.

4. **Acute Kidney Injury**: In patients with pre-existing kidney conditions, mannitol can precipitate acute kidney injury.

5. **Headache, Nausea, and Vomiting**: Common due to rapid shifts in fluid balance.

Mechanisms of Side Effects

1. **Electrolyte Imbalances**: Caused by changes in the osmolarity of body fluids and the differential excretion of water and electrolytes.

2. **Volume Overload**: The rapid influx of fluid into the bloodstream can overwhelm the cardiovascular system.

3. **Dehydration**: Excessive loss of body water without adequate replacement.

Monitoring and Management

1. **Electrolytes**: Frequent monitoring of blood sodium, potassium, and other electrolytes.

2. **Renal Function**: Monitoring serum creatinine and blood urea nitrogen (BUN) to assess kidney function.

3. **Fluid Balance**: Monitoring input and output to detect signs of volume overload or dehydration.

4. **Neurological Status**: For patients with cerebral edema, monitoring for changes in intracranial pressure and neurological signs.

Drug Interactions

1. **Nephrotoxic Agents**: Concurrent use can increase the risk of kidney damage.

2. **Lithium**: Can increase the excretion of lithium, reducing its effectiveness.

3. **Other Diuretics**: Combined use with other diuretics can exacerbate electrolyte imbalances and dehydration.

Mechanism of Action of Diuretics

The mechanism of action of diuretics involves altering the handling of electrolytes and water in the nephron, the functional unit of the kidney, to promote increased urine production. Each class of diuretics acts on a specific segment of the nephron, leading to distinctive effects on electrolyte reabsorption and excretion. Here's a detailed exploration of the mechanisms of action for the various classes of diuretics:

1. Thiazide Diuretics

Site of Action: Distal convoluted tubule

Mechanism:

a. Thiazide diuretics inhibit the sodium-chloride symporter (NCC) in the distal convoluted tubule.

b. This inhibition reduces the reabsorption of sodium (Na+) and chloride (Cl-) ions, leading to increased excretion of these ions in the urine.

c. The resultant reduction in sodium reabsorption also decreases water reabsorption, thus increasing urine volume.

d. Thiazides also promote potassium excretion indirectly, which can lead to hypokalemia.

Effects:

a. Increased sodium and water excretion

b. Reduction in blood volume and blood pressure

c. Potential hypokalemia and metabolic alkalosis

2. Loop Diuretics

Site of Action: Thick ascending limb of the loop of Henle

Mechanism:

a. Loop diuretics inhibit the sodium-potassium-chloride cotransporter (NKCC2) in the thick ascending limb of the loop of Henle.

b. This inhibition leads to a significant increase in the excretion of sodium, chloride, and potassium, along with water.

c. By disrupting the reabsorption of these ions, loop diuretics effectively prevent the kidneys from concentrating the urine, resulting in large volumes of dilute urine.

d. The action of loop diuretics also reduces the reabsorption of calcium and magnesium.

Effects:

a. Profound diuresis and natriuresis (sodium excretion)

b. Reduction in blood volume and edema

c. Potential hypokalemia, hypocalcemia, hypomagnesemia, and metabolic alkalosis

d. Possible ototoxicity with high doses or rapid administration

3. Potassium-Sparing Diuretics

Site of Action: Distal convoluted tubule and collecting duct

Mechanism:

a. **Aldosterone antagonists (e.g., Spironolactone, Eplerenone)**:

    i. These drugs block the action of aldosterone at mineralocorticoid receptors in the distal convoluted tubule and collecting duct.

    ii. Aldosterone promotes sodium reabsorption and potassium excretion, so its inhibition leads to decreased sodium reabsorption and reduced potassium excretion.

b. **Sodium channel blockers (e.g., Amiloride, Triamterene)**:

    i. These drugs directly inhibit epithelial sodium channels (ENaC) in the distal convoluted tubule and collecting duct.

    ii. This reduces sodium reabsorption and potassium excretion.

Effects:

a. Increased sodium and water excretion

b. Retention of potassium, reducing the risk of hypokalemia

c. Potential hyperkalemia, particularly in patients with renal impairment or those taking other medications that increase potassium levels

4. Carbonic Anhydrase Inhibitors

Site of Action: Proximal convoluted tubule

Mechanism:

a. Carbonic anhydrase inhibitors (e.g., Acetazolamide) inhibit the enzyme carbonic anhydrase in the proximal convoluted tubule.

b. This enzyme is crucial for the reabsorption of bicarbonate (HCO_3^-) and sodium.

c. Inhibition of carbonic anhydrase leads to increased excretion of bicarbonate, sodium, and water, resulting in alkaline urine.

Effects:

   a. Mild diuresis and natriuresis

   b. Reduction in the reabsorption of bicarbonate, leading to metabolic acidosis

   c. Potential hypokalemia and renal stone formation

5. Osmotic Diuretics

Site of Action: Throughout the nephron, primarily the proximal convoluted tubule and loop of Henle

Mechanism:

   a. Osmotic diuretics (e.g., Mannitol) are filtered by the glomerulus but not reabsorbed by the renal tubules.

   b. Their presence in the filtrate increases the osmolarity of the tubular fluid, which hinders water reabsorption.

   c. This leads to an increase in urine volume as water is retained in the tubules to balance the osmotic pressure.

Effects:

   a. Increased urine output and excretion of electrolytes (sodium, potassium)

   b. Reduction in intracranial and intraocular pressure

   c. Potential for dehydration and electrolyte imbalances

Summary of Diuretic Actions

1. **Thiazide Diuretics**: Inhibit sodium-chloride symporter in the distal convoluted tubule, leading to moderate diuresis and potential hypokalemia.

2. **Loop Diuretics**: Inhibit sodium-potassium-chloride cotransporter in the thick ascending limb, causing profound diuresis and potential electrolyte imbalances including hypokalemia and hypocalcemia.

3. **Potassium-Sparing Diuretics**: Either antagonize aldosterone or block epithelial sodium channels in the distal tubule and collecting duct, leading to mild diuresis and potassium retention.

4. **Carbonic Anhydrase Inhibitors**: Inhibit carbonic anhydrase in the proximal convoluted tubule, causing increased bicarbonate excretion and mild diuresis.

5. **Osmotic Diuretics**: Increase tubular fluid osmolarity, preventing water reabsorption and leading to significant diuresis.

Clinical Implications

The choice of diuretic depends on the specific clinical scenario, the underlying condition being treated, and the patient's individual characteristics. Understanding the mechanisms of action helps in predicting the therapeutic effects and potential side effects, which is crucial for optimizing patient care and management.

Potential Side Effects

1. **Electrolyte Imbalance**: Hypokalemia, hyponatremia, hypocalcemia, hypomagnesemia.

2. **Dehydration**: Excessive diuresis can lead to dehydration and reduced blood volume.

3. **Metabolic Effects**: Hyperglycemia, hyperlipidemia, hyperuricemia.

4. **Ototoxicity**: Hearing loss, especially with loop diuretics.

5. **Other Effects**: Gynecomastia, menstrual irregularities, impotence, gastrointestinal disturbances.

Conclusion

Diuretics are crucial in managing various conditions related to fluid overload and hypertension. Their effectiveness and safety profile depend on the type of diuretic, the specific medical condition being treated, and individual patient factors. Understanding the mechanisms, uses, and potential side effects of diuretics is essential for their optimal therapeutic use.

ANTI-DIURETICS

Anti-diuretic drugs, also known as antidiuretics or antidiuretic hormones (ADHs), are medications or hormones that reduce urine production by increasing water reabsorption in the kidneys. The primary antidiuretic hormone in the body is vasopressin, also known as arginine vasopressin (AVP) or antidiuretic hormone (ADH). Synthetic analogs of vasopressin are used therapeutically to treat conditions associated with excessive urination and fluid imbalance. The most commonly used synthetic analog is desmopressin (DDAVP).

Classification of anti- diuretics:

Anti-diuretics, also known as antidiuretic agents or antidiuretic drugs, refer to medications or hormones that reduce urine production and promote water retention in the body. They are used to treat conditions where excessive urine output (polyuria) is problematic, such as diabetes insipidus or certain types of kidney disease. Anti-diuretics can be classified based on their mechanisms of action and include:

1. Vasopressin Analogues

Vasopressin (also known as antidiuretic hormone, ADH) and its analogues mimic the action of endogenous vasopressin in the body. Vasopressin acts on V2 receptors in the kidney to increase water reabsorption, thereby reducing urine output.

a. **Desmopressin (DDAVP):**

    i. **Mechanism**: Selective V2 receptor agonist.

    ii. **Clinical Use**: Diabetes insipidus, nocturnal enuresis (bedwetting), and in some cases of bleeding disorders (to promote clotting).

    iii. **Administration**: Can be given orally, intranasally, or intravenously.

2. V2 Receptor Agonists

These agents specifically target the V2 receptors in the kidneys, promoting water reabsorption without significant effects on vasoconstriction.

a. **Desmopressin (DDAVP)**: As mentioned above, it is a synthetic analogue of vasopressin.

3. Aquaretics

Aquaretics enhance water excretion without affecting electrolyte balance, often through mechanisms that differ from traditional diuretics.

a. **Aquaretics**: These are not commonly used clinically and are more often a topic of research.

Mechanism of Action

Anti-diuretics are agents that reduce urine production by promoting water reabsorption in the kidneys. The primary mechanism involves the action of the hormone vasopressin (antidiuretic hormone, ADH) and its analogues. The detailed mechanisms are outlined below:

Vasopressin and Vasopressin Analogues

1. Vasopressin (Antidiuretic Hormone, ADH):

a. **Source**: Produced in the hypothalamus and released from the posterior pituitary gland.

b. **Receptors**: Acts on V2 receptors located in the renal collecting ducts.

Mechanism:

a. **Binding to V2 Receptors**:
   i. Vasopressin binds to V2 receptors on the basolateral membrane of the renal collecting duct cells.

b. **Activation of Adenylate Cyclase**:
   i. This binding activates the enzyme adenylate cyclase, which increases the intracellular concentration of cyclic AMP (cAMP).

c. **Activation of Protein Kinase A (PKA)**:
   i. The rise in cAMP activates protein kinase A (PKA).

d. **Translocation of Aquaporin-2 Channels**:
   i. PKA phosphorylates specific proteins that lead to the insertion of aquaporin-2 (AQP2) water channels into the apical (luminal) membrane of the collecting duct cells.

e. **Increased Water Reabsorption**:

      i.   Aquaporin-2 channels facilitate the reabsorption of water from the tubular fluid into the cells, and then into the bloodstream, reducing urine volume.

  f. **Concentrated Urine**:

      i.   As a result, water is reabsorbed, leading to a decrease in urine volume and an increase in urine concentration.

Desmopressin (DDAVP):

a. **Type**: Synthetic analogue of vasopressin.

b. **Receptors**: Highly selective for V2 receptors, with minimal activity on V1 receptors (which mediate vasoconstriction).

c. **Use**: Preferred in treating conditions like central diabetes insipidus, nocturnal enuresis, and certain bleeding disorders.

Mechanism: Similar to that of vasopressin, desmopressin increases water reabsorption by promoting the insertion of AQP2 channels in the collecting ducts.

Indications for Anti-Diuretic Use

1. **Central Diabetes Insipidus**: A condition characterized by a deficiency of vasopressin, leading to excessive urine production and dehydration. Desmopressin is used to replace the missing hormone.

2. **Nocturnal Enuresis**: Bedwetting in children and adults. Desmopressin helps reduce nighttime urine production.

3. **Postoperative Polyuria**: Excessive urine output following surgery, particularly in patients with central diabetes insipidus.

4. **Hemophilia A and von Willebrand Disease**: Desmopressin can increase the levels of clotting factors.

Adverse Effects and Monitoring

Adverse Effects:

a. **Hyponatremia**: Excessive water reabsorption can dilute blood sodium levels, leading to hyponatremia.

b. **Water Intoxication**: Severe hyponatremia can lead to cerebral edema and seizures.

c. **Allergic Reactions**: Rare but possible, particularly with synthetic analogues.

Monitoring:

a. **Serum Sodium Levels**: Regular monitoring to prevent and detect hyponatremia.

b. **Fluid Balance**: Monitoring of fluid intake and output.

c. **Clinical Symptoms**: Observing for signs of water intoxication, such as headaches, confusion, and seizures.

A. Desmopressin (DDAVP)

Desmopressin, also known as DDAVP (1-deamino-8-D-arginine vasopressin), is a synthetic analogue of the natural hormone vasopressin (antidiuretic hormone, ADH). It is primarily used as an anti-diuretic agent to reduce urine production and promote water retention in the body. Desmopressin has specific pharmacological properties that make it effective in treating conditions characterized by excessive urine output and in managing certain bleeding disorders.

Mechanism of Action

1. Receptor Specificity:

a. **V2 Receptors**: Desmopressin predominantly acts on V2 receptors located in the renal collecting ducts.

2. Activation of V2 Receptors:

a. When desmopressin binds to V2 receptors, it activates adenylate cyclase through G-protein coupling.

3. Increase in cAMP:

a. Adenylate cyclase activation leads to an increase in intracellular cyclic adenosine monophosphate (cAMP).

4. Protein Kinase A Activation:

    a. Elevated cAMP levels activate protein kinase A (PKA), which phosphorylates specific proteins involved in the translocation and insertion of aquaporin-2 (AQP2) water channels into the apical membrane of collecting duct cells.

5. Water Reabsorption:

    a. The insertion of AQP2 channels allows for enhanced reabsorption of water from the tubular fluid into the bloodstream, reducing urine volume.

6. Concentrated Urine Production:

    a. As a result, desmopressin promotes the production of concentrated urine, which helps in conserving water and maintaining hydration.

Clinical Uses

1. **Central Diabetes Insipidus:**

    a. Desmopressin is the treatment of choice for central diabetes insipidus, a condition characterized by a deficiency of endogenous vasopressin. It helps reduce excessive urine output and prevent dehydration.

2. **Nocturnal Enuresis (Bedwetting):**

    a. In children and adults with nocturnal enuresis, desmopressin is used to reduce nighttime urine production and improve sleep quality.

3. **Postoperative Polyuria:**

    a. After surgery, particularly in patients with central diabetes insipidus, desmopressin can manage postoperative polyuria by promoting water reabsorption.

4. **Bleeding Disorders:**

    a. Desmopressin stimulates the release of von Willebrand factor (vWF) and factor VIII from endothelial cells, making it useful in treating bleeding disorders like mild hemophilia A and von Willebrand disease.

Administration

1. **Routes**: Desmopressin can be administered orally, intranasally, or intravenously, depending on the clinical indication and severity of the condition.

2. **Intranasal Spray**: This is a common and convenient method for treating central diabetes insipidus and nocturnal enuresis.

3. **Tablets**: Used for long-term management in some cases of central diabetes insipidus.

4. **Injection**: Reserved for situations requiring rapid onset of action or when oral administration is not feasible.

Adverse Effects

1. **Hyponatremia**: Excessive water retention and reduced urine output can lead to hyponatremia (low blood sodium levels), which can be severe and potentially life-threatening if not monitored and managed properly.

2. **Fluid Overload**: Particularly in patients at risk of fluid retention, such as those with cardiovascular diseases.

3. **Nasal Irritation**: Mild irritation or congestion may occur with intranasal administration.

4. **Allergic Reactions**: Rarely, allergic reactions such as rash or itching can occur.

Monitoring and Management

1. **Fluid Intake and Output**: Monitoring fluid balance is crucial to prevent overhydration or dehydration.

2. **Serum Sodium Levels**: Regular monitoring of blood sodium levels to detect and manage hyponatremia.

3. **Clinical Symptoms**: Monitoring for signs of fluid overload or hyponatremia, such as headache, confusion, nausea, and seizures.

4. **Dosage Adjustment**: Adjusting the dosage based on individual response and clinical indications to optimize therapeutic outcomes while minimizing adverse effects.

B. Vasopressin

Vasopressin, also known as antidiuretic hormone (ADH), is a natural hormone produced in the hypothalamus and released from the posterior pituitary gland. It plays a crucial role in regulating water balance and reducing urine production through its actions on the kidneys. Here's a detailed look at vasopressin as an anti-diuretic agent:

Mechanism of Action

1. **Receptor Specificity**:
    a. **V2 Receptors**: Vasopressin primarily acts on V2 receptors located in the renal collecting ducts.

2. **Activation of V2 Receptors**:
    a. When vasopressin binds to V2 receptors, it stimulates adenylate cyclase activity through G-protein coupling.

3. **Increase in cAMP**:
    a. Adenylate cyclase activation leads to an increase in intracellular cyclic adenosine monophosphate (cAMP) levels.

4. **Protein Kinase A Activation**:
    a. Elevated cAMP levels activate protein kinase A (PKA), which phosphorylates proteins involved in the translocation and insertion of aquaporin-2 (AQP2) water channels into the apical membrane of collecting duct cells.

5. **Water Reabsorption**:
    a. The insertion of AQP2 channels allows for increased reabsorption of water from the tubular fluid into the bloodstream.

6. **Concentrated Urine Production**:

a. By promoting water reabsorption, vasopressin reduces urine volume and helps in the production of concentrated urine, thereby conserving body water.

Clinical Uses

1. **Central Diabetes Insipidus**:
   a. Vasopressin is essential in the treatment of central diabetes insipidus, a condition where there is a deficiency of endogenous vasopressin. It helps to reduce excessive urine output and prevent dehydration.

2. **Nocturnal Enuresis (Bedwetting)**:
   a. In children and adults with nocturnal enuresis, vasopressin analogues are sometimes used to reduce nighttime urine production and improve sleep quality.

3. **Hemorrhagic Shock**:
   a. In cases of severe hemorrhagic shock, vasopressin may be administered to help maintain blood pressure and reduce urine output.

Administration

1. **Routes**: Vasopressin can be administered intravenously for acute conditions or used in synthetic analogue forms like desmopressin (DDAVP) for longer-term management, including intranasal or oral routes.

Adverse Effects

1. **Fluid Retention**: Excessive use of vasopressin can lead to fluid retention and potentially cause hyponatremia (low blood sodium levels).

2. **Cardiovascular Effects**: In high doses, vasopressin can lead to vasoconstriction and affect blood pressure.

3. **Allergic Reactions**: Some individuals may experience allergic reactions to vasopressin or its analogues.

Monitoring and Management

1. **Fluid Balance**: Close monitoring of fluid intake and output to prevent overhydration or dehydration.

2. **Serum Sodium Levels**: Regular monitoring of blood sodium levels to detect and manage any abnormalities.

3. **Clinical Symptoms**: Monitoring for signs of fluid overload or electrolyte imbalances.

4. **Dosage Adjustment**: Adjusting the dosage based on individual response and clinical indications to optimize therapeutic outcomes while minimizing adverse effects.

Other Agents with Antidiuretic Properties

Thiazide Diuretics: Paradoxically, in conditions like nephrogenic diabetes insipidus (NDI), where the kidneys are unresponsive to ADH, thiazide diuretics can reduce urine volume. They do this by causing mild hypovolemia, which increases proximal tubular reabsorption of sodium and water, reducing the volume of filtrate reaching the distal tubules and collecting ducts.

Monitoring and Safety

Hyponatremia Management: A critical aspect of using antidiuretic drugs is the risk of hyponatremia, particularly with desmopressin. Patients must be monitored for signs of low sodium, such as headache, confusion, seizures, and in severe cases, coma. Regular blood tests to monitor sodium levels are essential, especially in the initial phase of treatment.

Fluid Intake: Patients on desmopressin should be advised to moderate their fluid intake to avoid water intoxication. Fluid intake recommendations depend on the condition being treated and individual patient factors.

Multiple Choice Questions (MCQs)

1. What is the primary mechanism of action of Thiazide diuretics?

    A) Inhibition of carbonic anhydrase

    B) Inhibition of the sodium-chloride symporter in the distal convoluted tubule

    C) Blockade of alpha-1 adrenergic receptors

D) Inhibition of the sodium-potassium pump

2. Which class of drugs is primarily used to treat overactive bladder?

    A) Alpha-blockers

    B) Beta-blockers

    C) Anticholinergics

    D) Diuretics

3. What is the primary adverse effect of loop diuretics?

    A) Hyperkalemia

    B) Hypokalemia

    C) Hyperglycemia

    D) Hypoglycemia

4. Which medication is a phosphodiesterase-5 inhibitor used to treat BPH?

    A) Tadalafil

    B) Finasteride

    C) Tamsulosin

    D) Doxazosin

5. Desmopressin is primarily used to treat which condition?

    A) Urinary tract infections

    B) Nocturnal enuresis

    C) Hypertension

    D) Heart failure

6. Which of the following is not a common side effect of anticholinergic drugs?

    A) Dry mouth

    B) Constipation

    C) Diarrhea

    D) Blurred vision

7. Alpha-blockers such as tamsulosin are used to treat symptoms of what condition?

    A) Diabetes mellitus

B) Benign prostatic hyperplasia

C) Cardiac arrhythmias

D) Glaucoma

8. What is the primary action of 5-alpha reductase inhibitors?

A) Block beta-adrenergic receptors

B) Inhibit the conversion of testosterone to dihydrotestosterone

C) Enhance the activity of nitric oxide in the bladder

D) Inhibit phosphodiesterase-5

9. Which diuretic is known for causing significant ototoxicity when used in high doses?

A) Hydrochlorothiazide

B) Furosemide

C) Spironolactone

D) Amiloride

10. Fosfomycin is primarily used to treat what type of infections?

A) Respiratory infections

B) Urinary tract infections

C) Gastrointestinal infections

D) Skin infections

11. The mechanism of action of potassium-sparing diuretics includes:

A) Inhibition of the sodium-potassium-chloride cotransporter

B) Inhibition of carbonic anhydrase

C) Blockage of epithelial sodium channels

D) Blockage of calcium channels

12. Which agent is a synthetic analog of the hormone vasopressin?

A) Oxybutynin

B) Furosemide

C) Desmopressin

D) Ciprofloxacin

13. Antimicrobials used in treating UTIs work by:

  A) Inhibiting bacterial cell wall synthesis

  B) Enhancing potassium excretion

  C) Blocking muscarinic receptors

  D) Increasing sodium absorption

14. What is the primary use of carbonic anhydrase inhibitors in the treatment of glaucoma?

  A) Increase aqueous humor production

  B) Reduce intraocular pressure

  C) Increase blood flow to the optic nerve

  D) Reduce pupil size

15. What adverse effect is common with the use of alpha-blockers in treating BPH?

  A) Orthostatic hypotension

  B) Hypertension

  C) Bradycardia

  D) Tachycardia

16. Which drug is used to reduce the size of the prostate gland in BPH treatment?

  A) Finasteride

  B) Oxybutynin

  C) Furosemide

  D) Tamsulosin

17. What is a potential side effect of desmopressin?

  A) Hyponatremia

  B) Hyperkalemia

  C) Hypernatremia

  D) Hypocalcemia

18. Loop diuretics act on which part of the kidney?

A) Distal convoluted tubule

B) Proximal convoluted tubule

C) Glomerulus

D) Thick ascending limb of the loop of Henle

19. Which type of diuretic is least likely to cause hypokalemia?

A) Thiazide diuretics

B) Loop diuretics

C) Potassium-sparing diuretics

D) Osmotic diuretics

20. What is the therapeutic action of alpha-blockers in BPH?

A) Reduce prostate size

B) Increase urine flow

C) Decrease bladder capacity

D) Increase bladder contractions

Short Answer Type Questions (Subjective)

1. What are the main therapeutic uses of Thiazide diuretics?

2. Describe the mechanism of action of loop diuretics.

3. What are the potential adverse effects of potassium-sparing diuretics?

4. How do anticholinergics help in managing overactive bladder?

5. What role do alpha-blockers play in the treatment of benign prostatic hyperplasia (BPH)?

6. Explain how 5-alpha reductase inhibitors reduce the symptoms of BPH.

7. What is the primary mechanism of action of phosphodiesterase-5 inhibitors in the treatment of BPH?

8. How does desmopressin treat nocturnal enuresis?

9. Identify the common antimicrobial agents used to treat urinary tract infections (UTIs) and their mechanisms.

10. What are the indications for using carbonic anhydrase inhibitors?

11. Discuss the clinical uses of osmotic diuretics.

12. What are the side effects associated with loop diuretics?

13. How do potassium-sparing diuretics differ from thiazide diuretics in their mechanism of action?

14. Describe the mechanism by which anticholinergics reduce urinary urgency.

15. What adverse effects are associated with alpha-blockers?

16. How do phosphodiesterase-5 inhibitors alleviate symptoms in BPH patients?

17. Explain the significance of water reabsorption in the action of anti-diuretic drugs.

18. What monitoring is required for patients taking desmopressin?

19. Describe the action of vasopressin in the kidneys.

20. What are the potential risks of using osmotic diuretics in patients with renal failure?

Long Answer Type Questions (Subjective)

1. Discuss the pharmacokinetics and pharmacodynamics of Thiazide diuretics and their impact on hypertension management.

2. Explain the role of loop diuretics in managing acute pulmonary edema and their effects on electrolyte balance.

3. Compare and contrast the mechanisms of action and clinical uses of potassium-sparing diuretics and carbonic anhydrase inhibitors.

4. Describe in detail how anticholinergic drugs manage symptoms of overactive bladder and the potential cognitive effects in elderly patients.

5. Analyze the treatment strategies using alpha-blockers for BPH, including their pharmacological effects on urinary obstruction.

6. Discuss the dual role of phosphodiesterase-5 inhibitors in treating erectile dysfunction and BPH, focusing on their mechanism of action within the lower urinary tract.

7. Explain how desmopressin works as an anti-diuretic agent and its application in treating central diabetes insipidus and nocturnal enuresis.

8. Discuss the use of antimicrobial agents in treating UTIs, focusing on the selection criteria based on the mechanism of action and resistance patterns.

9. Describe the clinical implications of using osmotic diuretics in the treatment of cerebral edema, including the mechanisms of action and potential side effects.

10. Explore the use of vasopressin and its analogues in managing disorders characterized by polyuria, detailing the mechanisms by which they reduce urine output and their therapeutic applications.

Answer Key for MCQs

1. (B) Inhibition of the sodium-chloride symporter in the distal convoluted tubule

2. (C) Anticholinergics

3. (B) Hypokalemia

4. (A) Tadalafil

5. (B) Nocturnal enuresis

6. (C) Diarrhea

7. (B) Benign prostatic hyperplasia

8. (B) Inhibit the conversion of testosterone to dihydrotestosterone

9. (B) Furosemide

10. (B) Urinary tract infections

11. (C) Blockage of epithelial sodium channels

12. (C) Desmopressin

13.(A) Inhibiting bacterial cell wall synthesis

14.(B) Reduce intraocular pressure

15.(A) Orthostatic hypotension

16.(A) Finasteride

17.(A) Hyponatremia

18.(D) Thick ascending limb of the loop of Henle

19.(C) Potassium-sparing diuretics

20.(B) Increase urine flow

CHAPTER – 4

AUTOCOIDS AND RELATED DRUGS

INTRODUCTION TO AUTACOIDS AND CLASSIFICATION

Introduction to Autacoids

Definition: Autacoids (from the Greek "autos" meaning self and "akos" meaning remedy) are locally acting bioactive molecules that exert their effects close to the site of their synthesis and release. They are involved in various physiological and pathological processes, including inflammation, pain, allergic reactions, and the regulation of smooth muscle tone and vascular permeability.

Characteristics:

1. **Local Action:** Autacoids typically act near their site of release rather than being transported through the bloodstream to distant targets.

2. **Short Duration:** Their actions are often short-lived due to rapid metabolism and degradation.

3. **Wide Range of Effects:** They can affect various systems, including the cardiovascular, respiratory, gastrointestinal, and nervous systems.

Classification of Autacoids

Autacoids can be classified based on their chemical nature and functions into several major categories:

1. Biogenic Amines

Histamine:

    a. **Synthesis and Storage:** Derived from histidine and stored in mast cells, basophils, and neurons.

    b. **Receptors:** H1, H2, H3, H4.

    c. **Functions:** Involved in allergic responses, gastric acid secretion, neurotransmission, and immune modulation.

Serotonin (5-Hydroxytryptamine, 5-HT):

a. **Synthesis and Storage:** Derived from tryptophan and stored in enterochromaffin cells, platelets, and neurons.

b. **Receptors:** Multiple subtypes (5-HT1 to 5-HT7).

c. **Functions:** Regulates mood, sleep, appetite, vascular tone, and gastrointestinal motility.

2. Lipid-Derived Autacoids

Prostaglandins:

a. **Synthesis:** From arachidonic acid via the cyclooxygenase (COX) pathway.

b. **Receptors:** Diverse receptors (e.g., EP, FP, IP, TP).

c. **Functions:** Mediate inflammation, pain, fever, regulation of blood flow, and protection of the gastric mucosa.

Leukotrienes:

a. **Synthesis:** From arachidonic acid via the lipoxygenase (LOX) pathway.

b. **Receptors:** CysLT1, CysLT2, BLT.

c. **Functions:** Involved in bronchoconstriction, increased vascular permeability, and chemotaxis of immune cells.

Thromboxanes:

a. **Synthesis:** From arachidonic acid via the COX pathway.

b. **Receptors:** TP receptors.

c. **Functions:** Promote platelet aggregation and vasoconstriction.

Platelet-Activating Factor (PAF):

a. **Synthesis:** Derived from membrane phospholipids.

b. **Receptors:** PAF receptor.

c. **Functions:** Involved in inflammation, bronchoconstriction, and platelet aggregation.

3. Polypeptides

Bradykinin:

a. **Synthesis:** Generated from kininogen by kallikrein.

b. **Receptors:** B1, B2.

c. **Functions:** Causes vasodilation, increased vascular permeability, pain, and contraction of smooth muscles.

Angiotensin:

a. **Synthesis:** Formed from angiotensinogen by renin and then converted to active angiotensin II by ACE.

b. **Receptors:** AT1, AT2.

c. **Functions:** Regulates blood pressure, fluid balance, and aldosterone secretion.

4. Gaseous Autacoids

Nitric Oxide (NO):

a. **Synthesis:** Produced from L-arginine by nitric oxide synthase (NOS).

b. **Receptors:** Acts via the cyclic GMP pathway.

c. **Functions:** Vasodilation, neurotransmission, and immune defense.

Hydrogen Sulfide (H2S):

a. **Synthesis:** Produced from cysteine by enzymes like cystathionine-γ-lyase.

b. **Receptors:** Modulates ion channels and signaling pathways.

c. **Functions:** Vasodilation, cytoprotection, and neurotransmission.

HISTAMINE, 5-HT AND THEIR ANTAGONISTS

Histamine

Synthesis and Storage:

1. Histamine is synthesized from the amino acid histidine by the enzyme histidine decarboxylase.

2. It is stored primarily in mast cells and basophils, but also in certain neurons in the central nervous system (CNS) and enterochromaffin-like (ECL) cells in the stomach.

Mechanism of Action:

1. Histamine exerts its effects through binding to four types of histamine receptors: H1, H2, H3, and H4.

H1 Receptors:

   a. Located in smooth muscle, endothelium, and CNS.

   b. **Effects:** Vasodilation, increased vascular permeability (leading to edema), bronchoconstriction, pruritus, and wakefulness.

2. **H2 Receptors:**

   a. Found in the gastric parietal cells, heart, and various other tissues.

   b. **Effects:** Stimulation of gastric acid secretion, vasodilation, and increased heart rate.

3. **H3 Receptors:**

   a. Present in the CNS and some peripheral nerves.

   b. **Effects:** Modulation of neurotransmitter release (e.g., histamine, acetylcholine, norepinephrine), thus playing a role in sleep and cognition.

4. **H4 Receptors:**

   a. Expressed in bone marrow, leukocytes, and other immune cells.

   b. **Effects:** Regulation of immune cell chemotaxis and cytokine production.

Pharmacological Effects:

1. Histamine plays a significant role in allergic reactions, gastric acid secretion, neurotransmission, and immune response modulation.

Related Drugs (Antihistamines):

H1 Antagonists:

1. **First-generation:** Diphenhydramine, chlorpheniramine.

   a. **Characteristics:** Cross the blood-brain barrier, causing sedation and anticholinergic effects.

   b. **Uses:** Allergic reactions, motion sickness, insomnia.

2. **Second-generation:** Loratadine, cetirizine, fexofenadine.

a. **Characteristics:** Less likely to cross the blood-brain barrier, causing fewer central side effects.

b. **Uses:** Allergic rhinitis, chronic urticaria.

H2 Antagonists:

1. **Examples:** Ranitidine, famotidine, cimetidine.

    a. **Mechanism of Action:** Block H2 receptors on gastric parietal cells, reducing acid secretion.

    b. **Uses:** Treatment of peptic ulcers, gastroesophageal reflux disease (GERD), and Zollinger-Ellison syndrome.

H3 Antagonists:

1. **Examples:** Betahistine (used in Ménière's disease).

    a. **Mechanism of Action:** Blocks H3 receptors, increasing histamine release and improving blood flow in the inner ear.

    b. **Uses:** Vertigo, Ménière's disease.

H4 Antagonists:

- **Examples:** Still largely experimental, under investigation for their roles in inflammation and immune modulation.

Serotonin (5-HT)

Synthesis and Storage:

1. Serotonin is synthesized from the amino acid tryptophan via a two-step process involving the enzymes tryptophan hydroxylase and aromatic L-amino acid decarboxylase.

2. It is stored in enterochromaffin cells of the gut, platelets, and certain neurons in the CNS.

Mechanism of Action:

1. Serotonin acts through multiple receptor subtypes, classified into seven families (5-HT1 to 5-HT7), each with distinct subtypes and functions.

    5-HT1 Receptors:

    a. **Effects:** Vasoconstriction, inhibition of neurotransmitter release.

    b. **Subtypes:** 5-HT1A, 5-HT1B, 5-HT1D, etc.

    c. **Drugs:** Buspirone (5-HT1A agonist) for anxiety; Sumatriptan (5-HT1B/1D agonist) for migraines.

2. **5-HT2 Receptors:**

    a. **Effects:** Smooth muscle contraction, platelet aggregation, modulation of mood and behavior.

    b. **Subtypes:** 5-HT2A, 5-HT2B, 5-HT2C.

    c. **Drugs:** Risperidone, olanzapine (5-HT2 antagonists) for schizophrenia and bipolar disorder.

3. **5-HT3 Receptors:**

    a. **Effects:** Nausea and vomiting (chemoreceptor trigger zone).

    b. **Drugs:** Ondansetron, granisetron (5-HT3 antagonists) for chemotherapy-induced nausea and vomiting.

4. **5-HT4 Receptors:**

    a. **Effects:** Gastrointestinal motility.

    b. **Drugs:** Metoclopramide (5-HT4 agonist) for gastroparesis.

5. **5-HT5, 5-HT6, 5-HT7 Receptors:**

    a. **Effects:** Less well understood, involved in CNS functions including mood, cognition, and circadian rhythm regulation.

Pharmacological Effects:

1. Serotonin regulates mood, anxiety, sleep, appetite, temperature, cardiovascular function, and gastrointestinal motility.

Related Drugs:

Selective Serotonin Reuptake Inhibitors (SSRIs):

1. **Examples:** Fluoxetine, sertraline, citalopram.

    a. **Mechanism of Action:** Inhibit the reuptake of serotonin into presynaptic neurons, increasing serotonin availability.

    b. **Uses:** Depression, anxiety disorders, OCD.

Serotonin-Norepinephrine Reuptake Inhibitors (SNRIs):

1. **Examples:** Venlafaxine, duloxetine.

   a. **Mechanism of Action:** Inhibit the reuptake of both serotonin and norepinephrine.

   b. **Uses:** Depression, anxiety disorders, chronic pain.

Tricyclic Antidepressants (TCAs):

1. **Examples:** Amitriptyline, nortriptyline.

   a. **Mechanism of Action:** Inhibit the reuptake of serotonin and norepinephrine; also antagonize several receptors.

   b. **Uses:** Depression, neuropathic pain, migraine prophylaxis.

5-HT1 Agonists:

1. **Examples:** Sumatriptan, rizatriptan.

   a. **Mechanism of Action:** Agonists at 5-HT1B/1D receptors, leading to vasoconstriction of intracranial blood vessels.

   b. **Uses:** Acute treatment of migraines.

5-HT2 Antagonists:

1. **Examples:** Risperidone, clozapine.

   a. **Mechanism of Action:** Antagonists at 5-HT2A receptors, among other actions.

   b. **Uses:** Schizophrenia, bipolar disorder.

5-HT3 Antagonists:

1. **Examples:** Ondansetron, granisetron.

   a. **Mechanism of Action:** Block 5-HT3 receptors in the chemoreceptor trigger zone and gastrointestinal tract.

   b. **Uses:** Prevention of nausea and vomiting associated with chemotherapy, radiation, and surgery.

5-HT4 Agonists:

1. **Examples:** Cisapride (withdrawn in many countries), metoclopramide.

   a. **Mechanism of Action:** Agonists at 5-HT4 receptors, enhancing gastrointestinal motility.

b. **Uses:** Gastroesophageal reflux disease (GERD), gastroparesis.

PROSTAGLANDINS

Prostaglandins Overview

Synthesis and Storage:

1. Prostaglandins are lipid-derived autacoids synthesized from arachidonic acid, a polyunsaturated fatty acid present in cell membrane phospholipids.
2. The synthesis begins with the release of arachidonic acid by the enzyme phospholipase A2, followed by its conversion to prostaglandin H2 (PGH2) through the action of cyclooxygenase enzymes (COX-1 and COX-2).
3. PGH2 is then further converted into various specific prostaglandins (e.g., PGE2, PGI2, PGD2, PGF2α, TXA2) by specific synthase enzymes.

Mechanism of Action:

1. Prostaglandins exert their effects by binding to specific G-protein coupled receptors (GPCRs) on target cells. The main prostaglandin receptors include EP (for PGE2), IP (for PGI2), DP (for PGD2), FP (for PGF2α), and TP (for TXA2).

Pharmacological Effects:

1. **PGE2 (Prostaglandin E2):**
   a. **Receptors:** EP1, EP2, EP3, EP4.
   b. **Effects:**
      i. Vasodilation and increased vascular permeability (inflammation).
      ii. Fever induction (pyrogenic effect).
      iii. Inhibition of gastric acid secretion and stimulation of mucus and bicarbonate secretion in the stomach (gastric protection).
      iv. Uterine contraction (labor induction).

2. **PGI2 (Prostacyclin):**
   a. **Receptor:** IP.
   b. **Effects:**

i. Potent vasodilator.

ii. Inhibition of platelet aggregation (antithrombotic effect).

iii. Regulation of renal blood flow and glomerular filtration.

3. **PGD2 (Prostaglandin D2):**

a. **Receptor:** DP1, DP2.

b. **Effects:**

i. Bronchoconstriction.

ii. Involvement in allergic responses.

iii. Regulation of sleep-wake cycle.

4. **PGF2α (Prostaglandin F2α):**

a. **Receptor:** FP.

b. **Effects:**

i. Uterine contraction (used to induce labor or abortion).

ii. Regulation of intraocular pressure (used in glaucoma treatment).

5. **TXA2 (Thromboxane A2):**

a. **Receptor:** TP.

b. **Effects:**

i. Potent vasoconstrictor.

ii. Promotes platelet aggregation (prothrombotic effect).

Related Drugs

Prostaglandin analogs and inhibitors are used therapeutically to modulate the effects of prostaglandins in various conditions.

Prostaglandin Analogs:

1. **Misoprostol (PGE1 Analog):**

a. **Uses:** Prevention of NSAID-induced gastric ulcers, induction of labor, medical abortion in combination with mifepristone.

b. **Mechanism of Action:** Mimics the action of PGE1, providing gastric mucosal protection and inducing uterine contractions.

2. **Alprostadil (PGE1 Analog):**

   a. **Uses:** Treatment of erectile dysfunction, maintenance of ductus arteriosus patency in neonates with congenital heart defects.

   b. **Mechanism of Action:** Vasodilation and smooth muscle relaxation.

3. **Dinoprostone (PGE2 Analog):**

   a. **Uses:** Cervical ripening and induction of labor.

   b. **Mechanism of Action:** Softens the cervix and stimulates uterine contractions.

4. **Carboprost (PGF2α Analog):**

   a. **Uses:** Control of postpartum hemorrhage, second-trimester abortion.

   b. **Mechanism of Action:** Induces strong uterine contractions.

5. **Latanoprost, Travoprost, Bimatoprost (PGF2α Analogs):**

   a. **Uses:** Treatment of glaucoma.

   b. **Mechanism of Action:** Reduces intraocular pressure by increasing the outflow of aqueous humor.

Prostaglandin Inhibitors (NSAIDs):

1. **Non-Selective COX Inhibitors:**

   a. **Examples:** Aspirin, ibuprofen, naproxen.

   b. **Mechanism of Action:** Inhibit both COX-1 and COX-2 enzymes, reducing the synthesis of prostaglandins.

   c. **Uses:** Pain relief, anti-inflammatory, antipyretic, and antithrombotic effects.

2. **Selective COX-2 Inhibitors:**

   a. **Examples:** Celecoxib, etoricoxib.

   b. **Mechanism of Action:** Selectively inhibit COX-2, which is primarily involved in inflammation and pain.

   c. **Uses:** Management of chronic inflammatory conditions like osteoarthritis and rheumatoid arthritis, with a lower risk of gastrointestinal side effects compared to non-selective NSAIDs.

Leukotriene Inhibitors (Related to Prostaglandin Pathway):

1. **Leukotriene Receptor Antagonists:**
   a. **Examples:** Montelukast, zafirlukast.
   b. **Mechanism of Action:** Block leukotriene receptors, reducing inflammation and bronchoconstriction.
   c. **Uses:** Management of asthma and allergic rhinitis.

2. **5-Lipoxygenase Inhibitors:**
   a. **Example:** Zileuton.
   b. **Mechanism of Action:** Inhibits the 5-lipoxygenase enzyme, reducing leukotriene synthesis.
   c. **Uses:** Management of asthma.

THROMBOXANES

Thromboxanes Overview

Synthesis and Storage:

1. Thromboxanes are synthesized from arachidonic acid via the cyclooxygenase (COX) pathway.
2. The pathway begins with the conversion of arachidonic acid to prostaglandin H2 (PGH2) by COX enzymes (COX-1 and COX-2).
3. PGH2 is then specifically converted to thromboxane A2 (TXA2) by thromboxane synthase.
4. Thromboxane A2 is not stored but synthesized on demand, mainly by platelets.

Mechanism of Action:

1. Thromboxane A2 (TXA2) exerts its effects by binding to thromboxane receptors (TP receptors), which are G-protein coupled receptors.
2. There are two isoforms of TP receptors: TPa and TPb, both involved in the physiological actions of TXA2.

Pharmacological Effects:

1. **Platelet Aggregation:** TXA2 is a potent promoter of platelet aggregation, essential for blood clot formation.

2. **Vasoconstriction:** It induces vasoconstriction, which helps reduce blood flow to an area and aids in clot formation.

3. **Smooth Muscle Contraction:** TXA2 can cause contraction of smooth muscles in the respiratory and vascular systems.

Related Drugs

Given the significant role of thromboxanes in hemostasis and vascular function, targeting the thromboxane pathway is crucial in various therapeutic contexts, particularly in cardiovascular diseases.

Thromboxane Synthesis Inhibitors:

1. **Aspirin (Acetylsalicylic Acid):**

    a. **Mechanism of Action:** Aspirin irreversibly inhibits COX-1 and COX-2, leading to decreased synthesis of TXA2 in platelets.

    b. **Uses:** Prevention of myocardial infarction, stroke, and other thromboembolic events. Aspirin's antiplatelet effect is primarily due to its inhibition of TXA2 synthesis, which reduces platelet aggregation.

2. **Other NSAIDs (Non-Steroidal Anti-Inflammatory Drugs):**

    a. **Examples:** Ibuprofen, naproxen.

    b. **Mechanism of Action:** Reversible inhibition of COX enzymes, leading to reduced thromboxane production.

    c. **Uses:** Pain relief, anti-inflammatory effects, and mild antiplatelet effects. However, they are not as effective as aspirin in preventing thromboembolic events due to their reversible action.

Thromboxane Receptor Antagonists:

1. **Terutroban:**

    a. **Mechanism of Action:** Selective antagonist of the TP receptor, inhibiting the effects of TXA2 on platelet aggregation and vasoconstriction.

b. **Uses:** Investigational drug for preventing thrombotic events in cardiovascular diseases. It has shown potential in reducing the risk of stroke and myocardial infarction.

2. **Ifetroban:**

   a. **Mechanism of Action:** TP receptor antagonist that blocks the action of thromboxane A2 on platelets and smooth muscle cells.

   b. **Uses:** Under investigation for treating conditions like pulmonary arterial hypertension and other thromboembolic disorders.

Dual Pathway Inhibitors:

1. Some drugs target both the thromboxane pathway and other pathways involved in platelet aggregation.

2. **Example:** Vorapaxar.

   a. **Mechanism of Action:** PAR-1 antagonist (Protease-Activated Receptor-1), which inhibits thrombin-induced platelet aggregation. It also has effects on the thromboxane pathway.

   b. **Uses:** Secondary prevention of thrombotic cardiovascular events in patients with a history of myocardial infarction or peripheral arterial disease.

LEUKOTRIENES

Leukotrienes Overview

Synthesis and Storage:

1. Leukotrienes are synthesized from arachidonic acid via the lipoxygenase (LOX) pathway.

2. The process begins with the action of 5-lipoxygenase (5-LOX) on arachidonic acid to produce 5-hydroperoxyeicosatetraenoic acid (5-HPETE), which is then converted to leukotriene A4 (LTA4).

3. LTA4 can be further metabolized into leukotriene B4 (LTB4) or converted into cysteinyl leukotrienes (LTC4, LTD4, and LTE4) by the addition of glutathione and subsequent enzymatic actions.

4. Leukotrienes are not stored; they are synthesized and released by leukocytes (such as neutrophils, eosinophils, and mast cells) upon cellular activation.

Mechanism of Action:

1. Leukotrienes exert their effects by binding to specific G-protein coupled receptors.

    a. **LTB4 Receptors:** BLT1 and BLT2.

    b. **Cysteinyl Leukotriene Receptors:** CysLT1 and CysLT2.

Pharmacological Effects:

1. **LTB4:**

    a. **Receptors:** BLT1 and BLT2.

    b. **Effects:**

        i. Potent chemotactic agent for neutrophils.

        ii. Promotes neutrophil adhesion and migration to sites of inflammation.

        iii. Increases the production of reactive oxygen species by neutrophils.

2. **Cysteinyl Leukotrienes (LTC4, LTD4, LTE4):**

    a. **Receptors:** CysLT1 and CysLT2.

    b. **Effects:**

        i. Potent bronchoconstrictors, leading to airway constriction.

        ii. Increase vascular permeability, contributing to edema.

        iii. Promote mucus secretion and eosinophil recruitment in the airways.

Related Drugs

Leukotriene Receptor Antagonists:

1. **Montelukast:**

    a. **Mechanism of Action:** Selective antagonist of the CysLT1 receptor, blocking the actions of LTC4, LTD4, and LTE4.

    b. **Uses:**

i. Management of asthma, including prevention of exercise-induced bronchoconstriction.

ii. Treatment of allergic rhinitis.

iii. Beneficial in chronic asthma control by reducing airway inflammation, bronchoconstriction, and mucus production.

c. **Side Effects:** Generally well-tolerated, with possible side effects including headache, gastrointestinal disturbances, and, rarely, neuropsychiatric effects (e.g., mood changes).

2. **Zafirlukast:**

a. **Mechanism of Action:** Selective antagonist of the CysLT1 receptor.

b. **Uses:**

i. Management of chronic asthma.

ii. Improves symptoms and pulmonary function.

c. **Side Effects:** Similar to montelukast, with possible liver enzyme elevation and gastrointestinal symptoms.

5-Lipoxygenase Inhibitors:

1. **Zileuton:**

a. **Mechanism of Action:** Inhibits 5-lipoxygenase, preventing the formation of leukotrienes from arachidonic acid.

b. **Uses:**

i. Management of chronic asthma.

ii. Reduces the production of both LTB4 and cysteinyl leukotrienes.

c. **Side Effects:** Elevated liver enzymes, potential hepatotoxicity, headache, and dyspepsia. Liver function monitoring is recommended during therapy.

ANGIOTENSIN

Angiotensin Overview

Synthesis and Storage:

1. Angiotensin is a peptide hormone system critical in regulating blood pressure and fluid balance.

2. The renin-angiotensin-aldosterone system (RAAS) controls angiotensin synthesis.

    a. **Renin**, an enzyme released by the kidneys in response to low blood pressure, converts angiotensinogen (produced by the liver) into angiotensin I.

    b. **Angiotensin-Converting Enzyme (ACE)**, primarily found in the lungs and endothelial cells, converts angiotensin I into angiotensin II, the active form.

Mechanism of Action:

1. **Angiotensin II** binds to specific receptors to exert its physiological effects:

    a. **AT1 Receptors**: Mediate most known actions of angiotensin II, including vasoconstriction, aldosterone secretion, increased sympathetic activity, and cell growth.

    b. **AT2 Receptors**: Generally oppose AT1 receptor actions, promoting vasodilation, anti-proliferation, and apoptosis.

Pharmacological Effects:

1. **Vasoconstriction:**

    a. Angiotensin II causes potent vasoconstriction, leading to increased blood pressure.

2. **Aldosterone Secretion:**

    a. Stimulates the adrenal cortex to release aldosterone, which increases sodium and water reabsorption in the kidneys, raising blood volume and pressure.

3. **Sympathetic Nervous System Activation:**

    a. Enhances norepinephrine release and inhibits its reuptake, further increasing blood pressure.

4. **Cell Growth and Proliferation:**
   a. Promotes growth of vascular smooth muscle cells and cardiac myocytes, contributing to hypertrophy and remodeling.

Related Drugs

Given the crucial role of angiotensin in cardiovascular health, several classes of drugs target the RAAS to manage hypertension, heart failure, and other cardiovascular diseases.

Angiotensin-Converting Enzyme Inhibitors (ACE Inhibitors):

1. **Examples:** Lisinopril, enalapril, ramipril.
   a. **Mechanism of Action:** Inhibit ACE, reducing the conversion of angiotensin I to angiotensin II.
   b. **Uses:** Hypertension, heart failure, post-myocardial infarction, diabetic nephropathy.
   c. **Side Effects:** Cough (due to bradykinin accumulation), hyperkalemia, angioedema, hypotension.

Angiotensin II Receptor Blockers (ARBs):

1. **Examples:** Losartan, valsartan, candesartan.
   a. **Mechanism of Action:** Block AT1 receptors, preventing angiotensin II from exerting its effects.
   b. **Uses:** Hypertension, heart failure, chronic kidney disease, post-myocardial infarction.
   c. **Side Effects:** Hyperkalemia, hypotension, less likely to cause cough or angioedema compared to ACE inhibitors.

Direct Renin Inhibitors:

1. **Example:** Aliskiren.
   a. **Mechanism of Action:** Inhibits renin, reducing the conversion of angiotensinogen to angiotensin I, thereby decreasing levels of angiotensin II.
   b. **Uses:** Hypertension.

c. **Side Effects:** Hyperkalemia, hypotension, diarrhea, potential renal impairment.

Aldosterone Antagonists (Mineralocorticoid Receptor Antagonists):

1. **Examples:** Spironolactone, eplerenone.
   a. **Mechanism of Action:** Block the action of aldosterone at its receptor, reducing sodium and water reabsorption.
   b. **Uses:** Heart failure, hypertension, primary aldosteronism, edema associated with liver cirrhosis.
   c. **Side Effects:** Hyperkalemia, gynecomastia (spironolactone), menstrual irregularities, hypotension.

Combination Therapies:

1. **ACE Inhibitors or ARBs with Diuretics:**
   a. **Example:** Lisinopril with hydrochlorothiazide.
   b. **Mechanism of Action:** Combination enhances blood pressure reduction by combining RAAS inhibition with diuretic-induced volume reduction.
   c. **Uses:** Hypertension.
   d. **Side Effects:** Combination of those seen with individual components, with enhanced risk of electrolyte imbalances.
2. **ACE Inhibitors or ARBs with Calcium Channel Blockers:**
   a. **Example:** Valsartan with amlodipine.
   b. **Mechanism of Action:** Provides complementary mechanisms of action, reducing blood pressure more effectively.
   c. **Uses:** Hypertension.
   d. **Side Effects:** Combination of those seen with individual components, with an improved side effect profile due to balanced mechanisms.

BRADYKININ

Bradykinin Overview

Synthesis and Storage:

1. Bradykinin is a peptide autacoid that is part of the kallikrein-kinin system.

2. It is produced from kininogen, a protein substrate, through the enzymatic action of kallikreins (plasma kallikrein and tissue kallikrein).

3. Bradykinin is not stored but synthesized and released locally in response to stimuli such as tissue injury, inflammation, and certain enzymatic activations.

Mechanism of Action:

1. Bradykinin exerts its effects by binding to bradykinin receptors, which are G-protein coupled receptors:

    a. **B1 Receptors:** Induced in response to tissue injury and inflammation.

    b. **B2 Receptors:** Constitutively expressed in many tissues and mediate most of the physiological effects of bradykinin.

Pharmacological Effects:

1. **Vasodilation:**

    a. Bradykinin induces vasodilation by stimulating the release of nitric oxide (NO), prostacyclin (PGI2), and endothelium-derived hyperpolarizing factor (EDHF) from endothelial cells.

    b. Results in reduced blood pressure and increased blood flow.

2. **Increased Vascular Permeability:**

    a. Enhances the permeability of capillaries, leading to plasma protein and fluid extravasation, contributing to edema and swelling in inflammatory conditions.

3. **Pain and Inflammation:**

    a. Bradykinin sensitizes sensory nerve endings, causing pain.

    b. It is involved in the inflammatory response by promoting the release of other inflammatory mediators such as prostaglandins and histamine.

4. **Smooth Muscle Contraction:**

    a. Causes contraction of non-vascular smooth muscles, such as those in the bronchi, leading to bronchoconstriction.

Related Drugs

Drugs targeting the bradykinin pathway are used to manage conditions associated with excessive bradykinin activity or to leverage its beneficial effects in certain therapeutic contexts.

Bradykinin Receptor Antagonists:

1. **Icatibant:**
    a. **Mechanism of Action:** Selective B2 receptor antagonist.
    b. **Uses:** Treatment of acute attacks of hereditary angioedema (HAE), a condition characterized by excessive bradykinin activity leading to swelling.
    c. **Side Effects:** Injection site reactions, fever, dizziness, elevated liver enzymes.

Angiotensin-Converting Enzyme Inhibitors (ACE Inhibitors):

1. **Examples:** Lisinopril, enalapril, ramipril.
    a. **Mechanism of Action:** ACE inhibitors prevent the degradation of bradykinin by inhibiting angiotensin-converting enzyme (ACE), which breaks down bradykinin.
    b. **Uses:** Hypertension, heart failure, chronic kidney disease.
    c. **Side Effects:** Increased bradykinin levels can lead to a persistent dry cough and, in rare cases, angioedema.

Kallikrein Inhibitors:

1. **Ecallantide:**
    a. **Mechanism of Action:** Inhibits plasma kallikrein, reducing the production of bradykinin.
    b. **Uses:** Treatment of acute attacks of hereditary angioedema (HAE).
    c. **Side Effects:** Headache, nausea, injection site reactions, hypersensitivity reactions.

2. **Lanadelumab:**

a. **Mechanism of Action:** Monoclonal antibody that inhibits plasma kallikrein.

b. **Uses:** Prophylactic treatment of hereditary angioedema (HAE).

c. **Side Effects:** Injection site reactions, upper respiratory infections, dizziness, hypersensitivity reactions.

Combination Therapies:

1. **ACE Inhibitors with Diuretics:**

   a. **Examples:** Lisinopril with hydrochlorothiazide.

   b. **Mechanism of Action:** Combination enhances blood pressure reduction by combining RAAS inhibition with diuretic-induced volume reduction.

   c. **Uses:** Hypertension.

   d. **Side Effects:** Combination of those seen with individual components, with enhanced risk of electrolyte imbalances.

SUBSTANCE P

Substance P Overview

Synthesis and Storage:

1. Substance P is an 11-amino acid neuropeptide, part of the tachykinin family of neuropeptides.

2. It is synthesized in neurons and stored in synaptic vesicles.

3. It is released from nerve endings in response to various stimuli, such as stress, injury, and inflammation.

Mechanism of Action:

1. Substance P exerts its effects by binding to neurokinin (NK) receptors, primarily the NK1 receptor.

   a. **NK1 Receptor:** The primary receptor for Substance P, a G-protein coupled receptor that mediates most of its physiological and pathological effects.

b. **NK2 and NK3 Receptors:** Bind other tachykinins, such as neurokinin A and neurokinin B.

Pharmacological Effects:

1. **Pain Transmission:**
   a. Substance P is a key neurotransmitter in pain pathways, especially in the central and peripheral nervous systems.
   b. It promotes pain transmission by sensitizing pain receptors and enhancing the release of other pain-related neurotransmitters.

2. **Inflammation:**
   a. Involved in the inflammatory response, it induces the release of pro-inflammatory cytokines and chemokines.
   b. Increases vascular permeability and promotes the accumulation of immune cells at sites of inflammation.

3. **Smooth Muscle Contraction:**
   a. Causes contraction of smooth muscles in the respiratory and gastrointestinal tracts, leading to bronchoconstriction and increased gut motility.

4. **Vasodilation:**
   a. Induces vasodilation, leading to increased blood flow and edema in inflamed tissues.

5. **Modulation of Immune Response:**
   a. Affects the activity of immune cells, including macrophages and T cells, contributing to the regulation of immune responses.

Related Drugs

Drugs targeting the Substance P pathway are primarily focused on managing pain and certain psychiatric conditions. The main class of drugs used to modulate Substance P activity are NK1 receptor antagonists.

NK1 Receptor Antagonists:

1. **Aprepitant:**

a. **Mechanism of Action:** Selective NK1 receptor antagonist, blocking the binding of Substance P to its receptor.

b. **Uses:** Prevention of chemotherapy-induced nausea and vomiting (CINV), postoperative nausea and vomiting.

c. **Side Effects:** Fatigue, dizziness, hiccups, constipation.

2. **Fosaprepitant:**

   a. **Mechanism of Action:** Prodrug of aprepitant, converted to aprepitant in the body, also acting as an NK1 receptor antagonist.

   b. **Uses:** Prevention of chemotherapy-induced nausea and vomiting (CINV), postoperative nausea and vomiting.

   c. **Side Effects:** Similar to aprepitant, including fatigue, dizziness, hiccups, and constipation.

3. **Rolapitant:**

   a. **Mechanism of Action:** Long-acting NK1 receptor antagonist, blocking Substance P from binding to its receptor.

   b. **Uses:** Prevention of delayed chemotherapy-induced nausea and vomiting (CINV).

   c. **Side Effects:** Neutropenia, hiccups, decreased appetite, dizziness.

Potential Future Therapies:

1. Research is ongoing to explore the use of NK1 receptor antagonists and other modulators of the Substance P pathway in the treatment of chronic pain conditions, depression, anxiety, and other psychiatric disorders.

NON-STEROIDAL ANTI-INFLAMMATORY AGENTS

Overview of NSAIDs

Non-steroidal anti-inflammatory drugs (NSAIDs) are a class of medications that provide analgesic (pain-relieving), anti-inflammatory, and antipyretic (fever-reducing) effects. They are widely used for the treatment of acute and chronic conditions involving pain and inflammation.

Mechanism of Action:

1. NSAIDs primarily work by inhibiting cyclooxygenase (COX) enzymes, which are key in the biosynthesis of prostaglandins from arachidonic acid. Prostaglandins are autacoids involved in inflammation, pain, and fever.
2. There are two main isoforms of COX enzymes:
    a. **COX-1:** Constitutively expressed in most tissues and involved in the regulation of normal cellular processes such as gastric mucosal protection, platelet aggregation, and renal blood flow.
    b. **COX-2:** Inducible enzyme, mainly expressed at sites of inflammation and responsible for the production of pro-inflammatory prostaglandins.

Classification of NSAIDs

NSAIDs can be classified based on their chemical structure and their selectivity for COX-1 and COX-2 enzymes.

Non-Selective COX Inhibitors:

1. Inhibit both COX-1 and COX-2 enzymes, leading to anti-inflammatory, analgesic, and antipyretic effects but also potential gastrointestinal and renal side effects.

Examples:

1. **Aspirin (Acetylsalicylic Acid):**
    a. **Mechanism of Action:** Irreversible inhibitor of both COX-1 and COX-2.
    b. **Uses:** Pain relief, fever reduction, anti-inflammatory effects, and prevention of thrombotic events (due to its antiplatelet effect).
    c. **Side Effects:** Gastrointestinal ulcers, bleeding, tinnitus, and Reye's syndrome in children.
2. **Ibuprofen:**
    a. **Mechanism of Action:** Reversible inhibitor of COX-1 and COX-2.
    b. **Uses:** Pain relief, fever reduction, and anti-inflammatory effects in conditions like arthritis, dysmenorrhea, and musculoskeletal injuries.

c. **Side Effects:** Gastrointestinal disturbances, renal impairment, and cardiovascular risks with long-term use.

3. **Naproxen:**

   a. **Mechanism of Action:** Reversible inhibitor of COX-1 and COX-2.

   b. **Uses:** Similar to ibuprofen, used for pain, inflammation, and fever.

   c. **Side Effects:** Gastrointestinal disturbances, renal impairment, and cardiovascular risks.

COX-2 Selective Inhibitors (Coxibs):

1. Selectively inhibit COX-2 enzyme, aiming to provide anti-inflammatory and analgesic effects with reduced gastrointestinal side effects.

Examples:

1. **Celecoxib:**

   a. **Mechanism of Action:** Selective COX-2 inhibitor.

   b. **Uses:** Osteoarthritis, rheumatoid arthritis, acute pain, and dysmenorrhea.

   c. **Side Effects:** Reduced gastrointestinal risk compared to non-selective NSAIDs, but potential cardiovascular risks.

2. **Etoricoxib:**

   a. **Mechanism of Action:** Selective COX-2 inhibitor.

   b. **Uses:** Osteoarthritis, rheumatoid arthritis, ankylosing spondylitis, and acute pain.

   c. **Side Effects:** Reduced gastrointestinal risk compared to non-selective NSAIDs, but potential cardiovascular risks.

Partially Selective NSAIDs:

1. Exhibit some preference for COX-2 inhibition but still affect COX-1 to a significant degree.

Examples:

1. **Meloxicam:**

   a. **Mechanism of Action:** Preferentially inhibits COX-2 over COX-1.

b. **Uses:** Osteoarthritis, rheumatoid arthritis, and other inflammatory conditions.

c. **Side Effects:** Lower gastrointestinal risk compared to non-selective NSAIDs but potential for renal and cardiovascular effects.

2. **Diclofenac:**

   a. **Mechanism of Action:** Preferentially inhibits COX-2 over COX-1.

   b. **Uses:** Pain and inflammation in conditions like osteoarthritis, rheumatoid arthritis, and musculoskeletal injuries.

   c. **Side Effects:** Gastrointestinal disturbances, renal impairment, and cardiovascular risks.

Clinical Applications and Considerations

Therapeutic Uses:

1. **Pain Management:** Effective in managing mild to moderate pain from various causes, including musculoskeletal injuries, dental pain, and post-operative pain.

2. **Inflammatory Conditions:** Widely used in chronic inflammatory diseases such as osteoarthritis, rheumatoid arthritis, and ankylosing spondylitis.

3. **Fever Reduction:** NSAIDs like ibuprofen and aspirin are commonly used to reduce fever.

Adverse Effects:

1. **Gastrointestinal:** Risk of gastric ulcers, bleeding, and perforation, especially with non-selective NSAIDs and long-term use.

2. **Renal:** Potential for renal impairment, particularly in patients with pre-existing kidney conditions or those using NSAIDs chronically.

3. **Cardiovascular:** Increased risk of cardiovascular events (e.g., heart attack and stroke) with selective COX-2 inhibitors and some non-selective NSAIDs.

4. **Hematologic:** Prolonged bleeding time due to platelet inhibition, especially with aspirin.

Contraindications and Cautions:

1. **Gastrointestinal Disorders:** Patients with a history of peptic ulcer disease or gastrointestinal bleeding should use NSAIDs cautiously and may require protective agents (e.g., proton pump inhibitors).

2. **Renal and Hepatic Impairment:** Dose adjustments and monitoring may be necessary in patients with renal or hepatic dysfunction.

3. **Cardiovascular Disease:** Patients with cardiovascular risk factors should avoid COX-2 selective inhibitors and use non-selective NSAIDs with caution.

4. **Pregnancy:** NSAIDs are generally avoided during pregnancy, particularly in the third trimester, due to potential adverse effects on fetal circulation and renal function.

ANTI-GOUT DRUGS

Gout is a type of arthritis characterized by the deposition of monosodium urate crystals in joints and tissues, leading to inflammation, pain, and swelling. The management of gout involves both acute treatment to relieve symptoms during attacks and long-term strategies to prevent recurrent episodes and reduce uric acid levels.

Overview of Anti-Gout Drugs

1. Non-Steroidal Anti-Inflammatory Drugs (NSAIDs):

a. **Mechanism of Action:** NSAIDs inhibit cyclooxygenase enzymes (COX-1 and COX-2), which reduces the production of prostaglandins and alleviates pain and inflammation associated with gout attacks.

b. **Examples:**

   i. **Indomethacin:** Often used for acute gout attacks due to its potent anti-inflammatory effects. It helps in reducing pain, swelling, and inflammation in affected joints.

   ii. **Naproxen, ibuprofen:** These NSAIDs are also effective for managing acute gout attacks.

c. **Side Effects:** Gastrointestinal upset (e.g., nausea, dyspepsia), potential renal impairment, and cardiovascular risks are associated with NSAID use. These drugs should be used with caution in patients with peptic ulcer disease, renal insufficiency, or cardiovascular disease.

2. Colchicine:

a. **Mechanism of Action:** Colchicine disrupts microtubule polymerization, inhibiting neutrophil migration and phagocytosis of urate crystals, thereby reducing inflammation during acute gout attacks.

b. **Uses:**

  i. **Acute Gout:** Colchicine is highly effective for treating acute gout attacks when taken early in the attack.

  ii. **Prophylaxis:** Low-dose colchicine is used for prophylaxis to prevent recurrent gout attacks in patients with frequent episodes.

c. **Side Effects:** Common side effects include gastrointestinal symptoms such as diarrhea, nausea, and abdominal pain. Colchicine toxicity can lead to severe gastrointestinal symptoms and even multi-organ failure, so dosing should be carefully monitored.

3. Corticosteroids:

a. **Mechanism of Action:** Corticosteroids reduce inflammation and suppress the immune response, providing rapid relief from pain and swelling during acute gout attacks.

b. **Administration:** They can be administered orally (e.g., prednisone), intra-articularly (into the affected joint), or intramuscularly (e.g., methylprednisolone) depending on the severity and location of the gout attack.

c. **Side Effects:** Long-term use of corticosteroids can lead to significant systemic side effects, including immunosuppression, osteoporosis, hyperglycemia, and hypertension. Short-term use for acute gout is generally safer but should be monitored carefully.

4. Urate-Lowering Therapy (ULT):

    a. **Mechanism of Action:** ULT aims to lower serum uric acid levels, thereby preventing the formation and deposition of urate crystals in joints and tissues.

    b. **Examples:**

        i. **Allopurinol:** Inhibits xanthine oxidase, the enzyme responsible for converting hypoxanthine to xanthine and then to uric acid. By reducing uric acid production, allopurinol helps prevent gout attacks and tophi formation.

        ii. **Febuxostat:** Another xanthine oxidase inhibitor used for ULT in patients who cannot tolerate allopurinol or do not achieve adequate uric acid control with allopurinol.

        iii. **Probenecid:** Increases uric acid excretion by inhibiting its reabsorption in the kidneys, thus lowering serum uric acid levels. It is used in patients with under-excretion of uric acid.

    c. **Side Effects:** Allopurinol and febuxostat can cause hypersensitivity reactions and potentially severe skin reactions (e.g., Stevens-Johnson syndrome). Probenecid may lead to nephrolithiasis (kidney stones) and gastrointestinal disturbances.

5. Other Therapies:

    a. **Pegloticase:** A recombinant uricase enzyme that converts uric acid into allantoin, a more soluble compound excreted by the kidneys. Pegloticase is used for refractory gout, where other treatments have failed.

    b. **Side Effects:** Infusion reactions, including anaphylaxis, are significant risks associated with pegloticase therapy.

Clinical Considerations

1. **Acute Gout Management:** NSAIDs, colchicine, and corticosteroids are typically used to manage acute gout attacks, with NSAIDs and colchicine being first-line options.

2. **Chronic Gout Management:** Long-term ULT with medications like allopurinol or febuxostat is essential to lower uric acid levels and prevent recurrent gout attacks and tophi formation.

3. **Monitoring:** Regular monitoring of serum uric acid levels and renal function is crucial during ULT to adjust doses and prevent adverse effects.

4. **Patient Education:** Lifestyle modifications, including dietary changes (e.g., reducing purine-rich foods, alcohol intake) and weight management, are important adjuncts to pharmacological therapy in managing gout.

ANTIRHEUMATIC DRUGS

Antirheumatic drugs encompass a diverse group of medications used to manage rheumatic diseases, which include autoimmune inflammatory conditions affecting joints, connective tissues, and other organs. These drugs aim to reduce inflammation, alleviate symptoms, prevent disease progression, and improve quality of life for patients with rheumatic diseases.

Classification of Antirheumatic Drugs

Antirheumatic drugs can be classified based on their mechanism of action and their specific targets in the immune and inflammatory pathways.

1. Non-Steroidal Anti-Inflammatory Drugs (NSAIDs):

a. **Mechanism of Action:** NSAIDs inhibit cyclooxygenase enzymes (COX-1 and COX-2), which are involved in the production of prostaglandins from arachidonic acid. This inhibition leads to anti-inflammatory, analgesic, and antipyretic effects.

b. **Uses:** NSAIDs are commonly used to manage symptoms of inflammation and pain in rheumatic diseases such as rheumatoid arthritis, osteoarthritis, and ankylosing spondylitis.

c. **Examples:** Ibuprofen, naproxen, diclofenac, celecoxib.

d. **Side Effects:** Gastrointestinal side effects (e.g., ulceration, bleeding), renal impairment, cardiovascular risks (especially with long-term use), and potential hepatotoxicity.

2. Disease-Modifying Antirheumatic Drugs (DMARDs):

DMARDs are a critical class of drugs that modify the underlying disease process in rheumatic diseases, particularly autoimmune inflammatory conditions like rheumatoid arthritis.

a. Conventional Synthetic DMARDs (csDMARDs):

a. **Mechanism of Action:** csDMARDs exert their effects by modulating immune responses, reducing inflammation, and inhibiting joint damage.

b. **Examples:**

   i. **Methotrexate:** Inhibits dihydrofolate reductase, leading to decreased purine and pyrimidine synthesis and anti-inflammatory effects.

   ii. **Sulfasalazine:** Anti-inflammatory and immunomodulatory effects, particularly effective in rheumatoid arthritis.

   iii. **Hydroxychloroquine:** Inhibits lysosomal activity and interferes with antigen presentation, used in systemic lupus erythematosus and rheumatoid arthritis.

c. **Uses:** Methotrexate is considered first-line in rheumatoid arthritis and is also used in psoriatic arthritis and other autoimmune diseases. Sulfasalazine and hydroxychloroquine are used in rheumatoid arthritis and systemic lupus erythematosus.

d. **Side Effects:** Methotrexate can cause hepatotoxicity, bone marrow suppression, and gastrointestinal disturbances. Sulfasalazine may cause gastrointestinal upset and rarely hematologic abnormalities. Hydroxychloroquine can lead to ocular toxicity with long-term use.

b. Biologic DMARDs (bDMARDs):

a. **Mechanism of Action:** bDMARDs target specific molecules involved in the inflammatory process, such as cytokines, cell surface receptors, or signaling pathways.

b. **Examples:**

i. **Tumor Necrosis Factor (TNF) Inhibitors:** Infliximab, adalimumab, etanercept.

ii. **Interleukin-6 (IL-6) Inhibitors:** Tocilizumab, sarilumab.

iii. **B-cell Depletion Therapy:** Rituximab (anti-CD20 monoclonal antibody).

iv. **T-cell Co-stimulation Blockers:** Abatacept.

c. **Uses:** bDMARDs are used in moderate to severe rheumatoid arthritis, psoriatic arthritis, ankylosing spondylitis, and other autoimmune diseases refractory to csDMARDs.

d. **Side Effects:** Increased risk of infections (especially with TNF inhibitors), infusion reactions, development of antibodies, and rare but serious adverse events such as demyelinating disorders or heart failure.

3. Targeted Synthetic DMARDs (tsDMARDs):

a. **Mechanism of Action:** tsDMARDs inhibit specific molecules involved in the immune response, similar to biologic DMARDs but with a small-molecule structure.

b. **Examples:** Janus kinase (JAK) inhibitors such as tofacitinib, baricitinib, and upadacitinib.

c. **Uses:** Used in moderate to severe rheumatoid arthritis and other autoimmune diseases as second-line or alternative therapies.

d. **Side Effects:** Increased risk of infections, gastrointestinal perforations, liver enzyme elevations, and cardiovascular events.

Clinical Considerations

1. **Treatment Goals:** Antirheumatic therapy aims to achieve remission or low disease activity, relieve pain and inflammation, prevent joint damage and disability, and improve quality of life.

2. **Monitoring:** Regular monitoring of disease activity, inflammatory markers, and potential side effects (e.g., laboratory tests, imaging studies) is essential to guide treatment adjustments and ensure safety.

3. **Combination Therapy:** Combination of DMARDs (e.g., methotrexate with a biologic or targeted therapy) may be used to enhance efficacy and reduce the risk of developing antibodies and treatment resistance.

4. **Safety Considerations:** Individualize therapy based on disease severity, comorbidities (e.g., infections, cardiovascular risk), and patient preferences. Consider potential drug interactions and monitor for adverse effects during treatment.

5. **Patient Education:** Educate patients about the importance of adherence to therapy, monitoring for side effects, and lifestyle modifications (e.g., smoking cessation, weight management) to optimize treatment outcomes.

Multiple Choice Questions (MCQs)

1. What type of receptor does histamine act through?
   A) G-protein coupled receptors
   B) Ion channels
   C) Enzyme-linked receptors
   D) Nuclear receptors

2. What is the primary action of serotonin in the gastrointestinal tract?
   A) Decreases motility
   B) Increases acid secretion
   C) Increases motility
   D) Decreases absorption

3. Which enzyme is involved in the synthesis of prostaglandins?
   A) Cyclooxygenase
   B) Lipoxygenase
   C) Phospholipase A2
   D) Nitric oxide synthase

4. Which drug is a prostaglandin E1 analog used to prevent NSAID-induced gastric ulcers?

A) Misoprostol

B) Alprostadil

C) Latanoprost

D) Dinoprostone

5. What is the primary function of bradykinin?

   A) Reduces inflammation

   B) Promotes inflammation

   C) Decreases blood pressure

   D) Increases blood clotting

6. What receptor does Angiotensin II primarily act on to exert most of its physiological effects?

   A) AT1

   B) AT2

   C) AP1

   D) AP2

7. Which medication is used as an antagonist for leukotriene receptors in managing asthma?

   A) Zileuton

   B) Montelukast

   C) Indomethacin

   D) Alprostadil

8. What is the primary action of thromboxane A2?

   A) Decreases platelet aggregation

   B) Increases platelet aggregation

   C) Acts as a vasodilator

   D) Inhibits inflammation

9. Which of the following is NOT a serotonin receptor antagonist?

   A) Ondansetron

   B) Granisetron

C) Risperidone

D) Buspirone

10. Which drug is a COX-2 selective inhibitor?

A) Aspirin

B) Ibuprofen

C) Celecoxib

D) Acetaminophen

11. Which enzyme does Aliskiren directly inhibit?

A) Angiotensin-converting enzyme

B) Renin

C) Adenylate cyclase

D) Phosphodiesterase

12. Which prostaglandin is involved in protecting the gastric mucosa?

A) PGD2

B) PGE2

C) PGF2α

D) TXA2

13. What effect does nitric oxide primarily have on the blood vessels?

A) Vasoconstriction

B) Vasodilation

C) Increases blood viscosity

D) Decreases blood flow

14. Which drug is used for the acute treatment of migraines by agonizing 5-HT1 receptors?

A) Duloxetine

B) Sumatriptan

C) Fluoxetine

D) Olanzapine

15. Which of the following is a characteristic of autacoids?

A) Act globally

B) Have long-lasting effects

C) Act near the site of their synthesis

D) Stored in large quantities

16. What is the primary use of H2 antagonists?

A) Treat allergic rhinitis

B) Inhibit gastric acid secretion

C) Manage depression

D) Prevent platelet aggregation

17. Prostaglandins have which of the following effects on the uterus?

A) Relaxation

B) Contraction

C) No effect

D) Reduces sensitivity

18. How does capsaicin function as an analgesic?

A) Blocks NK1 receptors

B) Activates opioid receptors

C) Depletes Substance P

D) Inhibits COX enzymes

19. Which leukotriene pathway inhibitor specifically blocks the 5-lipoxygenase enzyme? A) Montelukast

B) Zafirlukast

C) Zileuton

D) Omalizumab

20. The use of which antirheumatic drug category involves monitoring for liver function due to potential hepatotoxicity?

A) NSAIDs

B) Biologic DMARDs

C) csDMARDs

D) Corticosteroids

Short Answer Type Questions (Subjective)

1. Define autacoids.
2. What are the primary functions of histamine in the body?
3. How do prostaglandins affect inflammation?
4. What role does serotonin play in the central nervous system?
5. Describe the mechanism of action of NSAIDs.
6. What is the significance of COX enzymes in prostaglandin synthesis?
7. Explain how leukotrienes contribute to asthma.
8. What is the therapeutic use of thromboxanes?
9. How do selective serotonin reuptake inhibitors (SSRIs) work?
10. What are the clinical applications of H2 antagonists?
11. Describe the role of nitric oxide in the cardiovascular system.
12. How does bradykinin cause pain?
13. What are the therapeutic applications of angiotensin II receptor blockers (ARBs)?
14. List two adverse effects of corticosteroids.
15. How does colchicine work to treat gout?
16. What is the mechanism of action of ACE inhibitors?
17. What are the uses of prostaglandin analogs in medicine?
18. How do disease-modifying antirheumatic drugs (DMARDs) work?
19. What are the side effects associated with the long-term use of NSAIDs?
20. Explain how leukotriene receptor antagonists help manage asthma symptoms.

Long Answer Type Questions (Subjective)

1. Discuss the synthesis, storage, and functions of histamine in the human body.

2. Explain the role of serotonin in gastrointestinal motility and how drugs targeting serotonin receptors can be used in clinical practice.

3. Describe the synthesis pathway of prostaglandins and their role in inflammation and pain, including the mechanism of action of NSAIDs.

4. Provide a detailed overview of the role of thromboxanes in vascular function and platelet aggregation, including therapeutic approaches to modulate their effects.

5. Explain the role of angiotensin in blood pressure regulation and discuss the pharmacological interventions used to modulate the renin-angiotensin system.

6. Describe the pharmacological effects of bradykinin and the clinical use of drugs that modulate its pathway.

7. Discuss the synthesis, effects, and therapeutic targeting of leukotrienes in inflammatory and allergic conditions.

8. Elaborate on the clinical applications of drugs that target serotonin receptors, with a focus on their use in psychiatric and gastrointestinal disorders.

9. Discuss the therapeutic strategies involving prostaglandin analogs and inhibitors in the treatment of various diseases, including their mechanisms of action and clinical uses.

10. Describe the mechanism of action, uses, and potential side effects of non-steroidal anti-inflammatory drugs (NSAIDs), with a focus on their role in managing pain and inflammation.

Answer Key for MCQs

1. (A) G-protein coupled receptors
2. (C) Increases motility
3. (A) Cyclooxygenase
4. (A) Misoprostol

5. (B) Promotes inflammation

6. (A) AT1

7. (B) Montelukast

8. (B) Increases platelet aggregation

9. (D) Buspirone

10.(C) Celecoxib

11.(B) Renin

12.(B) PGE2

13.(B) Vasodilation

14.(B) Sumatriptan

15.(C) Act near the site of their synthesis

16.(B) Inhibit gastric acid secretion

17.(B) Contraction

18.(C) Depletes Substance P

19.(C) Zileuton

20.(C) csDMARDs

CHAPTER – 5

PHARMACOLOGY OF DRUGS ACTING ON ENDOCRINE SYSTEM

INTRODUCTION:

Pharmacology of drugs acting on the endocrine system involves understanding how various medications affect the hormonal systems in the body to treat endocrine disorders. Here is a detailed introduction to this field:

1. Overview of the Endocrine System

The endocrine system comprises glands that secrete hormones directly into the bloodstream. These hormones regulate various bodily functions, including metabolism, growth, reproduction, and mood. Major endocrine glands include:

a. **Hypothalamus**

b. **Pituitary gland**

c. **Thyroid gland**

d. **Parathyroid glands**

e. **Adrenal glands**

f. **Pancreas**

g. **Gonads (ovaries and testes)**

2. Classes of Endocrine Drugs

Drugs affecting the endocrine system can be broadly categorized based on the gland or hormone they target:

a. Hypothalamic and Pituitary Drugs

i. **Hypothalamic Hormones**: Examples include gonadotropin-releasing hormone (GnRH) analogs (leuprolide, goserelin) used in the treatment of hormone-sensitive cancers and precocious puberty.

ii. **Pituitary Hormones**: Drugs like somatropin (growth hormone) are used in growth hormone deficiency, while vasopressin and desmopressin are used for diabetes insipidus.

b. Thyroid and Antithyroid Drugs

  i. **Thyroid Hormones**: Levothyroxine (T4) and liothyronine (T3) are used to treat hypothyroidism.

  ii. **Antithyroid Drugs**: Methimazole and propylthiouracil are used to treat hyperthyroidism by inhibiting thyroid hormone synthesis.

c. Adrenal Hormones

  i. **Corticosteroids**: Glucocorticoids (e.g., prednisone, dexamethasone) are used for their anti-inflammatory and immunosuppressive effects, while mineralocorticoids (e.g., fludrocortisone) are used in Addison's disease.

  ii. **Adrenal Medulla**: Drugs like epinephrine and norepinephrine are used in acute settings such as anaphylaxis and cardiac arrest.

d. Pancreatic Hormones

  i. **Insulin**: Various forms of insulin (rapid-acting, short-acting, intermediate-acting, and long-acting) are used in the management of diabetes mellitus.

  ii. **Oral Hypoglycemic Agents**: Includes sulfonylureas, biguanides (metformin), thiazolidinediones, DPP-4 inhibitors, and SGLT2 inhibitors.

e. Gonadal Hormones

  i. **Estrogens and Progestins**: Used in hormone replacement therapy, contraception, and certain cancers.

  ii. **Androgens**: Testosterone and its derivatives are used in androgen deficiency.

  iii. **Antiandrogens**: Used in conditions like prostate cancer (e.g., flutamide, bicalutamide).

3. Mechanism of Action

  a. **Hormone Replacement**: Directly supplementing deficient hormones (e.g., levothyroxine for hypothyroidism).

  b. **Inhibition of Hormone Synthesis or Action**: Blocking the synthesis or effects of excess hormones (e.g., antithyroid drugs like methimazole).

c. **Modulation of Receptor Sensitivity**: Enhancing or diminishing the body's sensitivity to hormones (e.g., insulin sensitizers like metformin).

4. Pharmacokinetics and Pharmacodynamics

Understanding the absorption, distribution, metabolism, and excretion (ADME) of endocrine drugs is crucial:

a. **Absorption**: Oral vs. parenteral routes, bioavailability.

b. **Distribution**: Protein binding, volume of distribution.

c. **Metabolism**: Liver metabolism (cytochrome P450 enzymes).

d. **Excretion**: Renal and hepatic pathways.

5. Clinical Applications and Side Effects

a. **Therapeutic Uses**: Management of hormone deficiencies, hypersecretion conditions, and certain cancers.

b. **Side Effects**: Vary widely depending on the drug and hormone system involved. For example, corticosteroids can cause osteoporosis, hyperglycemia, and immune suppression.

6. Recent Advances and Research

a. **Novel Drug Delivery Systems**: Developments in sustained-release formulations, transdermal patches, and implantable devices.

b. **Biologics and Biosimilars**: Introduction of monoclonal antibodies and biosimilar hormones.

c. **Gene Therapy**: Exploring genetic approaches to treat endocrine disorders.

BASIC CONCEPTS IN ENDOCRINE PHARMACOLOGY

Understanding the pharmacology of drugs acting on the endocrine system requires a grasp of several fundamental concepts. These concepts include the physiology of the endocrine system, the mechanisms by which drugs can influence hormone levels and actions, and the clinical applications of these drugs. Here is a detailed breakdown:

Endocrine Physiology

Endocrine physiology forms the foundation upon which the pharmacology of drugs acting on the endocrine system is built. Understanding the physiological principles governing hormone synthesis, secretion, and action is crucial for comprehending how pharmacological interventions can modulate these processes to treat endocrine disorders effectively. Here's an in-depth exploration of key aspects of endocrine physiology relevant to pharmacology:

1. Endocrine Glands and Hormones

a. **Endocrine Glands**: Include glands such as the pituitary, thyroid, adrenal glands, pancreas, parathyroid glands, and gonads.

b. **Hormones**: Chemical messengers secreted directly into the bloodstream to target distant organs or tissues.

2. Hormone Synthesis and Regulation

a. **Synthesis**: Hormones are synthesized within specific endocrine glands in response to various stimuli, including:

   i. **Pituitary Hormones**: Controlled by hypothalamic releasing and inhibiting factors.

   ii. **Thyroid Hormones**: Synthesized from iodine and tyrosine within the thyroid gland.

   iii. **Adrenal Hormones**: Cortisol and aldosterone synthesized in response to adrenocorticotropic hormone (ACTH) from the pituitary.

   iv. **Pancreatic Hormones**: Insulin and glucagon synthesized in response to blood glucose levels.

b. **Regulation**: Hormone secretion is tightly regulated by feedback mechanisms:

   i. **Negative Feedback**: Maintains hormone levels within a normal range (e.g., thyroid hormones regulated by thyroid-stimulating hormone).

ii. **Positive Feedback**: Occurs in specific instances to amplify hormone secretion (e.g., oxytocin during childbirth).

3. Mechanisms of Hormone Action

a. **Receptor-Mediated Action**: Hormones bind to specific receptors on target cells, initiating signaling cascades that regulate cellular functions.

   i. **Steroid Hormones**: Lipophilic hormones that diffuse through cell membranes and bind to intracellular receptors to modulate gene expression (e.g., cortisol).

   ii. **Peptide Hormones**: Hydrophilic hormones that bind to cell surface receptors, activating second messenger systems (e.g., insulin).

4. Feedback Loops in Hormone Regulation

a. **Hypothalamic-Pituitary Axis**: Controls the secretion of many hormones:

   i. **Hypothalamus**: Produces releasing and inhibiting factors that regulate pituitary hormone secretion.

   ii. **Pituitary Gland**: Secretes hormones that regulate other endocrine glands (e.g., thyroid-stimulating hormone, adrenocorticotropic hormone).

5. Endocrine Disorders and Pharmacological Interventions

a. **Hypothyroidism**: Insufficient thyroid hormone production treated with synthetic thyroid hormone (levothyroxine).

b. **Hyperthyroidism**: Excess thyroid hormone production managed with antithyroid medications (methimazole, propylthiouracil).

c. **Diabetes Mellitus**: Deficient insulin production or insulin resistance treated with insulin or oral hypoglycemic agents.

6. Pharmacological Interventions

a. **Mechanisms**: Drugs may act as agonists (mimicking hormone action), antagonists (blocking hormone action), or modulators (affecting hormone synthesis or release).

b. **Therapeutic Targets**: Targeting specific enzymes (e.g., aromatase inhibitors in breast cancer) or receptors (e.g., selective estrogen receptor modulators) involved in hormone regulation.

Mechanisms of Hormone Action

Understanding the mechanisms of hormone action is fundamental to comprehending how pharmacological agents interact with the endocrine system to treat various disorders. Hormones exert their effects through specific mechanisms that involve binding to receptors and initiating signaling pathways within target cells. Here's a detailed exploration of the mechanisms of hormone action in endocrine pharmacology:

1. General Mechanisms of Hormone Action

a. **Receptor Binding**: Hormones bind to specific receptors on target cells, triggering a series of biochemical events.

b. **Signal Transduction**: Initiation of signaling cascades that ultimately regulate cellular functions such as gene transcription, protein synthesis, or metabolic processes.

2. Types of Hormone Receptors

a. **Intracellular Receptors**: Found inside the cell, typically for lipophilic (lipid-soluble) hormones such as steroids.

   i. **Mechanism**: Hormones diffuse through the cell membrane and bind to intracellular receptors (often in the nucleus), altering gene expression.

   ii. **Example**: Cortisol and thyroid hormones act via intracellular receptors.

b. **Cell Surface Receptors**: Located on the cell membrane, typically for hydrophilic (water-soluble) hormones such as peptides and catecholamines.

   i. **Mechanism**: Hormones bind to cell surface receptors, activating second messenger systems that relay signals inside the cell.

   ii. **Examples**: Insulin (tyrosine kinase receptors), glucagon (GPCR receptors).

3. Signal Transduction Pathways

a. **Second Messenger Systems**: Mediate hormone effects by transmitting signals from the cell membrane to intracellular targets.

   1. **cAMP (Cyclic Adenosine Monophosphate) Pathway**: Activated by hormones binding to G-protein coupled receptors (GPCRs).

      i. **Example**: Activation of beta-adrenergic receptors by adrenaline leading to cAMP production.

   2. **Phosphoinositide Pathway**: Involves hydrolysis of phosphoinositides and subsequent activation of protein kinase C (PKC).

      i. **Example**: Action of vasopressin on renal tubules via V2 receptors.

b. **Tyrosine Kinase Pathway**: Activation of receptor tyrosine kinases leads to phosphorylation cascades that regulate gene transcription and cellular processes.

   1. **Example**: Insulin signaling through insulin receptor tyrosine kinase.

4. Feedback Mechanisms

a. **Negative Feedback**: Regulatory mechanism where the end product of a pathway inhibits its own production.

   i. **Example**: Hypothalamic-pituitary-thyroid axis regulation by thyroid hormones.

b. **Positive Feedback**: Amplifies hormone secretion in response to specific stimuli.

   i. **Example**: Oxytocin release during childbirth.

5. Clinical Implications

a. **Drug Development**: Understanding receptor types and signaling pathways helps in developing drugs that can mimic or block hormone actions.

b. **Therapeutic Targets**: Targeting specific steps in hormone action pathways for treating endocrine disorders (e.g., insulin analogues for diabetes mellitus).

6. Pharmacological Interventions

a. **Agonists**: Drugs that mimic hormone action by binding to receptors and activating the same pathways.

   i. **Example**: Levothyroxine as an analogue of thyroid hormone for hypothyroidism.

b. **Antagonists**: Drugs that block hormone action by competing with hormones for receptor binding or inhibiting downstream signaling.

   i. **Example**: Tamoxifen as an estrogen receptor antagonist in breast cancer.

Pharmacokinetics and Pharmacodynamics

Pharmacokinetics and pharmacodynamics are essential concepts in understanding how drugs interact with the endocrine system, influencing hormone levels and physiological responses. These principles help elucidate how drugs are absorbed, distributed, metabolized, and excreted, as well as how they exert their effects on hormone receptors and signaling pathways. Here's a detailed exploration of pharmacokinetics and pharmacodynamics in the context of endocrine pharmacology:

1. Pharmacokinetics

Pharmacokinetics refers to the study of how the body affects a drug, including its absorption, distribution, metabolism, and excretion (ADME).

a. **Absorption**:

    i. **Route**: Endocrine drugs can be administered orally (e.g., thyroid hormones), intravenously (e.g., insulin), or via other routes (e.g., transdermal patches for hormone replacement).

    ii. **Factors**: Absorption depends on factors such as drug formulation, gastrointestinal pH, and presence of food or other medications.

b. **Distribution**:

    i. **Tissue Penetration**: Endocrine drugs distribute throughout the body via the bloodstream, reaching target tissues with varying degrees of permeability.

    ii. **Protein Binding**: Many hormones and their analogues bind to plasma proteins (e.g., thyroxine-binding globulin for thyroid hormones), affecting their distribution and availability.

c. **Metabolism**:

    i. **Liver Metabolism**: Endocrine drugs are often metabolized in the liver by enzymes (e.g., cytochrome P450 enzymes), converting active drugs into inactive metabolites or active metabolites.

    ii. **First-Pass Effect**: Some drugs undergo significant metabolism during their first pass through the liver after oral administration, affecting bioavailability.

d. **Excretion**:

    i. **Renal Clearance**: Endocrine drugs and their metabolites are primarily excreted through the kidneys via urine.

    ii. **Biliary Excretion**: Some drugs may undergo excretion into bile and subsequently into feces.

2. Pharmacodynamics

Pharmacodynamics involves the study of how drugs exert their effects on the body, including the mechanisms of action and their physiological and biochemical effects.

    a. **Mechanisms of Action**:

        i. **Receptor Binding**: Hormones and their analogues bind to specific receptors on target cells, initiating signal transduction pathways that regulate gene expression, enzyme activity, or ion channel function.

        ii. **Enzyme Inhibition**: Some drugs inhibit enzymes involved in hormone synthesis or metabolism (e.g., aromatase inhibitors in breast cancer therapy).

        iii. **Ion Channel Modulation**: Drugs may affect ion channels, altering cellular membrane potential and hormone secretion (e.g., potassium channel modulators in insulin secretion).

    b. **Dose-Response Relationship**:

        i. **Efficacy**: Relationship between drug concentration and magnitude of effect.

        ii. **Potency**: Measure of drug concentration required to produce a specific effect.

    c. **Time Course of Action**:

        i. **Onset and Duration**: Pharmacodynamics also includes the time course of drug action, including onset of action, peak effects, and duration of therapeutic effects.

3. Clinical Implications

    a. **Individual Variability**: Understanding pharmacokinetic and pharmacodynamic variability among patients helps in individualizing drug therapy.

    b. **Drug Interactions**: Recognition of potential interactions with other medications affecting hormone levels or metabolism.

c. **Therapeutic Monitoring**: Regular assessment of hormone levels and clinical response to optimize drug dosing and efficacy.

4. Safety Considerations

a. **Adverse Effects**: Monitoring for adverse drug reactions related to hormone imbalance or excessive pharmacological effects (e.g., hypoglycemia with insulin therapy).

b. **Drug Metabolism**: Considerations for hepatic impairment or renal dysfunction affecting drug clearance.

c. **Long-Term Effects**: Evaluation of potential long-term effects on endocrine function and overall health.

Therapeutic Uses of Endocrine Drugs

Endocrine drugs play a pivotal role in managing a wide range of endocrine disorders by restoring hormonal balance, alleviating symptoms, and improving quality of life for patients. Understanding their therapeutic uses involves recognizing their mechanisms of action, clinical indications, and considerations for effective treatment. Here's an in-depth exploration of the therapeutic uses of endocrine drugs:

1. Thyroid Hormones

a. **Levothyroxine (T4)**:

1. **Mechanism**: Synthetic form of thyroxine (T4) that replaces deficient thyroid hormone.

2. **Therapeutic Uses**:

   i. **Hypothyroidism**: Primary treatment to restore thyroid hormone levels in individuals with inadequate thyroid function.

   ii. **Goiter**: Shrinks goiter by suppressing thyroid-stimulating hormone (TSH) secretion.

   iii. **Thyroid Cancer**: Used in conjunction with surgery or radioactive iodine therapy to suppress TSH levels.

b. **Liothyronine (T3)**:

1. **Mechanism**: Synthetic triiodothyronine (T3) used for rapid correction of severe hypothyroidism or when conversion of T4 to T3 is impaired.

2. **Therapeutic Uses**: Limited use due to shorter half-life compared to T4; sometimes used in combination with levothyroxine.

2. Antithyroid Agents

a. **Methimazole and Propylthiouracil (PTU)**:

1. **Mechanism**: Inhibit thyroid peroxidase enzyme, thereby reducing synthesis of thyroid hormones T4 and T3.

2. **Therapeutic Uses**:

   i. **Hyperthyroidism**: Primary treatment to reduce thyroid hormone levels in Graves' disease, toxic nodular goiter, and thyroid storm.

   ii. **Preoperative Preparation**: Control thyroid hormone levels before thyroidectomy.

3. Glucocorticoids

a. **Prednisone, Dexamethasone**:

1. **Mechanism**: Synthetic analogues of cortisol that bind to glucocorticoid receptors, influencing gene transcription and exerting anti-inflammatory and immunosuppressive effects.

2. **Therapeutic Uses**:

   i. **Adrenal Insufficiency**: Replace deficient cortisol in primary adrenal insufficiency (Addison's disease) or secondary adrenal insufficiency.

   ii. **Autoimmune Diseases**: Manage inflammatory conditions such as rheumatoid arthritis, lupus, and inflammatory bowel disease.

iii. **Allergic Reactions**: Control severe allergic reactions and anaphylaxis.

4. Mineralocorticoids

a. **Fludrocortisone**:

1. **Mechanism**: Synthetic analogue of aldosterone that acts on mineralocorticoid receptors, regulating electrolyte balance and blood pressure.

2. **Therapeutic Uses**:

i. **Addison's Disease**: Replace deficient aldosterone in combination with glucocorticoid replacement therapy.

5. Insulin and Oral Hypoglycemic Agents

a. **Insulin (Various Preparations)**:

1. **Mechanism**: Hormone that regulates glucose metabolism by facilitating glucose uptake into cells.

2. **Therapeutic Uses**:

i. **Diabetes Mellitus Type 1**: Essential for managing blood glucose levels in individuals with autoimmune destruction of pancreatic beta cells.

ii. **Diabetes Mellitus Type 2**: Used when lifestyle modifications and oral medications are insufficient to control blood glucose.

b. **Oral Hypoglycemic Agents** (e.g., Metformin, Sulfonylureas, DPP-4 Inhibitors, SGLT-2 Inhibitors):

1. **Mechanism**: Act through various mechanisms to lower blood glucose levels (e.g., enhancing insulin secretion, improving insulin sensitivity, inhibiting glucose reabsorption).

2. **Therapeutic Uses**: Management of diabetes mellitus type 2 to improve glycemic control and prevent complications.

6. Sex Hormones

   a. **Estrogen, Progesterone, Testosterone**:

      1. **Mechanism**: Regulate secondary sexual characteristics, reproductive functions, and bone metabolism.

      2. **Therapeutic Uses**:

         i. **Hormone Replacement Therapy**: Manage symptoms of menopause (e.g., hot flashes, vaginal dryness) and prevent osteoporosis in postmenopausal women.

        ii. **Hypogonadism**: Replace deficient sex hormones in conditions such as primary ovarian or testicular failure.

7. Bone Metabolism Regulators

   a. **Calcitonin, Bisphosphonates, Denosumab**:

      1. **Mechanism**: Act on bone metabolism to regulate calcium balance and bone density.

      2. **Therapeutic Uses**:

         i. **Osteoporosis**: Prevent bone loss and reduce fracture risk by increasing bone density and inhibiting bone resorption.

8. Pituitary Hormones and Analogues

   a. **Growth Hormone (Somatotropin)**:

      i. **Mechanism**: Stimulate growth, cell reproduction, and regeneration.

      ii. **Therapeutic Uses**: Growth hormone deficiency in children and adults, Turner syndrome, and chronic kidney disease.

   b. **Others**: Includes pituitary hormone analogues such as vasopressin analogues (desmopressin) for diabetes insipidus and gonadotropin-releasing hormone analogues for hormone-sensitive cancers.

Regulation of Endocrine Function

The regulation of endocrine function involves complex mechanisms that maintain hormonal balance and coordinate physiological processes throughout the body. Understanding these regulatory mechanisms is crucial in pharmacology to develop effective treatments for endocrine disorders. Here's a detailed exploration of how endocrine function is regulated:

1. Hypothalamic-Pituitary Axis

The hypothalamus and pituitary gland play central roles in regulating many endocrine functions through the production and release of various hormones:

a. **Hypothalamus**:

    1. **Hormones**: Produces releasing and inhibiting hormones that control the secretion of pituitary hormones.

    2. **Examples**: Thyrotropin-releasing hormone (TRH), gonadotropin-releasing hormone (GnRH), corticotropin-releasing hormone (CRH).

b. **Pituitary Gland**:

    1. **Anterior Pituitary**: Secretes hormones in response to hypothalamic signals.

        i. **Examples**: Thyroid-stimulating hormone (TSH), adrenocorticotropic hormone (ACTH), follicle-stimulating hormone (FSH), luteinizing hormone (LH).

    2. **Posterior Pituitary**: Stores and releases hormones produced by the hypothalamus.

        i. **Examples**: Oxytocin, vasopressin (antidiuretic hormone, ADH).

2. Feedback Mechanisms

Feedback loops are essential in regulating hormone secretion and maintaining homeostasis:

a. **Negative Feedback**:

    i. **Mechanism**: End product of a pathway inhibits further hormone release.

ii. **Example**: Thyroid hormones inhibit TRH and TSH release through negative feedback loops.

b. **Positive Feedback**:

i. **Mechanism**: Amplifies hormone secretion in response to certain stimuli.

ii. **Example**: Estrogen feedback on gonadotropin secretion during the menstrual cycle.

3. Peripheral Hormone Regulation

Endocrine glands throughout the body respond to central and local signals to regulate hormone production:

a. **Thyroid Gland**:

i. **Regulation**: Controlled by TSH from the pituitary gland in response to circulating thyroid hormone levels.

b. **Adrenal Glands**:

i. **Cortisol Regulation**: Regulated by ACTH from the pituitary gland, influenced by stress and circadian rhythms.

c. **Pancreas**:

i. **Insulin and Glucagon**: Secretion regulated by blood glucose levels, with insulin released in response to high glucose and glucagon in response to low glucose.

d. **Gonads**:

i. **Sex Hormones**: Regulated by gonadotropins (LH and FSH) from the pituitary gland, modulated by feedback from sex steroids.

4. Role of Feedback in Pharmacology

Understanding feedback mechanisms is critical in pharmacology for designing treatments that modulate hormone levels effectively:

a. **Agonists and Antagonists**: Drugs can mimic (agonists) or block (antagonists) hormone actions at receptors, influencing feedback loops.

b. **Enzyme Inhibitors**: Target enzymes involved in hormone synthesis or metabolism, altering feedback signals.

c. **Modulators**: Drugs that affect hormone release or receptor sensitivity, modifying feedback responses.

5. Clinical Implications

Effective management of endocrine disorders relies on understanding regulatory mechanisms:

a. **Diagnostic Tools**: Hormonal tests assess feedback mechanisms to diagnose endocrine disorders (e.g., dexamethasone suppression test for Cushing's syndrome).

b. **Therapeutic Monitoring**: Monitoring hormone levels and clinical response helps adjust pharmacological treatments to optimize outcomes.

c. **Treatment Strategies**: Individualized treatment plans consider feedback mechanisms to minimize side effects and achieve therapeutic goals.

6. Drug Classes and Their Actions

a. **Hypothalamic and Pituitary Drugs**: Include analogs of releasing hormones (e.g., GnRH agonists) and pituitary hormones (e.g., somatropin for growth hormone deficiency).

b. **Thyroid Drugs**: Levothyroxine for thyroid hormone replacement; antithyroid drugs like methimazole inhibit thyroid hormone synthesis.

c. **Adrenal Cortex Drugs**: Glucocorticoids (e.g., prednisone) for anti-inflammatory and immunosuppressive effects; mineralocorticoids (e.g., fludrocortisone) for adrenal insufficiency.

d. **Pancreatic Drugs**: Insulins and oral hypoglycemic agents (e.g., sulfonylureas, biguanides) for diabetes management.

e. **Gonadal Hormones and Modulators**: Estrogens, progestins, androgens, and their antagonists for conditions like hormone replacement, contraception, and certain cancers.

7. Adverse Effects and Monitoring

a. **Adverse Effects**: Hormone therapies can have significant side effects due to their widespread actions in the body. For example, glucocorticoids can cause osteoporosis, hyperglycemia, and increased infection risk.

b. **Monitoring**: Regular monitoring of hormone levels and clinical symptoms is essential to adjust dosages and ensure therapeutic efficacy while minimizing side effects.

ANTERIOR PITUITARY HORMONES- ANALOGUES AND THEIR INHIBITORS

The anterior pituitary gland secretes several hormones that regulate various physiological processes, including growth, metabolism, and reproduction. Drugs that act on the anterior pituitary can be either analogues of these hormones or inhibitors that regulate their secretion or action. Here is a detailed examination of these drugs:

1. Growth Hormone (GH)

a. **Analogues**:

   i. **Somatropin**: Recombinant human growth hormone used for GH deficiency, Turner syndrome, chronic renal insufficiency, and cachexia associated with AIDS.

b. **Inhibitors**:

   i. **Somatostatin Analogs**: Octreotide, lanreotide, and pasireotide inhibit GH release and are used to treat acromegaly and neuroendocrine tumors.

2. Thyroid-Stimulating Hormone (TSH)

a. **Analogues**:

   i. **Thyrotropin alfa**: Recombinant human TSH used in diagnostic testing for thyroid function and to enhance radioactive iodine uptake in thyroid cancer treatment.

b. **Inhibitors**:

i. There are no direct inhibitors of TSH, but thyroid hormone replacement (levothyroxine) can suppress TSH secretion via negative feedback in conditions like hypothyroidism.

3. Adrenocorticotropic Hormone (ACTH)

a. **Analogues**:

i. **Cosyntropin**: Synthetic ACTH used primarily for diagnostic purposes in adrenal insufficiency.

b. **Inhibitors**:

i. **Pasireotide**: A somatostatin analog that inhibits ACTH secretion in Cushing's disease.

ii. **Glucocorticoids**: Such as dexamethasone can suppress ACTH production via negative feedback.

4. Gonadotropins (LH and FSH)

a. **Analogues**:

i. **Human Menopausal Gonadotropin (hMG)**: Contains both LH and FSH used for fertility treatments.

ii. **Follitropin alfa and beta**: Recombinant FSH used for controlled ovarian stimulation and infertility.

iii. **Lutropin alfa**: Recombinant LH used in combination with follitropin alfa for infertility.

b. **Inhibitors**:

i. **GnRH Agonists**: Leuprolide, goserelin, nafarelin, and triptorelin initially stimulate but then suppress LH and FSH secretion through receptor downregulation. Used in prostate cancer, endometriosis, and precocious puberty.

ii. **GnRH Antagonists**: Cetrorelix and ganirelix directly inhibit GnRH receptors to prevent premature LH surge in assisted reproductive technologies.

5. Prolactin (PRL)

a. **Analogues**:

   i. There are no therapeutic prolactin analogues as prolactin deficiency is rare and usually asymptomatic.

b. **Inhibitors**:

   i. **Dopamine Agonists**: Bromocriptine and cabergoline inhibit prolactin release by activating dopamine receptors. Used in hyperprolactinemia, prolactinomas, and Parkinson's disease.

Mechanisms of Action and Clinical Applications

a. Growth Hormone Analogues and Inhibitors

   i. **Somatropin**: Mimics endogenous GH, stimulating growth and cell reproduction.

   ii. **Octreotide**: Mimics somatostatin, inhibiting GH, insulin, and glucagon secretion.

b. TSH Analogues and Inhibitors

   i. **Thyrotropin alfa**: Stimulates thyroid gland function and increases iodine uptake.

   ii. **Thyroid hormone replacement**: Suppresses TSH via negative feedback.

c. ACTH Analogues and Inhibitors

   i. **Cosyntropin**: Stimulates adrenal cortex to produce cortisol.

   ii. **Pasireotide and glucocorticoids**: Inhibit ACTH secretion, reducing cortisol production in conditions like Cushing's disease.

d. Gonadotropin Analogues and Inhibitors

   i. **hMG, Follitropin, Lutropin**: Stimulate ovarian follicle development and spermatogenesis.

   ii. **GnRH agonists and antagonists**: Control the release of LH and FSH, managing hormone-related conditions.

e. Prolactin Inhibitors

i. **Bromocriptine and Cabergoline**: Reduce prolactin secretion by stimulating dopamine receptors, addressing conditions like hyperprolactinemia and prolactinomas.

Pharmacokinetics and Pharmacodynamics

Understanding the ADME profile (Absorption, Distribution, Metabolism, Excretion) of these drugs is crucial:

a. **Analogues**: Often administered via injection due to poor oral bioavailability.

b. **Inhibitors**: Can be oral or injectable, depending on the drug and condition treated.

Adverse Effects

a. **Somatropin**: Joint pain, insulin resistance, edema.

b. **Somatostatin analogs**: Gastrointestinal disturbances, gallstones.

c. **GnRH analogs**: Initial hormone surge (flare), long-term suppression effects (e.g., osteoporosis).

d. **Dopamine agonists**: Nausea, orthostatic hypotension, psychiatric effects.

THYROID HORMONES- ANALOGUES AND THEIR INHIBITORS

Thyroid hormones play a critical role in regulating metabolism, growth, and development. Pharmacological agents that act on the thyroid gland include both analogues that replace or supplement thyroid hormones and inhibitors that reduce thyroid hormone synthesis or action. Here is a detailed exploration of these drugs:

Thyroid Hormones and Their Analogues

Thyroid hormones, primarily thyroxine (T4) and triiodothyronine (T3), are essential for regulating metabolism, growth, and development throughout the body. This section provides a comprehensive overview of thyroid hormones and their analogues, including their pharmacology, mechanisms of action, clinical uses, pharmacokinetics, and therapeutic implications in the context of thyroid disorders.

Thyroid Hormones: T4 and T3

1. **Natural Thyroid Hormones**:
    a. **Thyroxine (T4)**: Produced by the thyroid gland, T4 is the prohormone that is converted peripherally to the active hormone T3.
    b. **Triiodothyronine (T3)**: The biologically active form of thyroid hormone, T3 is more potent than T4 and directly influences cellular metabolism.

2. **Mechanisms of Action**:
    a. **Nuclear Receptors**: T3 binds to nuclear thyroid hormone receptors (TRs) in target tissues, forming hormone-receptor complexes that regulate gene transcription.
    b. **Metabolic Effects**: Thyroid hormones increase basal metabolic rate, heat production (thermogenesis), protein synthesis, and oxygen consumption in tissues.

3. **Regulation of Metabolism**:
    a. **Calorigenic Effects**: Thyroid hormones stimulate ATP-dependent sodium-potassium pumps, increasing cellular oxygen consumption and heat production.
    b. **Lipid and Carbohydrate Metabolism**: They enhance lipolysis and glycogenolysis, mobilizing fats and glucose for energy production.

Clinical Uses and Analogues

1. **Hypothyroidism Treatment**:
    a. **Levothyroxine (T4)**: Synthetic analogue of T4, levothyroxine is the standard treatment for hypothyroidism.
        i. **Mechanism**: Converted to T3 peripherally, providing replacement therapy for deficient thyroid hormone production.

ii. **Administration**: Oral administration, typically taken once daily in the morning.

iii. **Monitoring**: Regular monitoring of thyroid function tests (TSH, T4, and sometimes T3) to adjust dosage and ensure euthyroid state.

2. **Hyperthyroidism Treatment**:

    a. **Thionamides (Methimazole, Propylthiouracil)**: Inhibit thyroid hormone synthesis by blocking iodine incorporation and thyroid peroxidase activity.

        i. **Clinical Uses**: Used in the treatment of hyperthyroidism, particularly as a preparatory treatment before surgery or radioiodine therapy.

3. **Thyroid Hormone Analogue: Liothyronine (T3)**:

    a. **Clinical Role**: Synthetic T3 analogue used in the treatment of hypothyroidism, especially when conversion of T4 to T3 is impaired.

    b. **Administration**: Oral or intravenous administration; more potent than T4 but shorter duration of action.

    c. **Monitoring**: Similar to levothyroxine, requires monitoring of thyroid function tests.

Pharmacokinetics

1. **Absorption**: Oral administration of thyroid hormones is well absorbed in the gastrointestinal tract.

2. **Distribution**: Thyroid hormones bind extensively to plasma proteins (thyroxine-binding globulin, albumin).

3. **Metabolism**: Liver and peripheral tissues metabolize thyroid hormones, with T4 converting to T3.

4. **Excretion**: Metabolites are primarily excreted in the urine.

Adverse Effects

1. **Hypothyroidism Treatment**: Over-replacement can lead to symptoms of hyperthyroidism (e.g., palpitations, weight loss, heat intolerance).

2. **Hyperthyroidism Treatment**: Thionamides can cause agranulocytosis, hepatotoxicity, and other rare adverse effects.

3. **Cardiovascular Effects**: Thyroid hormones can affect cardiovascular function, including heart rate and contractility.

Thyroid Hormone Synthesis Inhibitors

Thyroid hormone synthesis inhibitors are medications used primarily in the treatment of hyperthyroidism to reduce the production of thyroid hormones by interfering with various steps in thyroid hormone synthesis. This section provides a detailed overview of thyroid hormone synthesis inhibitors, including their mechanisms of action, clinical uses, pharmacokinetics, and therapeutic implications.

Mechanisms of Action

Thyroid hormone synthesis inhibitors work by targeting key enzymes and processes involved in the synthesis of thyroid hormones, predominantly thyroxine (T4) and triiodothyronine (T3). These medications interfere with iodine uptake, thyroid peroxidase activity, and thyroid hormone release, thereby reducing the production and secretion of thyroid hormones from the thyroid gland.

1. **Thyroid Peroxidase Inhibitors**:

   a. **Methimazole (MMI) and Propylthiouracil (PTU)**:

      i. **Mechanism**: Inhibit thyroid peroxidase enzyme, which is essential for iodination of tyrosine residues in thyroglobulin (Tg) and coupling of iodotyrosine residues to form T3 and T4.

      ii. **Clinical Uses**: Treatment of hyperthyroidism, Graves' disease, and as preparatory therapy before thyroidectomy or radioactive iodine therapy.

2. **Iodine Uptake Inhibitors**:

   a. **Potassium Iodide (KI)**:

      i. **Mechanism**: High doses of iodide inhibit iodine uptake by the thyroid gland, thereby reducing thyroid hormone synthesis and release.

      ii. **Clinical Uses**: Short-term treatment of thyrotoxic crisis (thyroid storm) and as adjunctive therapy in preparation for thyroidectomy or radioactive iodine therapy.

Clinical Uses

1. **Hyperthyroidism Management**:

   a. **Graves' Disease**: First-line treatment to control symptoms of hyperthyroidism, including tremors, palpitations, heat intolerance, and weight loss.

   b. **Thyroid Storm**: Rapid control of severe hyperthyroidism symptoms to stabilize the patient's condition before definitive treatment.

2. **Preoperative Preparation**:

   a. **Thyroidectomy**: Reduces thyroid hormone levels preoperatively to minimize the risk of perioperative complications such as thyroid storm.

   b. **Radioactive Iodine Therapy**: Prepares patients by decreasing thyroid hormone levels before administering radioactive iodine to destroy thyroid tissue.

Pharmacokinetics

1. **Absorption**: Generally well absorbed after oral administration.

2. **Distribution**: Methimazole and PTU cross the placenta and are excreted in breast milk.

3. **Metabolism**: Methimazole is primarily metabolized in the liver, while PTU undergoes extensive hepatic metabolism.

4. **Excretion**: Both medications and their metabolites are excreted renally.

Monitoring and Adjustments

1. **Thyroid Function Tests**: Monitor serum levels of thyroid-stimulating hormone (TSH), free T4 (FT4), and free T3 (FT3) to assess thyroid function and adjust dosage accordingly.

2. **Liver Function Tests**: Regular monitoring of liver enzymes (especially with PTU) to detect potential hepatotoxicity.

Adverse Effects

1. **Methimazole**: Common adverse effects include rash, pruritus, arthralgia, and gastrointestinal disturbances. Rare but serious adverse effects include agranulocytosis and hepatotoxicity.

2. **Propylthiouracil (PTU)**: Can cause agranulocytosis, hepatotoxicity, and rarely, severe vasculitis.

3. **Potassium Iodide (KI)**: Adverse effects include gastrointestinal upset, hypersensitivity reactions, and iodism (metallic taste, soreness of teeth and gums, frontal headache, and coryza).

Mechanisms and Clinical Implications

Thyroid hormones and their analogues, along with inhibitors of thyroid hormone synthesis, are critical components in the management of thyroid disorders. This section provides an in-depth exploration of their mechanisms of action, clinical implications, and therapeutic applications in pharmacology.

1. Thyroid Hormones: T4 and T3

Mechanisms of Action:

a. **Nuclear Receptors**: Both thyroxine (T4) and triiodothyronine (T3) bind to nuclear thyroid hormone receptors (TRs) in target cells.

b. **Gene Transcription**: Hormone-receptor complexes modulate gene transcription, influencing cellular metabolism, growth, and development.

c. **Metabolic Effects**: Thyroid hormones increase basal metabolic rate, protein synthesis, and oxygen consumption in tissues.

Clinical Implications:

a. **Hypothyroidism**: Replacement therapy with synthetic T4 (levothyroxine) or T3 (liothyronine) is essential for managing hypothyroidism and preventing associated symptoms such as fatigue, weight gain, and cold intolerance.

b. **Monitoring**: Regular monitoring of thyroid function tests (TSH, T4, and T3 levels) ensures adequate hormone replacement and optimal therapeutic outcomes.

2. Thyroid Hormone Analogues

Mechanisms of Action:

a. **Levothyroxine (T4)**: Synthetic T4 analogue that serves as a prohormone converted peripherally to T3.

   i. **Clinical Use**: Primary treatment for hypothyroidism, providing stable and sustained thyroid hormone replacement.

b. **Liothyronine (T3)**: Synthetic T3 analogue with more rapid onset and shorter duration of action than T4.

   i. **Clinical Use**: Sometimes used in combination with levothyroxine for patients with impaired T4 to T3 conversion or when rapid correction of hypothyroidism is needed.

Clinical Implications:

a. **Dosing**: Individualized dosing based on patient response and thyroid function tests.

b. **Bioequivalence**: Ensuring bioequivalence and consistency in hormone levels through proper administration and monitoring.

3. Thyroid Hormone Synthesis Inhibitors

Mechanisms of Action:

a. **Thyroid Peroxidase Inhibitors (Methimazole, Propylthiouracil)**:

i. **Mechanism**: Inhibit thyroid peroxidase enzyme, reducing iodine oxidation and organification, thereby decreasing thyroid hormone synthesis.

ii. **Clinical Use**: Treatment of hyperthyroidism, Graves' disease, and thyroid storm.

b. **Iodine Uptake Inhibitors (Potassium Iodide)**:

i. **Mechanism**: High doses of iodide inhibit thyroid gland uptake of iodine, temporarily reducing thyroid hormone synthesis and release.

ii. **Clinical Use**: Short-term management of thyroid storm and preparation for thyroidectomy or radioactive iodine therapy.

Clinical Implications:

a. **Efficacy**: Effective in controlling hyperthyroid symptoms and preparing patients for definitive therapies.

b. **Adverse Effects**: Monitoring for adverse effects such as agranulocytosis (with thionamides), hepatotoxicity (with PTU), and potential iodine-induced thyroid dysfunction (with potassium iodide).

4. Pharmacokinetics and Monitoring

a. **Absorption and Distribution**: Varied absorption rates and protein binding affect pharmacokinetics and dosing schedules.

b. **Metabolism and Excretion**: Metabolized primarily in the liver and excreted in the urine.

c. **Monitoring**: Regular thyroid function tests (TSH, T4, T3) and liver function tests (especially with PTU) are crucial for adjusting therapy and monitoring for adverse effects.

HORMONES REGULATING PLASMA CALCIUM LEVEL- PARATHORMONE, CALCITONIN AND VITAMIN- D, INSULIN

The regulation of plasma calcium levels is essential for numerous physiological processes, including bone health, neuromuscular function, and blood coagulation. The key hormones involved in calcium homeostasis are parathyroid hormone (PTH), calcitonin, and vitamin D. While insulin primarily regulates glucose metabolism, it can have indirect effects on calcium metabolism as well. Here is a detailed exploration of these hormones in the context of pharmacology:

1. Parathyroid Hormone (PTH)

Parathyroid hormone (PTH), also known as parathormone, is a crucial regulator of calcium and phosphate metabolism in the body. Produced by the parathyroid glands, PTH acts through various mechanisms to maintain extracellular calcium concentrations within a narrow physiological range. This section provides an in-depth exploration of the pharmacology of PTH, including its mechanisms of action, clinical significance, therapeutic uses, pharmacokinetics, and associated disorders.

Mechanisms of Action

1. **Calcium Homeostasis**:
    a. **Bone Resorption**: PTH stimulates osteoclast activity in bones, leading to the breakdown of bone matrix and release of calcium and phosphate into the bloodstream.
    b. **Renal Effects**: PTH enhances renal tubular reabsorption of calcium in the distal convoluted tubules, thereby reducing urinary calcium excretion.
    c. **Activation of Vitamin D**: PTH indirectly stimulates the kidneys to produce active vitamin D (calcitriol), which enhances intestinal absorption of calcium.

2. **Phosphate Regulation**:
    a. **Renal Effects**: PTH decreases phosphate reabsorption in the proximal renal tubules, increasing phosphate excretion in urine.
    b. **Direct Effects on Bone**: PTH inhibits osteoblast activity, which indirectly reduces bone formation and phosphate deposition.

3. **Calcium-Sensing Receptor (CaSR)**:

   a. PTH regulates its own secretion via feedback mechanisms involving the CaSR, which senses changes in extracellular calcium levels.

Clinical Significance

1. **Hypoparathyroidism**:

   a. **Causes**: Surgical removal of parathyroid glands, autoimmune disorders, or genetic mutations.

   b. **Consequences**: Low PTH levels lead to hypocalcemia (low blood calcium levels) and hyperphosphatemia (high blood phosphate levels), resulting in symptoms like muscle cramps, tetany, and seizures.

2. **Hyperparathyroidism**:

   a. **Primary Hyperparathyroidism**: Overproduction of PTH due to adenoma or hyperplasia of parathyroid glands.

   b. **Secondary Hyperparathyroidism**: Increased PTH secretion in response to chronic hypocalcemia or vitamin D deficiency.

   c. **Consequences**: Hypercalcemia (high blood calcium levels), which can lead to kidney stones, bone pain, and gastrointestinal disturbances.

Therapeutic Uses

1. **Treatment of Hypoparathyroidism**:

   a. **PTH Replacement Therapy**: Recombinant human PTH (teriparatide) is used to increase blood calcium levels in patients with severe hypocalcemia due to hypoparathyroidism.

2. **Osteoporosis Treatment**:

   a. **Teriparatide**: Intermittent administration of teriparatide stimulates bone formation, making it useful in the treatment of osteoporosis in postmenopausal women and men at high risk of fractures.

Pharmacokinetics

1. **Administration**: Teriparatide is administered subcutaneously once daily.

2. **Absorption**: Rapid absorption after subcutaneous injection.

3. **Distribution**: Binds to PTH receptors on bone cells and kidneys.

4. **Metabolism**: Metabolized in the liver and excreted primarily in the urine.

5. **Half-Life**: Approximately 1 hour for teriparatide.

Monitoring and Adjustments

1. **Monitoring**: Assess serum calcium and phosphate levels regularly during PTH replacement therapy.

2. **Adjustments**: Titrate the dose of teriparatide based on clinical response and laboratory values to achieve target calcium levels without inducing hypercalcemia.

Adverse Effects

1. **Hypercalcemia**: The most significant adverse effect of PTH therapy, leading to potential kidney stones, nausea, vomiting, and bone pain.

2. **Orthostatic Hypotension**: Due to transient reductions in blood pressure after injection.

2. Calcitonin

Calcitonin is a hormone primarily involved in the regulation of calcium and phosphate metabolism in the body. Produced by the parafollicular cells (C cells) of the thyroid gland, calcitonin works antagonistically to parathyroid hormone (PTH) to decrease blood calcium levels. This section provides a comprehensive overview of the pharmacology of calcitonin, including its mechanisms of action, clinical uses, pharmacokinetics, and associated therapeutic implications.

Mechanism of Action

1. **Inhibition of Bone Resorption**:

    a. Calcitonin binds to specific receptors on osteoclasts, inhibiting their activity and reducing bone resorption.

b. This leads to decreased release of calcium and phosphate from bones into the bloodstream.

2. **Renal Effects**:

   a. Calcitonin increases renal excretion of calcium and phosphate by inhibiting their reabsorption in the kidneys.

   b. This further contributes to lowering blood calcium levels.

3. **Overall Effect**:

   a. Calcitonin opposes the actions of PTH, which predominantly increases blood calcium levels through bone resorption and renal calcium reabsorption.

Clinical Uses

1. **Osteoporosis**:

   a. **Therapeutic Role**: Calcitonin is used as a treatment option for osteoporosis, especially in postmenopausal women who cannot tolerate or do not respond adequately to other therapies.

   b. **Mechanism**: By inhibiting bone resorption, calcitonin helps preserve bone mass and reduce the risk of fractures.

2. **Hypercalcemia**:

   a. **Emergency Treatment**: Calcitonin can be used in the acute management of hypercalcemia, such as in hyperparathyroidism or certain cancers that cause excessive calcium release from bones.

Pharmacokinetics

1. **Administration**: Calcitonin can be administered intranasally, subcutaneously, or intramuscularly.

2. **Absorption**: Intranasal administration provides rapid absorption through the nasal mucosa.

3. **Distribution**: Calcitonin has a short duration of action and is mainly distributed to bone and kidney tissues.

4. **Metabolism**: Metabolized in various tissues, with a short half-life requiring frequent dosing.

5. **Excretion**: Metabolites are excreted primarily in urine.

Monitoring and Adjustments

1. **Monitoring**: Evaluate bone mineral density and serum calcium levels periodically during calcitonin therapy.

2. **Adjustments**: Adjust dosage based on clinical response and serum calcium levels to achieve optimal therapeutic outcomes.

Adverse Effects

1. **Nasal Formulation**: Nasal irritation or discomfort may occur with intranasal calcitonin.

2. **Hypocalcemia**: Excessive use of calcitonin can lead to transient hypocalcemia, necessitating monitoring of serum calcium levels.

Controversies and Considerations

1. **Efficacy Concerns**: The efficacy of calcitonin in osteoporosis treatment has been debated, with some studies suggesting modest benefits in bone density preservation but uncertain effects on fracture risk reduction.

2. **Alternative Therapies**: Due to concerns over efficacy and availability of other osteoporosis treatments (e.g., bisphosphonates, denosumab), calcitonin is generally considered a second-line option.

3. Vitamin D

Vitamin D is a unique hormone-like substance that plays a crucial role in calcium and phosphate homeostasis, bone health, and various physiological processes throughout the body. This section provides a detailed exploration of the pharmacology of vitamin D, including its synthesis, metabolism, mechanisms of action, clinical uses, and therapeutic implications in the context of calcium regulation and beyond.

Synthesis and Metabolism

1. **Synthesis**:

a. **Cutaneous Synthesis**: UVB radiation converts 7-dehydrocholesterol in the skin to previtamin D3, which is subsequently converted to vitamin D3 (cholecalciferol).

b. **Dietary Sources**: Vitamin D2 (ergocalciferol) and vitamin D3 are obtained from dietary sources such as fortified foods (e.g., dairy products, cereals) and supplements.

2. **Activation**:

a. Vitamin D undergoes hydroxylation in the liver to form 25-hydroxyvitamin D [25(OH)D], the major circulating form.

b. Further hydroxylation in the kidneys by 1-alpha-hydroxylase (regulated by PTH) converts 25(OH)D to the active form, 1,25-dihydroxyvitamin D [1,25(OH)2D], also known as calcitriol.

Mechanisms of Action

1. **Intestinal Absorption of Calcium and Phosphate**:

a. Calcitriol stimulates the expression of proteins involved in intestinal absorption of calcium (and phosphate) from the diet.

b. This enhances calcium and phosphate uptake from the gut into circulation, maintaining adequate serum levels.

2. **Bone Remodeling**:

a. Calcitriol promotes bone mineralization by regulating osteoblast and osteoclast activity.

b. It supports bone formation by stimulating osteoblasts and regulating the release of calcium and phosphate from bone stores.

3. **Renal Effects**:

a. Calcitriol enhances renal reabsorption of calcium and phosphate, thereby conserving these minerals and maintaining serum levels.

Clinical Uses

1. **Treatment and Prevention of Vitamin D Deficiency**:

a. **Supplementation**: Vitamin D supplements (ergocalciferol or cholecalciferol) are prescribed to correct deficiencies and maintain adequate serum levels.

b. **Prevention**: Recommended for individuals at risk of deficiency due to insufficient sunlight exposure, dietary factors, or malabsorption disorders.

2. **Osteoporosis Management**:

a. **Adjunctive Therapy**: Used in combination with bisphosphonates or other anti-resorptive agents to enhance bone mineral density and reduce fracture risk in osteoporosis.

3. **Secondary Hyperparathyroidism**:

a. **Management**: Calcitriol or vitamin D analogs may be used to suppress PTH secretion in chronic kidney disease (CKD) patients with secondary hyperparathyroidism.

Pharmacokinetics

1. **Absorption**: Vitamin D is absorbed from the small intestine along with dietary fats.

2. **Distribution**: Vitamin D and its metabolites circulate bound to vitamin D-binding protein (DBP).

3. **Metabolism**: Metabolized in the liver and kidneys to active forms (1,25(OH)2D).

4. **Excretion**: Excreted primarily in bile and urine.

Monitoring and Adjustments

1. **Monitoring**: Measure serum 25(OH)D levels to assess vitamin D status; monitor serum calcium and phosphate levels during therapy.

2. **Adjustments**: Adjust vitamin D supplementation based on serum levels and clinical response to maintain optimal bone health and calcium metabolism.

Adverse Effects

1. **Hypercalcemia**: Excessive vitamin D supplementation can lead to hypercalcemia, characterized by symptoms such as nausea, vomiting, weakness, and kidney stones.
2. **Hypervitaminosis D**: Rare condition resulting from prolonged high-dose vitamin D supplementation, causing hypercalcemia and potential toxicity.

4. Insulin

Insulin is a peptide hormone critical for glucose homeostasis, but it also plays a role in calcium metabolism indirectly through its effects on other hormones and metabolic pathways. This section provides insights into the pharmacology of insulin, its interactions with hormones involved in calcium regulation (parathyroid hormone, calcitonin, and vitamin D), clinical implications, and therapeutic uses.

Mechanisms of Action

1. **Glucose Homeostasis**:
   a. Insulin promotes glucose uptake into cells, particularly muscle and adipose tissue, by facilitating the translocation of glucose transporter proteins (GLUT-4) to the cell membrane.
   b. It stimulates glycogen synthesis in the liver and skeletal muscles, thereby reducing blood glucose levels postprandially.
2. **Lipid and Protein Metabolism**:
   a. Insulin promotes lipogenesis (synthesis of fatty acids) in adipose tissue and inhibits lipolysis (breakdown of fats).
   b. It enhances protein synthesis and inhibits protein breakdown, supporting cellular growth and repair.
3. **Calcium Regulation**:
   a. **Indirect Effects**: Insulin indirectly affects calcium metabolism through its interactions with other hormones such as PTH, calcitonin, and vitamin D.

b. **Calcium Homeostasis**: Insulin helps maintain calcium homeostasis by influencing bone metabolism indirectly through its effects on bone formation and remodeling processes.

Clinical Implications

1. **Hyperglycemia and Calcium Regulation**:

   a. **Hyperglycemia Effects**: Uncontrolled diabetes mellitus, particularly type 1 diabetes, can lead to disturbances in calcium metabolism due to alterations in insulin levels and action.

   b. **Secondary Effects**: Prolonged hyperglycemia can affect bone health and increase the risk of osteoporosis and fractures.

2. **Diabetes Mellitus and Bone Health**:

   a. **Type 1 Diabetes**: Insulin deficiency in type 1 diabetes can lead to impaired bone formation and increased bone resorption, affecting overall bone density and strength.

   b. **Type 2 Diabetes**: Insulin resistance in type 2 diabetes may contribute to disturbances in bone metabolism and increased fracture risk.

Therapeutic Uses

1. **Diabetes Management**:

   a. **Type 1 Diabetes**: Insulin replacement therapy is essential for managing blood glucose levels and preventing complications associated with insulin deficiency.

   b. **Type 2 Diabetes**: Insulin therapy may be initiated when other oral hypoglycemic agents are insufficient to control blood glucose levels.

2. **Bone Health Considerations**:

   a. **Importance**: Optimal management of diabetes, including glycemic control with insulin, is crucial for preserving bone health and reducing the risk of osteoporosis.

Pharmacokinetics

1. **Administration**: Insulin is administered subcutaneously due to its proteinaceous nature, which precludes oral administration.

2. **Absorption**: Absorbed relatively quickly after subcutaneous injection, with absorption rates influenced by injection site and technique.

3. **Distribution**: Circulates bound to insulin-binding proteins, with rapid distribution throughout the body.

4. **Metabolism**: Metabolized primarily in the liver and kidneys.

5. **Excretion**: Metabolites and inactive fragments are excreted in the urine.

Monitoring and Adjustments

1. **Blood Glucose Monitoring**: Regular monitoring of blood glucose levels is essential to adjust insulin doses and optimize glycemic control.

2. **Dosage Adjustments**: Insulin doses are adjusted based on individual insulin sensitivity, carbohydrate intake, physical activity, and other factors affecting glucose metabolism.

Adverse Effects

1. **Hypoglycemia**: The most common adverse effect of insulin therapy, characterized by symptoms such as sweating, tremors, confusion, and in severe cases, loss of consciousness.

2. **Weight Gain**: Insulin therapy can lead to weight gain due to enhanced glucose uptake and storage in adipose tissue.

ORAL HYPOGLYCEMIC AGENTS AND GLUCAGON

Management of diabetes mellitus, particularly type 2 diabetes, often involves the use of oral hypoglycemic agents. Additionally, glucagon is an essential hormone used to treat severe hypoglycemia. Here is a detailed overview of these agents, their mechanisms, clinical uses, and potential adverse effects.

Oral Hypoglycemic Agents

Oral hypoglycemic agents are medications used to manage diabetes mellitus type 2 by lowering blood glucose levels. They work through various mechanisms to enhance insulin secretion, improve insulin sensitivity, inhibit glucose production in the liver, or delay carbohydrate digestion and absorption. Understanding the pharmacology of these agents involves exploring their mechanisms of action, clinical uses, pharmacokinetics, and potential adverse effects.

Classification of Oral Hypoglycemic Agents

1. **Sulfonylureas**:
    a. **Examples**: Glibenclamide (glyburide), glipizide, gliclazide.
    b. **Mechanism of Action**: Stimulate insulin secretion from pancreatic beta cells by binding to sulfonylurea receptors on ATP-sensitive potassium channels, leading to depolarization and calcium influx, which triggers insulin release.
    c. **Clinical Uses**: Used as first-line agents for patients with type 2 diabetes mellitus (T2DM) who have adequate beta cell function.
    d. **Adverse Effects**: Hypoglycemia, weight gain, gastrointestinal disturbances.

2. **Biguanides**:
    a. **Examples**: Metformin.
    b. **Mechanism of Action**: Decreases hepatic glucose production by inhibiting gluconeogenesis and enhances insulin sensitivity in peripheral tissues (muscle and adipose tissue).
    c. **Clinical Uses**: First-line therapy for T2DM, particularly in overweight and obese patients.
    d. **Adverse Effects**: Gastrointestinal disturbances (e.g., diarrhea, nausea), rare risk of lactic acidosis.

3. **Thiazolidinediones (TZDs)**:
    a. **Examples**: Pioglitazone, rosiglitazone.

b. **Mechanism of Action**: Activates peroxisome proliferator-activated receptor gamma (PPAR-γ), improving insulin sensitivity in adipose tissue, skeletal muscle, and liver.

c. **Clinical Uses**: Used as monotherapy or in combination with other oral hypoglycemic agents in patients with T2DM.

d. **Adverse Effects**: Fluid retention, weight gain, increased risk of heart failure (especially with rosiglitazone).

4. **Alpha-Glucosidase Inhibitors**:

   a. **Examples**: Acarbose, miglitol.

   b. **Mechanism of Action**: Inhibit alpha-glucosidase enzymes in the intestine, delaying carbohydrate digestion and absorption, thereby reducing postprandial glucose spikes.

   c. **Clinical Uses**: Used mainly to control postprandial hyperglycemia in T2DM.

   d. **Adverse Effects**: Gastrointestinal disturbances (e.g., flatulence, diarrhea), rare risk of hepatotoxicity.

5. **Dipeptidyl Peptidase-4 (DPP-4) Inhibitors**:

   a. **Examples**: Sitagliptin, saxagliptin, linagliptin.

   b. **Mechanism of Action**: Inhibit the enzyme DPP-4, which degrades incretin hormones (GLP-1 and GIP). Incretins stimulate insulin secretion and inhibit glucagon release, leading to improved glucose control.

   c. **Clinical Uses**: Second-line or add-on therapy in T2DM.

   d. **Adverse Effects**: Generally well-tolerated; rare risk of pancreatitis.

6. **Sodium-Glucose Co-Transporter 2 (SGLT-2) Inhibitors**:

   a. **Examples**: Canagliflozin, dapagliflozin, empagliflozin.

   b. **Mechanism of Action**: Inhibit SGLT-2 in the proximal renal tubules, reducing renal glucose reabsorption and increasing urinary glucose excretion.

c. **Clinical Uses**: Used to improve glycemic control in T2DM, also associated with cardiovascular benefits.

d. **Adverse Effects**: Genital mycotic infections, urinary tract infections, increased risk of euglycemic diabetic ketoacidosis (DKA).

Pharmacokinetics of Oral Hypoglycemic Agents

1. **Absorption**: Oral hypoglycemic agents are generally well-absorbed from the gastrointestinal tract.

2. **Distribution**: They distribute throughout the body, exerting their effects on insulin secretion, sensitivity, or glucose metabolism in various tissues.

3. **Metabolism**: Metabolism occurs primarily in the liver and other tissues, with some agents undergoing extensive first-pass metabolism (e.g., sulfonylureas).

4. **Excretion**: Metabolites and unchanged drug are excreted in urine and feces.

Monitoring and Adjustments

a. **Baseline Assessments**: Before initiating therapy, assess renal function, liver function, blood pressure, and cardiovascular risk factors.

b. **Monitoring Parameters**:

   i. **Blood Glucose Levels**: Monitor fasting and postprandial glucose levels to assess efficacy and adjust therapy.

   ii. **Hemoglobin A1c (HbA1c)**: Measure every 3-6 months to evaluate long-term glycemic control.

   iii. **Renal Function**: Especially important for agents excreted renally (e.g., metformin, SGLT-2 inhibitors).

   iv. **Liver Function**: Monitor for potential hepatotoxicity with certain agents.

   v. **Body Weight**: Monitor for weight gain or loss, which may influence treatment choices.

   c. **Adjustments**:
   i.   **Dose Titration**: Adjust doses based on glycemic control, renal function, and tolerance.
   ii. **Combination Therapy**: Consider adding or switching to other agents based on treatment goals and individual patient response.
   iii. **Adverse Effects Management**: Address and manage adverse effects promptly to optimize treatment adherence and efficacy.

Glucagon

Glucagon is a peptide hormone produced by alpha cells of the pancreas and plays a crucial role in glucose homeostasis. Unlike oral hypoglycemic agents that lower blood glucose levels, glucagon acts to increase blood glucose levels, primarily by stimulating glycogenolysis (breakdown of glycogen to glucose) and gluconeogenesis (synthesis of glucose from non-carbohydrate sources) in the liver. This section provides a detailed overview of the pharmacology of glucagon, including its mechanisms of action, clinical uses, pharmacokinetics, and administration considerations.

Mechanism of Action

1. **Glycogenolysis**:
   a. Glucagon binds to specific receptors on hepatocytes, activating adenylate cyclase through G-protein coupled receptors (GPCRs).
   b. This leads to increased intracellular levels of cyclic AMP (cAMP), which activates protein kinase A (PKA).
   c. PKA phosphorylates enzymes involved in glycogenolysis, such as glycogen phosphorylase, promoting the breakdown of glycogen into glucose.

2. **Gluconeogenesis**:
   a. Glucagon also enhances gluconeogenesis by stimulating the transcription of key enzymes involved in this process, such as

phosphoenolpyruvate carboxykinase (PEPCK) and glucose-6-phosphatase.

   b. This results in increased synthesis of glucose from substrates like amino acids and glycerol, contributing to elevated blood glucose levels.

3. **Lipolysis**:

   a. Glucagon promotes lipolysis in adipose tissue, releasing free fatty acids into circulation.

   b. These fatty acids serve as alternative energy sources for tissues, thereby conserving glucose for the brain and red blood cells during fasting or hypoglycemia.

Pharmacokinetics

1. **Route of Administration**: Glucagon is primarily administered via intramuscular (IM), subcutaneous (SC), or intravenous (IV) injection.

2. **Absorption**: IM and SC injections have slower absorption compared to IV administration.

3. **Distribution**: Glucagon is distributed widely throughout the body but has a short half-life due to rapid metabolism.

4. **Metabolism**: Metabolized in the liver and kidneys.

5. **Excretion**: Metabolites are excreted in the urine.

Clinical Uses

1. **Treatment of Severe Hypoglycemia**:

   a. **Emergency Management**: Glucagon is used to rapidly increase blood glucose levels in patients with severe hypoglycemia who are unconscious or unable to take oral glucose.

   b. **Administration**: Given IM or SC by caregivers, emergency medical personnel, or even by patients themselves if trained.

2. **Diagnostic Use**:

a. **Glucagon Stimulation Test**: Used to assess alpha cell function in patients with suspected insulinomas (insulin-secreting tumors) or other pancreatic disorders.

b. **Administration**: Given intravenously to stimulate endogenous glucagon secretion and measure its effects on glucose and insulin levels.

Administration Considerations

1. **Dosage**: Standard doses for emergency treatment of hypoglycemia vary but typically range from 1 to 2 mg IM or SC.

2. **Response Time**: Glucagon acts quickly to increase blood glucose levels, usually within 10 to 15 minutes after administration.

3. **Monitoring**: After administration, monitor the patient's response, blood glucose levels, and potential adverse effects.

4. **Storage**: Glucagon kits should be stored properly according to manufacturer instructions to maintain potency.

Adverse Effects

1. **Gastrointestinal Disturbances**: Nausea and vomiting are common adverse effects of glucagon administration.

2. **Cardiovascular Effects**: Transient increases in heart rate and blood pressure may occur.

3. **Allergic Reactions**: Rarely, hypersensitivity reactions such as rash or anaphylaxis may occur.

ACTH AND CORTICOSTEROIDS

Adrenocorticotropic hormone (ACTH) and corticosteroids are critical components in the regulation of the body's response to stress, metabolism, immune function, and inflammation. This section provides a detailed overview of the pharmacology of ACTH and corticosteroids, including their mechanisms of action, clinical uses, and adverse effects.

Adrenocorticotropic Hormone (ACTH)

Adrenocorticotropic hormone (ACTH) is a pivotal hormone in the endocrine system, primarily involved in stimulating the production and release of corticosteroids from the adrenal cortex. Understanding the pharmacology of ACTH involves exploring its mechanisms of action, pharmacological preparations, clinical uses, and potential adverse effects.

Mechanism of Action

a. **Receptor Binding**: ACTH exerts its effects by binding to melanocortin-2 receptors (MC2R) on the surface of adrenal cortical cells.

b. **Signal Transduction**: Binding of ACTH to MC2R activates adenylate cyclase, leading to an increase in cyclic AMP (cAMP) levels within the cell.

c. **Steroidogenesis**: Elevated cAMP activates protein kinase A (PKA), which phosphorylates target proteins involved in the synthesis and secretion of corticosteroids. This includes the upregulation of enzymes like cholesterol side-chain cleavage enzyme (CYP11A1) that convert cholesterol to pregnenolone, the precursor of all steroid hormones.

d. **Hormone Release**: The primary hormones released in response to ACTH are glucocorticoids (mainly cortisol), but it also stimulates the production of mineralocorticoids (like aldosterone) and adrenal androgens.

Pharmacological Preparations

a. **Cosyntropin (Synthetic ACTH):**

   i. **Structure**: Cosyntropin is a synthetic peptide that mimics the biological activity of natural ACTH.

   ii. **Administration**: Available as an injection for intravenous or intramuscular use.

   iii. **Advantages**: Synthetic preparations like cosyntropin offer a consistent and reliable response in diagnostic testing and therapeutic use.

Clinical Uses

Diagnostic Uses

1. **ACTH Stimulation Test:**
   a. **Purpose**: To assess the function of the adrenal cortex and diagnose conditions like adrenal insufficiency (Addison's disease) or secondary adrenal insufficiency due to pituitary dysfunction.
   b. **Procedure**: Cosyntropin is administered, and cortisol levels are measured before and after the injection. A normal adrenal response involves a significant increase in cortisol levels, whereas a suboptimal or absent response indicates adrenal insufficiency.

Therapeutic Uses

2. **Infantile Spasms (West Syndrome):**
   a. **Treatment**: ACTH therapy is used to control seizures in infants with this condition. It is believed to work through both direct effects on the brain and indirect effects via adrenal steroid production.
   b. **Administration**: High-dose ACTH injections are given over a specified period.

3. **Multiple Sclerosis (MS) Exacerbations:**
   a. **Use**: ACTH may be used to treat acute exacerbations of MS when standard corticosteroid therapy is ineffective or contraindicated.

4. **Other Inflammatory and Autoimmune Conditions:**
   a. **Application**: In cases where corticosteroids are not suitable, ACTH can be an alternative, utilizing its broad immunomodulatory effects.

Adverse Effects

The adverse effects of ACTH are primarily due to its stimulation of cortisol and other adrenal steroids:

1. **Metabolic Effects**: Hyperglycemia, weight gain, and fat redistribution similar to Cushing's syndrome.

2. **Electrolyte Imbalances**: Sodium retention and potassium loss, leading to hypertension and hypokalemia.

3. **Musculoskeletal Effects**: Osteoporosis and muscle weakness.

4. **Gastrointestinal Effects**: Increased risk of peptic ulcers.

5. **Immune Suppression**: Increased susceptibility to infections.

6. **Psychiatric Effects**: Mood swings, insomnia, and potential for psychosis.

7. **HPA Axis Suppression**: Long-term use can suppress the hypothalamic-pituitary-adrenal axis, leading to adrenal insufficiency upon withdrawal.

Pharmacokinetics

1. **Absorption**: ACTH is administered parenterally due to its peptide nature, which would be degraded in the gastrointestinal tract.

2. **Distribution**: It is rapidly distributed to the adrenal glands and other tissues.

3. **Metabolism**: ACTH is metabolized in the liver and kidneys.

4. **Excretion**: Metabolites are excreted in the urine.

Monitoring and Administration

1. **Monitoring**: Patients receiving ACTH therapy, especially long-term, require regular monitoring of blood pressure, blood glucose levels, electrolytes, and signs of infection.

2. **Tapering**: Gradual tapering is necessary to avoid adrenal insufficiency due to HPA axis suppression.

Corticosteroids

Corticosteroids are steroid hormones produced by the adrenal cortex and play crucial roles in regulating inflammation, immune response, metabolism, and electrolyte balance. They are broadly classified into glucocorticoids and mineralocorticoids based on their predominant physiological effects. This section provides a detailed overview of the pharmacology of corticosteroids, including their mechanisms of action, pharmacokinetics, clinical uses, and potential adverse effects.

Classification of Corticosteroids

1. **Glucocorticoids**
   a. Primarily involved in regulating metabolism, immune response, and stress responses.
   b. Examples: Cortisol (hydrocortisone), prednisone, prednisolone, dexamethasone, betamethasone.
2. **Mineralocorticoids**
   a. Primarily involved in regulating sodium and water balance.
   b. Example: Aldosterone, fludrocortisone.

Mechanisms of Action

Glucocorticoids:

1. **Gene Regulation**: Glucocorticoids bind to intracellular glucocorticoid receptors (GR). The receptor-hormone complex then translocates to the nucleus, where it binds to glucocorticoid response elements (GREs) in the DNA, regulating the transcription of target genes. This leads to increased synthesis of anti-inflammatory proteins (e.g., lipocortin-1) and suppression of pro-inflammatory genes (e.g., cytokines, COX-2).
2. **Anti-inflammatory Effects**: Suppress the migration of leukocytes, reduce capillary permeability, inhibit the release of pro-inflammatory mediators (e.g., prostaglandins, leukotrienes), and decrease the activity of lymphocytes and macrophages.
3. **Metabolic Effects**: Increase gluconeogenesis, decrease glucose uptake in peripheral tissues, promote protein catabolism, and increase lipolysis.

Mineralocorticoids:

1. **Sodium and Water Retention**: Mineralocorticoids bind to mineralocorticoid receptors in the distal renal tubules, leading to increased reabsorption of sodium and water and excretion of potassium

and hydrogen ions. This process helps regulate blood pressure and plasma volume.

Pharmacokinetics

1. **Absorption**: Corticosteroids can be administered orally, intravenously, intramuscularly, intra-articularly, topically, or by inhalation. Oral corticosteroids are well absorbed from the gastrointestinal tract.

2. **Distribution**: They are widely distributed throughout the body, including the brain. They cross the placenta and are present in breast milk.

3. **Metabolism**: Primarily metabolized in the liver through reduction and conjugation.

4. **Excretion**: Metabolites are excreted in the urine.

Clinical Uses

Glucocorticoids:

1. **Inflammatory and Autoimmune Diseases**:
   a. Rheumatoid arthritis, systemic lupus erythematosus, inflammatory bowel disease, multiple sclerosis, and autoimmune hepatitis.

2. **Allergic Reactions**:
   a. Severe asthma, anaphylaxis, allergic rhinitis, and atopic dermatitis.

3. **Endocrine Disorders**:
   a. Adrenal insufficiency (e.g., Addison's disease), congenital adrenal hyperplasia, and secondary adrenal insufficiency.

4. **Oncologic Uses**:
   a. Part of chemotherapy regimens for hematologic cancers (e.g., lymphomas, leukemias) and to reduce inflammation caused by tumors.

5. **Organ Transplantation**:
   a. Prevention and treatment of graft rejection.

6. **Other Uses**:

a. Prevention of nausea and vomiting in chemotherapy, treatment of acute exacerbations of chronic obstructive pulmonary disease (COPD), and treatment of certain types of shock.

Mineralocorticoids:

1. **Adrenal Insufficiency:**

    a. Replacement therapy for aldosterone deficiency in conditions like Addison's disease and congenital adrenal hyperplasia.

2. **Orthostatic Hypotension:**

    a. Off-label use to increase blood volume and pressure.

Adverse Effects

Glucocorticoids:

1. **Metabolic Effects**: Hyperglycemia, insulin resistance, weight gain, and fat redistribution (e.g., moon face, buffalo hump).

2. **Cardiovascular Effects**: Hypertension, increased risk of atherosclerosis, and fluid retention.

3. **Musculoskeletal Effects**: Osteoporosis, muscle weakness, myopathy, and avascular necrosis.

4. **Gastrointestinal Effects**: Increased risk of peptic ulcers and gastrointestinal bleeding.

5. **Immune Effects**: Increased susceptibility to infections and impaired wound healing.

6. **Neuropsychiatric Effects**: Mood swings, insomnia, depression, and psychosis.

7. **Ophthalmic Effects**: Cataracts and glaucoma.

8. **Endocrine Effects**: Suppression of the hypothalamic-pituitary-adrenal (HPA) axis, leading to adrenal insufficiency upon withdrawal.

Mineralocorticoids:

1. **Electrolyte Imbalances**: Hypokalemia, hypernatremia.

2. **Fluid Retention**: Edema and hypertension.

3. **Metabolic Alkalosis**: Due to excessive loss of hydrogen ions.

Monitoring and Adjustments

1. **Regular Monitoring**: For patients on long-term corticosteroid therapy, regular monitoring of blood pressure, blood glucose levels, bone density, and electrolyte balance is essential.

2. **Tapering**: Gradual tapering is necessary to avoid adrenal insufficiency due to HPA axis suppression.

Pharmacokinetics

The pharmacokinetics of ACTH and corticosteroids involve the processes of absorption, distribution, metabolism, and excretion, which determine the onset, duration, and intensity of their effects. Understanding these processes is crucial for optimizing their therapeutic use and managing potential adverse effects.

Pharmacokinetics of ACTH

Absorption:

a. **Route of Administration**: ACTH is primarily administered parenterally (intravenous, intramuscular, or subcutaneous) because it is a peptide hormone and would be degraded in the gastrointestinal tract if taken orally.

b. **Onset of Action**: The onset of action is rapid, with plasma cortisol levels typically rising within 30 minutes to an hour after injection.

Distribution:

a. **Plasma Binding**: ACTH is rapidly distributed in the body, particularly to the adrenal glands. It binds minimally to plasma proteins.

b. **Volume of Distribution**: The volume of distribution is relatively low, indicating that ACTH remains primarily in the extracellular fluid compartment.

Metabolism:

a. **Degradation**: ACTH is metabolized primarily in the liver and kidneys. It has a short half-life, typically around 10-20 minutes, due to rapid enzymatic degradation.

b. **Active Metabolites**: No significant active metabolites are produced from ACTH degradation.

Excretion:

a. **Elimination**: The metabolites of ACTH are excreted in the urine.

Pharmacokinetics of Corticosteroids

Absorption:

a. **Oral Administration**: Corticosteroids are well absorbed from the gastrointestinal tract. Bioavailability varies among different corticosteroids, with most having high oral bioavailability.

b. **Parenteral Administration**: Intravenous and intramuscular injections provide rapid and complete absorption. Inhaled and topical formulations are also used for targeted effects.

c. **Onset of Action**: The onset of action can vary from minutes (for intravenous administration) to several hours (for oral administration).

Distribution:

a. **Plasma Binding**: Corticosteroids are extensively bound to plasma proteins, primarily corticosteroid-binding globulin (CBG) and, to a lesser extent, albumin. Only the unbound fraction is biologically active.

b. **Volume of Distribution**: They have a large volume of distribution, indicating widespread distribution throughout the body, including crossing the blood-brain barrier and the placenta.

Metabolism:

a. **Liver Metabolism**: Corticosteroids are primarily metabolized in the liver through reduction and conjugation reactions. They undergo extensive first-pass metabolism, especially when administered orally.

b. **Enzyme Involvement**: Cytochrome P450 enzymes, particularly CYP3A4, play a significant role in the metabolism of corticosteroids.

c. **Active Metabolites**: Some corticosteroids, like prednisone, are prodrugs that are converted to their active forms (prednisolone) in the liver.

Excretion:

a. **Renal Excretion**: Metabolites of corticosteroids are excreted in the urine. The half-lives of corticosteroids vary widely depending on their formulation and route of administration.

b. **Half-Life**:

   i. **Short-acting**: Hydrocortisone has a half-life of about 8-12 hours.

   ii. **Intermediate-acting**: Prednisone and prednisolone have half-lives of approximately 12-36 hours.

   iii. **Long-acting**: Dexamethasone and betamethasone have half-lives exceeding 36 hours.

Pharmacokinetic Parameters of Selected Corticosteroids

a. **Hydrocortisone (Cortisol)**:

   i. **Absorption**: Rapid and complete oral absorption.

   ii. **Half-Life**: 8-12 hours.

   iii. **Protein Binding**: High (approximately 90%).

b. **Prednisone/Prednisolone**:

   i. **Absorption**: Well absorbed orally.

   ii. **Half-Life**: 12-36 hours.

   iii. **Protein Binding**: Prednisone (70-90%), Prednisolone (90-95%).

c. **Dexamethasone**:

   i. **Absorption**: Excellent oral absorption.

   ii. **Half-Life**: 36-54 hours.

   iii. **Protein Binding**: Moderate (approximately 70-75%).

d. **Fludrocortisone**:

   i. **Absorption**: Well absorbed orally.

ii. **Half-Life**: Approximately 18-36 hours.

iii. **Protein Binding**: High (approximately 70%).

Clinical Implications of Pharmacokinetics

ACTH:

a. **Short Half-Life**: Requires frequent dosing or continuous infusion for sustained effects.

b. **Rapid Onset**: Suitable for acute diagnostic tests and emergency therapeutic use.

Corticosteroids:

a. **Bioavailability and Formulations**: Choice of oral, parenteral, inhaled, or topical formulations allows for tailored treatment based on the desired onset and duration of action.

b. **Dosing Frequency**: Short-acting corticosteroids may require multiple daily doses, whereas long-acting corticosteroids can be dosed less frequently.

c. **Monitoring**: Long-term corticosteroid therapy necessitates monitoring for side effects such as adrenal suppression, metabolic disturbances, and osteoporosis, influenced by the pharmacokinetic properties of the specific corticosteroid used.

Monitoring and Adjustments

Monitoring and adjustments in ACTH and corticosteroid therapy are crucial to optimize therapeutic outcomes, manage potential adverse effects, and ensure patient safety. This section discusses the key aspects of monitoring and necessary adjustments for both ACTH and corticosteroid treatments.

Monitoring in ACTH Therapy

1. Diagnostic Use (ACTH Stimulation Test):

a. **Purpose**: Assess adrenal gland function by measuring cortisol levels before and after administering cosyntropin (synthetic ACTH).

b. **Monitoring Parameters**:

i. **Baseline Cortisol Levels**: Measure before cosyntropin administration.

ii. **Post-Stimulation Cortisol Levels**: Measure at specified intervals (e.g., 30 minutes, 60 minutes) after cosyntropin administration.

iii. **Interpretation**: A normal response shows a significant rise in cortisol levels. A suboptimal or absent response suggests adrenal insufficiency.

2. Therapeutic Use:

a. **Infantile Spasms (West Syndrome)**:

i. **Monitoring**: Assess seizure frequency and response to ACTH therapy.

ii. **Adverse Effects**: Monitor for signs of hyperglycemia, hypertension, electrolyte imbalances, and infections.

Adjustments in ACTH Therapy

a. **Dosing**: Adjust based on clinical response and cortisol level measurements.

b. **Frequency**: Depending on the condition treated (e.g., infantile spasms), ACTH may be administered daily or in cycles with gradual tapering.

Monitoring in Corticosteroid Therapy

1. General Monitoring Parameters:

a. **Baseline Assessment**:

i. **Medical History**: Assess for contraindications (e.g., diabetes, hypertension, osteoporosis).

ii. **Physical Examination**: Monitor for signs of Cushing's syndrome (e.g., weight gain, central obesity, moon face).

iii. **Laboratory Tests**: Baseline measurements of blood glucose, electrolytes (especially potassium), renal function, liver function, and bone density (if long-term therapy is anticipated).

2. Ongoing Monitoring During Therapy:

a. **Clinical Assessment**:
   i. **Symptoms**: Monitor for improvement in symptoms related to the underlying condition (e.g., inflammation, autoimmune disease).
   ii. **Adverse Effects**: Regularly assess for signs of hyperglycemia, hypertension, fluid retention, osteoporosis, mood changes, and infections.

b. **Laboratory Monitoring**:
   i. **Blood Glucose**: Regular monitoring to detect hyperglycemia.
   ii. **Electrolytes**: Particularly potassium levels to detect hypokalemia.
   iii. **Renal and Liver Function**: Assess for abnormalities that may indicate metabolic disturbances or hepatotoxicity.
   iv. **Bone Density**: Consider baseline and periodic monitoring, especially for patients on long-term therapy.

3. Adjustments in Corticosteroid Therapy:

a. **Dose Titration**: Adjust corticosteroid dose based on clinical response and monitoring parameters.

b. **Tapering**: Gradual tapering is necessary to avoid adrenal insufficiency, especially after long-term therapy.

c. **Alternative Formulations**: Consider switching to alternate formulations (e.g., from oral to topical or inhalational) to minimize systemic side effects while maintaining therapeutic efficacy.

Special Considerations

a. **Pediatric and Geriatric Populations**: Monitor more closely due to potential differences in metabolism, susceptibility to adverse effects, and response to therapy.

b. **Long-Term Therapy**: Continuously reassess the need for ongoing therapy versus the risks of cumulative adverse effects, particularly bone density loss and metabolic disturbances.

Multiple choice question (MCQ):

1. What is the primary role of parathyroid hormone (PTH) in the body?

   A) Decreases calcium levels

   B) Regulates blood sugar

   C) Increases calcium levels

   D) Lowers phosphate levels

2. Which hormone is used in the treatment of osteoporosis and is administered subcutaneously?

   A) Insulin

   B) Calcitonin

   C) Teriparatide

   D) Glucagon

3. What is the main action of glucocorticoids in the body?

   A) Decrease glucose uptake

   B) Increase calcium absorption

   C) Regulate immune response and inflammation

   D) Stimulate glycogen breakdown

4. Which medication class is Methimazole a part of?

   A) Thyroid hormone analogues

   B) Thyroid hormone synthesis inhibitors

   C) Glucocorticoids

   D) Mineralocorticoids

5. Which drug is an oral hypoglycemic agent that increases insulin secretion from pancreatic beta cells?

   A) Metformin

   B) Glibenclamide

   C) Canagliflozin

   D) Dapagliflozin

6. ACTH stimulates the production of which type of hormones from the adrenal cortex? A) Thyroid hormones

   B) Corticosteroids

   C) Gonadal hormones

   D) Pancreatic hormones

7. Which of the following is NOT an adverse effect of corticosteroids?

   A) Hypoglycemia

   B) Osteoporosis

   C) Hyperglycemia

   D) Hypertension

8. What is the function of the ACTH stimulation test?

   A) To diagnose diabetes mellitus

   B) To assess adrenal gland function

   C) To evaluate thyroid function

   D) To check pancreatic function

9. Which hormone has a primary role in calcium homeostasis by lowering blood calcium levels?

   A) Insulin

   B) PTH

   C) Vitamin D

   D) Calcitonin

10. What is the primary clinical use of calcitonin?

    A) To treat diabetes mellitus

    B) To manage osteoporosis

    C) To stimulate insulin release

    D) To increase blood calcium levels

11. Which is a mechanism of action for biguanides in diabetes management?

    A) Stimulate insulin secretion

    B) Decrease hepatic glucose production

C) Increase glucagon secretion

D) Enhance glucose absorption

12. Glucagon acts to:

A) Lower blood glucose levels

B) Raise blood glucose levels

C) Decrease blood insulin levels

D) Increase glycogen synthesis

13. Which of the following hormones is involved in the regulation of sodium and water balance?

A) Cortisol

B) Aldosterone

C) Adrenaline

D) Thyroxine

14. What is the effect of mineralocorticoids?

A) Promote inflammation

B) Increase sodium reabsorption

C) Decrease glucose production

D) Enhance calcium excretion

15. How do thiazolidinediones work to manage diabetes?

A) By decreasing insulin sensitivity

B) By inhibiting pancreatic beta-cell function

C) By activating PPAR-γ, improving insulin sensitivity

D) By blocking carbohydrate absorption

16. Which hormone is used for rapid correction of severe hypothyroidism?

A) Levothyroxine

B) Liothyronine

C) Methimazole

D) Propylthiouracil

17. What is the primary function of DPP-4 inhibitors in diabetes management?

A) Increase glucagon secretion

B) Inhibit insulin secretion

C) Decrease insulin degradation

D) Enhance insulin resistance

18. What is the primary adverse effect of using somatostatin analogs like octreotide?

A) Hypoglycemia

B) Gallstones

C) Hypercalcemia

D) Hyperthyroidism

19. Which drug class does acarbose belong to?

A) Sulfonylureas

B) Biguanides

C) Alpha-glucosidase inhibitors

D) SGLT-2 inhibitors

20. Which of the following is NOT a clinical use of glucocorticoids?

A) Treatment of anaphylaxis

B) Increasing calcium absorption

C) Prevention of organ transplant rejection

D) Management of rheumatoid arthritis

Short Answer Type Questions

1. What is the primary function of parathyroid hormone (PTH)?

2. How does calcitonin affect bone metabolism?

3. Describe the role of vitamin D in calcium absorption.

4. What are the key actions of glucocorticoids in the body?

5. Explain the mechanism by which insulin affects glucose uptake in cells.

6. How does methimazole work to treat hyperthyroidism?

7. What is the clinical use of levothyroxine?

8. Identify one major side effect of corticosteroid use.

9. What role does aldosterone play in electrolyte balance?

10. How do bisphosphonates help in managing osteoporosis?

11. What is the effect of glucagon on blood glucose levels?

12. Explain the principle of negative feedback in hormone regulation.

13. How do thiazolidinediones affect insulin sensitivity?

14. What is the purpose of the ACTH stimulation test?

15. Describe how somatostatin analogs like octreotide are used clinically.

16. What are the pharmacokinetic properties of synthetic ACTH (cosyntropin)?

17. How do mineralocorticoids like fludrocortisone function in the body?

18. What is the mechanism of action of DPP-4 inhibitors in diabetes management?

19. Explain the clinical significance of PTH replacement therapy.

20. Describe the role of insulin in bone health indirectly.

Long Answer Type Questions

1. Discuss the pharmacological actions of thyroid hormones and their importance in metabolic regulation.

2. Describe the process of bone remodeling and the hormones involved in this process.

3. Explain the role of the hypothalamic-pituitary-adrenal (HPA) axis in stress response and how glucocorticoids modulate this process.

4. Detail the therapeutic uses of corticosteroids in autoimmune diseases and their potential side effects.

5. Discuss the mechanisms by which oral hypoglycemic agents manage diabetes mellitus type 2.

6. Explain how calcium homeostasis is maintained in the body and the roles of PTH, calcitonin, and vitamin D in this process.

7. Describe the pharmacokinetics and pharmacodynamics of insulin and its importance in diabetes management.

8. Analyze the role of drug therapy in the management of hyperthyroidism, including the actions of antithyroid drugs.

9. Discuss the impact of glucagon in treating severe hypoglycemia and its mechanism of action.

10. Explain the role and therapeutic uses of mineralocorticoids in managing disorders like Addison's disease.

Answer Key

1. C (Increases calcium levels)
2. C (Teriparatide)
3. C (Regulate immune response and inflammation)
4. B (Thyroid hormone synthesis inhibitors)
5. B (Glibenclamide)
6. B (Corticosteroids)
7. A (Hypoglycemia)
8. B (To assess adrenal gland function)
9. D (Calcitonin)
10. B (To manage osteoporosis)
11. B (Decrease hepatic glucose production)
12. B (Raise blood glucose levels)
13. B (Aldosterone)
14. B (Increase sodium reabsorption)
15. C (By activating PPAR-γ, improving insulin sensitivity)
16. B (Liothyronine)
17. C (Decrease insulin degradation)

18.B (Gallstones)

19.C (Alpha-glucosidase inhibitors)

20.B (Increasing calcium absorption)

CHAPTER – 6

PHARMACOLOGY OF DRUGS ACTING ON ENDOCRINE SYSTEM

INTRODUCTION:

Pharmacology of the endocrine system focuses on understanding how drugs interact with the body's hormonal systems to influence various physiological processes. The endocrine system is composed of glands that secrete hormones directly into the bloodstream, which regulate metabolism, growth, reproduction, and other vital functions. Drugs targeting the endocrine system can either mimic (agonists) or inhibit (antagonists) the actions of natural hormones.

Key Glands and Hormones in the Endocrine System

The endocrine system is a complex network of glands that produce and secrete hormones to regulate various physiological processes, including growth, metabolism, reproduction, and homeostasis. This section outlines the key glands and hormones involved in the endocrine system, highlighting their roles and the pharmacology of drugs that act on them.

1. Hypothalamus

Hormones:

a. **Releasing Hormones**: Gonadotropin-releasing hormone (GnRH), Thyrotropin-releasing hormone (TRH), Corticotropin-releasing hormone (CRH), Growth hormone-releasing hormone (GHRH).

b. **Inhibitory Hormones**: Somatostatin, Dopamine.

Functions:

a. The hypothalamus regulates the pituitary gland and acts as a link between the endocrine and nervous systems.

b. It controls the secretion of hormones from the anterior and posterior pituitary glands through releasing and inhibitory hormones.

Pharmacology:

a. **GnRH Agonists and Antagonists**: Used in the treatment of prostate cancer, endometriosis, and precocious puberty.

   i.   **Examples**: Leuprolide (agonist), Cetrorelix (antagonist).

b. **Somatostatin Analogues**: Used to treat acromegaly, carcinoid tumors, and other hormone-secreting tumors.

   i.   **Examples**: Octreotide, Lanreotide.

c. **Dopamine Agonists**: Used in the treatment of hyperprolactinemia.

   i.   **Examples**: Bromocriptine, Cabergoline.

2. Pituitary Gland

Hormones:

a. **Anterior Pituitary**: Growth hormone (GH), Thyroid-stimulating hormone (TSH), Adrenocorticotropic hormone (ACTH), Prolactin, Follicle-stimulating hormone (FSH), Luteinizing hormone (LH).

b. **Posterior Pituitary**: Oxytocin, Vasopressin (antidiuretic hormone, ADH).

Functions:

a. Regulates growth, metabolism, stress response, lactation, and reproductive functions.

b. The posterior pituitary stores and releases hormones produced by the hypothalamus.

Pharmacology:

a. **Growth Hormone (GH)**: Used to treat GH deficiency, Turner syndrome, and chronic renal insufficiency.

   i.   **Examples**: Somatropin.

b. **GH Antagonists**: Used to treat acromegaly.

   i.   **Examples**: Pegvisomant.

c. **TSH**: Used in diagnostic testing for thyroid function.

d. **ACTH**: Used in diagnostic testing for adrenal insufficiency.

i.   **Examples**: Cosyntropin.

e. **Vasopressin Analogues**: Used to treat diabetes insipidus and control bleeding in certain conditions.

i.   **Examples**: Desmopressin, Vasopressin.

f. **Oxytocin**: Used to induce labor and control postpartum hemorrhage.

3. Thyroid Gland

Hormones:

a. **Thyroxine (T4)**

b. **Triiodothyronine (T3)**

c. **Calcitonin**

Functions:

a. Regulates metabolism, growth, and development.

b. Calcitonin plays a role in calcium homeostasis.

Pharmacology:

a. **Thyroid Hormone Replacement**: Used to treat hypothyroidism.

i.   **Examples**: Levothyroxine (T4), Liothyronine (T3).

b. **Antithyroid Drugs**: Used to treat hyperthyroidism.

i.   **Examples**: Methimazole, Propylthiouracil.

c. **Radioactive Iodine**: Used to ablate thyroid tissue in hyperthyroidism and thyroid cancer.

d. **Calcitonin**: Used to treat hypercalcemia and Paget's disease of bone.

4. Parathyroid Glands

Hormones:

a. **Parathyroid Hormone (PTH)**

Functions:

a. Regulates calcium and phosphate metabolism by increasing blood calcium levels through its actions on the bones, kidneys, and intestines.

Pharmacology:

a. **PTH Analogues**: Used to treat hypoparathyroidism.

i.   **Examples**: Teriparatide.

b. **Calcimimetics**: Used to treat secondary hyperparathyroidism in chronic kidney disease.

i.   **Examples**: Cinacalcet.

5. Adrenal Glands

Hormones:

a. **Adrenal Cortex**: Cortisol, Aldosterone, Androgens.

b. **Adrenal Medulla**: Epinephrine, Norepinephrine.

Functions:

a. Cortisol regulates metabolism, immune response, and stress response.

b. Aldosterone regulates sodium and potassium balance.

c. Androgens contribute to secondary sex characteristics.

d. Catecholamines (epinephrine and norepinephrine) are involved in the fight-or-flight response.

Pharmacology:

a. **Glucocorticoids**: Used to treat inflammatory and autoimmune diseases, allergies, and adrenal insufficiency.

i.   **Examples**: Prednisone, Hydrocortisone, Dexamethasone.

b. **Mineralocorticoids**: Used to treat adrenal insufficiency.

i.   **Examples**: Fludrocortisone.

c. **Adrenal Androgens**: Supplementation in adrenal insufficiency.

d. **Catecholamines**: Used in emergency medicine to treat cardiac arrest, anaphylaxis, and severe asthma.

i.   **Examples**: Epinephrine, Norepinephrine.

6. Pancreas

Hormones:

a. **Insulin**

b. **Glucagon**

c. **Somatostatin**

Functions:

    a. Insulin lowers blood glucose levels by promoting glucose uptake in cells.

    b. Glucagon raises blood glucose levels by stimulating glycogenolysis and gluconeogenesis.

    c. Somatostatin inhibits the release of insulin and glucagon and regulates the digestive system.

Pharmacology:

    a. **Insulin**: Used to treat type 1 and type 2 diabetes mellitus.

        i. **Examples**: Regular insulin, Insulin glargine, Insulin lispro.

    b. **Oral Hypoglycemic Agents**: Used to treat type 2 diabetes mellitus.

        i. **Examples**: Metformin, Sulfonylureas (Glipizide), DPP-4 inhibitors (Sitagliptin), GLP-1 agonists (Exenatide).

    c. **Glucagon**: Used to treat severe hypoglycemia.

    d. **Somatostatin Analogues**: Used to treat hormone-secreting tumors.

        i. **Examples**: Octreotide.

7. Gonads

Hormones:

    a. **Ovaries**: Estrogens (Estradiol), Progesterone.

    b. **Testes**: Testosterone.

Functions:

    a. Regulate reproductive functions, secondary sexual characteristics, and menstrual cycle.

Pharmacology:

    a. **Estrogens and Progestins**: Used in hormone replacement therapy, contraception, and treatment of menstrual disorders.

        i. **Examples**: Ethinyl estradiol, Levonorgestrel, Progesterone.

    b. **Anti-estrogens**: Used in the treatment of estrogen receptor-positive breast cancer.

        i. **Examples**: Tamoxifen, Fulvestrant.

c. **Testosterone and Anabolic Steroids**: Used to treat hypogonadism and certain types of anemia.

   i. **Examples**: Testosterone enanthate, Nandrolone.

d. **Anti-androgens**: Used to treat prostate cancer and conditions like polycystic ovary syndrome (PCOS).

   i. **Examples**: Flutamide, Finasteride.

PHARMACOLOGICAL AGENTS ACTING ON THE ENDOCRINE SYSTEM

Pharmacological agents that act on the endocrine system are used to treat a variety of conditions by either mimicking or inhibiting the actions of endogenous hormones. These agents target specific glands and hormones to manage diseases such as diabetes, thyroid disorders, adrenal insufficiency, reproductive health issues, and more. This section provides a detailed overview of these agents, their mechanisms of action, therapeutic uses, and potential adverse effects.

1. Hypothalamic and Pituitary Hormones

Hypothalamic Hormones:

a. **Gonadotropin-Releasing Hormone (GnRH) Analogues:**

   1. **Agonists**: Leuprolide, Goserelin.

      i. **Mechanism**: Initially stimulate, then downregulate GnRH receptors, reducing LH and FSH secretion.

      ii. **Uses**: Prostate cancer, endometriosis, precocious puberty.

      iii. **Adverse Effects**: Hot flashes, bone density loss, sexual dysfunction.

   2. **Antagonists**: Cetrorelix, Ganirelix.

      i. **Mechanism**: Directly inhibit GnRH receptors, reducing LH and FSH secretion.

      ii. **Uses**: Prevention of premature LH surge in IVF.

      iii. **Adverse Effects**: Nausea, headache.

b. **Somatostatin Analogues**:

1. **Examples**: Octreotide, Lanreotide.

    i. **Mechanism**: Inhibit the release of growth hormone and other hormones.

    ii. **Uses**: Acromegaly, hormone-secreting tumors, esophageal variceal bleeding.

    iii. **Adverse Effects**: Gastrointestinal disturbances, gallstones, glucose metabolism alterations.

c. **Dopamine Agonists**:

1. **Examples**: Bromocriptine, Cabergoline.

    i. **Mechanism**: Inhibit prolactin secretion by stimulating dopamine receptors.

    ii. **Uses**: Hyperprolactinemia, prolactinomas, Parkinson's disease.

    iii. **Adverse Effects**: Nausea, orthostatic hypotension, headache.

Pituitary Hormones:

a. **Growth Hormone (GH) and GH Analogues**:

1. **Examples**: Somatropin.

    i. **Mechanism**: Mimics endogenous GH, stimulating growth and cell reproduction.

    ii. **Uses**: GH deficiency, Turner syndrome, chronic renal insufficiency.

    iii. **Adverse Effects**: Edema, joint pain, insulin resistance.

b. **GH Antagonists**:

1. **Examples**: Pegvisomant.

    i. **Mechanism**: Blocks GH receptors, reducing IGF-1 levels.

    ii. **Uses**: Acromegaly.

    iii. **Adverse Effects**: Liver enzyme elevations, injection site reactions.

c. **Vasopressin and Analogues**:

    1. **Examples**: Desmopressin.

        i. **Mechanism**: Acts on V2 receptors in the kidneys to promote water reabsorption.

        ii. **Uses**: Diabetes insipidus, nocturnal enuresis, von Willebrand disease.

        iii. **Adverse Effects**: Hyponatremia, fluid retention.

d. **Oxytocin**:

    1. **Mechanism**: Stimulates uterine contractions and milk ejection.

    2. **Uses**: Induction and augmentation of labor, postpartum hemorrhage.

    3. **Adverse Effects**: Uterine hyperstimulation, water intoxication.

2. Thyroid Hormones

a. **Thyroid Hormone Replacement**:

    1. **Examples**: Levothyroxine (T4), Liothyronine (T3).

        i. **Mechanism**: Mimics endogenous thyroid hormones, regulating metabolism and growth.

        ii. **Uses**: Hypothyroidism, myxedema coma.

        iii. **Adverse Effects**: Hyperthyroidism symptoms if overdosed, such as palpitations, weight loss, and anxiety.

b. **Antithyroid Drugs**:

    1. **Examples**: Methimazole, Propylthiouracil (PTU).

        i. **Mechanism**: Inhibit thyroid peroxidase, reducing thyroid hormone synthesis.

        ii. **Uses**: Hyperthyroidism, Graves' disease.

        iii. **Adverse Effects**: Agranulocytosis, hepatotoxicity (PTU), rash.

c. **Radioactive Iodine (I-131)**:

    1. **Mechanism**: Destroys thyroid tissue by emitting beta radiation.

2. **Uses**: Hyperthyroidism, thyroid cancer.

3. **Adverse Effects**: Hypothyroidism, radiation thyroiditis.

3. Adrenal Hormones

a. **Glucocorticoids**:

1. **Examples**: Prednisone, Hydrocortisone, Dexamethasone.

   i. **Mechanism**: Mimic cortisol, exerting anti-inflammatory and immunosuppressive effects.

   ii. **Uses**: Adrenal insufficiency, inflammatory and autoimmune conditions, allergies.

   iii. **Adverse Effects**: Cushingoid features, osteoporosis, hyperglycemia, increased infection risk.

b. **Mineralocorticoids**:

1. **Examples**: Fludrocortisone.

   i. **Mechanism**: Mimics aldosterone, promoting sodium retention and potassium excretion.

   ii. **Uses**: Addison's disease, orthostatic hypotension.

   iii. **Adverse Effects**: Hypertension, edema, hypokalemia.

c. **Catecholamines**:

1. **Examples**: Epinephrine, Norepinephrine.

   i. **Mechanism**: Stimulate alpha and beta-adrenergic receptors, increasing heart rate and vasoconstriction.

   ii. **Uses**: Anaphylaxis, cardiac arrest, severe asthma exacerbations.

   iii. **Adverse Effects**: Tachycardia, hypertension, arrhythmias.

4. Pancreatic Hormones

a. **Insulin**:

1. **Examples**: Regular insulin, Insulin glargine, Insulin lispro.

   i. **Mechanism**: Lowers blood glucose by facilitating cellular uptake of glucose.

ii. **Uses**: Type 1 and type 2 diabetes mellitus.

iii. **Adverse Effects**: Hypoglycemia, weight gain.

b. **Oral Hypoglycemic Agents**:

1. **Biguanides**: Metformin.

   i. **Mechanism**: Decreases hepatic glucose production and increases insulin sensitivity.

   ii. **Uses**: Type 2 diabetes mellitus.

   iii. **Adverse Effects**: Gastrointestinal disturbances, lactic acidosis (rare).

2. **Sulfonylureas**: Glipizide, Glyburide.

   i. **Mechanism**: Stimulate insulin release from pancreatic beta cells.

   ii. **Uses**: Type 2 diabetes mellitus.

   iii. **Adverse Effects**: Hypoglycemia, weight gain.

3. **DPP-4 Inhibitors**: Sitagliptin.

   i. **Mechanism**: Inhibits DPP-4 enzyme, prolonging the action of incretin hormones.

   ii. **Uses**: Type 2 diabetes mellitus.

   iii. **Adverse Effects**: Pancreatitis, joint pain.

4. **GLP-1 Agonists**: Exenatide.

   i. **Mechanism**: Mimics incretin hormones, enhancing glucose-dependent insulin secretion.

   ii. **Uses**: Type 2 diabetes mellitus.

   iii. **Adverse Effects**: Nausea, risk of thyroid C-cell tumors (in animals).

c. **Glucagon**:

1. **Mechanism**: Raises blood glucose by stimulating glycogenolysis and gluconeogenesis.

2. **Uses**: Severe hypoglycemia, diagnostic aid in radiology.

3. **Adverse Effects**: Nausea, vomiting.

5. Gonadal Hormones

a. **Estrogens**:

1. **Examples**: Ethinyl estradiol, Estradiol valerate.

   i. **Mechanism**: Mimic natural estrogen, regulating reproductive function and secondary sexual characteristics.

   ii. **Uses**: Hormone replacement therapy, contraception, menopausal symptoms.

   iii. **Adverse Effects**: Thromboembolism, breast tenderness, nausea.

b. **Progestins**:

1. **Examples**: Progesterone, Levonorgestrel.

   i. **Mechanism**: Mimic natural progesterone, regulating menstrual cycle and maintaining pregnancy.

   ii. **Uses**: Contraception, hormone replacement therapy, dysfunctional uterine bleeding.

   iii. **Adverse Effects**: Weight gain, mood changes, breast tenderness.

c. **Anti-estrogens**:

1. **Examples**: Tamoxifen, Fulvestrant.

   i. **Mechanism**: Block estrogen receptors, inhibiting estrogen-stimulated growth of breast cancer cells.

   ii. **Uses**: Estrogen receptor-positive breast cancer.

   iii. **Adverse Effects**: Hot flashes, risk of endometrial cancer (Tamoxifen).

d. **Testosterone and Anabolic Steroids**:

1. **Examples**: Testosterone enanthate, Nandrolone.

i. **Mechanism**: Mimic natural testosterone, promoting development of male secondary sexual characteristics and muscle growth.

ii. **Uses**: Hypogonadism, certain types of anemia.

iii. **Adverse Effects**: Liver toxicity, cardiovascular issues, masculinization in women.

e. **Anti-androgens**:

1. **Examples**: Flutamide, Finasteride.

i. **Mechanism**: Block androgen receptors or inhibit 5-alpha-reductase.

ii. **Uses**: Prostate cancer, benign prostatic hyperplasia, hirsutism.

iii. **Adverse Effects**: Gynecomastia, sexual dysfunction, liver toxicity.

Mechanisms of Action and Pharmacodynamics

Understanding the mechanisms of action (MOA) and pharmacodynamics (PD) of drugs acting on the endocrine system is crucial for comprehending how these medications interact with the body to achieve therapeutic effects. Here, I'll provide an overview of the mechanisms of action and pharmacodynamics of various classes of drugs used in endocrine pharmacology:

1. Hormone Replacement Therapies

Mechanisms of Action:

a. **Thyroid Hormones (e.g., Levothyroxine)**:

i. **MOA**: Synthetic T4 that converts to T3 in the body, replacing deficient thyroid hormone levels.

ii. **PD**: Acts on nuclear thyroid hormone receptors to regulate gene transcription and metabolism.

b. **Insulin (e.g., Insulin Glargine)**:

i. **MOA**: Mimics endogenous insulin, facilitating glucose uptake into cells and regulating blood glucose levels.

ii. **PD**: Binds to insulin receptors on cell surfaces, activating intracellular signaling pathways that increase glucose uptake and utilization.

2. Antithyroid Drugs

Mechanisms of Action:

a. **Thioamides (e.g., Methimazole)**:

i. **MOA**: Inhibit thyroid peroxidase enzyme, thereby blocking iodine organification and thyroid hormone synthesis.

ii. **PD**: Decreases production of T4 and T3 hormones, normalizing thyroid function.

3. Glucocorticoids

Mechanisms of Action:

a. **Prednisone, Dexamethasone**:

i. **MOA**: Bind to glucocorticoid receptors (GR) in the cytoplasm, translocate to the nucleus, and modulate gene expression.

ii. **PD**: Suppress inflammation and immune responses by altering transcription of anti-inflammatory proteins (e.g., lipocortins), and reducing production of cytokines and prostaglandins.

4. Gonadotropin-Releasing Hormone (GnRH) Analogues

Mechanisms of Action:

a. **GnRH Agonists (e.g., Leuprolide)**:

i. **MOA**: Initially stimulate GnRH receptors, leading to increased release of LH and FSH from the pituitary gland. Prolonged exposure desensitizes GnRH receptors, resulting in decreased LH and FSH release.

ii.   **PD**: Suppression of gonadal steroidogenesis by reducing LH and FSH levels, used in conditions requiring gonadal suppression (e.g., prostate cancer, endometriosis).

b. **GnRH Antagonists (e.g., Cetrorelix)**:

i.   **MOA**: Bind competitively to GnRH receptors, immediately blocking LH and FSH release from the pituitary gland.

ii.   **PD**: Rapid suppression of gonadal steroidogenesis, used in controlled ovarian stimulation for assisted reproduction.

5. Estrogen and Progestin Hormonal Therapies

Mechanisms of Action:

a. **Estrogens (e.g., Ethinyl Estradiol)**:

i.   **MOA**: Bind to estrogen receptors (ER) in target tissues, modulating gene transcription and cellular responses.

ii.   **PD**: Induce proliferation of endometrial tissue, maintain secondary sexual characteristics, and regulate menstrual cycle.

b. **Progestins (e.g., Levonorgestrel)**:

i.   **MOA**: Bind to progesterone receptors (PR) in target tissues, altering gene transcription and modulating endometrial changes.

ii.   **PD**: Induce secretory changes in endometrium, support pregnancy, and provide contraceptive effects.

6. Androgen and Anti-Androgen Therapies

Mechanisms of Action:

a. **Testosterone (e.g., Testosterone Enanthate)**:

i.   **MOA**: Binds to androgen receptors (AR) in target tissues, activating AR-mediated gene transcription.

ii.   **PD**: Promotes development and maintenance of male secondary sexual characteristics, muscle growth, and bone density.

b. **Anti-Androgens (e.g., Flutamide)**:

i. **MOA**: Competitively inhibit androgen binding to AR, blocking androgen-mediated gene transcription.

ii. **PD**: Used in the treatment of androgen-dependent conditions like prostate cancer and hirsutism.

7. Anti-diabetic Medications

Mechanisms of Action:

a. **Metformin**:

i. **MOA**: Reduces hepatic glucose production, enhances peripheral glucose uptake, and improves insulin sensitivity.

ii. **PD**: Decreases fasting and postprandial blood glucose levels, used in type 2 diabetes mellitus.

b. **Insulin Secretagogues (e.g., Sulfonylureas)**:

i. **MOA**: Stimulate insulin secretion from pancreatic beta cells by closing ATP-sensitive potassium channels.

ii. **PD**: Increase insulin release, lowering blood glucose levels in type 2 diabetes mellitus.

8. Parathyroid Hormone Analogs

Mechanisms of Action:

a. **Teriparatide (PTH analog)**:

i. **MOA**: Stimulates osteoblast activity, promoting bone formation and increasing bone mineral density.

ii. **PD**: Used in the treatment of osteoporosis to reduce fracture risk.

9. Antidiuretic Hormone Analogs

Mechanisms of Action:

a. **Desmopressin**:

i. **MOA**: Acts on V2 receptors in the kidneys, promoting water reabsorption and reducing urine output.

ii. **PD**: Used in diabetes insipidus and nocturnal enuresis.

Pharmacodynamics (PD)

a. **Binding Affinity**: Affinity of the drug for its receptor.

b. **Efficacy**: Ability of the drug-receptor complex to initiate a response.

c. **Potency**: Concentration of the drug required to produce a given effect.

d. **Duration of Action**: Length of time the drug produces its therapeutic effect.

e. **Dose-Response Relationship**: Relationship between drug dose and the magnitude of the response.

f. **Receptor Downregulation and Desensitization**: Adaptation of cells to prolonged exposure to drugs, leading to reduced responsiveness.

Clinical Applications and Considerations

Pharmacological agents that target the endocrine system have diverse clinical applications spanning various conditions, from hormonal imbalances to metabolic disorders and reproductive health issues. Understanding their clinical applications and considerations is crucial for optimizing treatment outcomes and minimizing adverse effects. Here's an in-depth exploration of the clinical applications and considerations for drugs acting on the endocrine system:

1. Thyroid Disorders

Clinical Applications:

a. **Hypothyroidism**: Thyroid hormone replacement therapy (e.g., Levothyroxine) is used to normalize thyroid hormone levels and alleviate symptoms such as fatigue, weight gain, and cold intolerance.

b. **Hyperthyroidism**: Antithyroid drugs (e.g., Methimazole) are employed to inhibit thyroid hormone synthesis and manage symptoms like rapid heartbeat, weight loss, and heat intolerance.

c. **Thyroid Cancer**: Radioactive iodine therapy (I-131) is utilized post-surgery to destroy remaining thyroid tissue or treat metastatic disease.

Considerations:

a. **Monitoring**: Regular monitoring of thyroid function tests (TSH, T4, T3) is essential to adjust medication dosage and ensure optimal hormone levels.

b. **Side Effects**: Potential side effects include thyroid hormone excess or deficiency, allergic reactions, and in the case of radioactive iodine, radiation-related effects.

2. Diabetes Mellitus

Clinical Applications:

a. **Type 1 Diabetes**: Insulin replacement therapy (various insulin formulations) is necessary to maintain blood glucose control and prevent complications.

b. **Type 2 Diabetes**: Oral hypoglycemic agents (e.g., Metformin, Sulfonylureas) and injectable therapies (e.g., GLP-1 agonists, SGLT-2 inhibitors) are used to improve insulin sensitivity, enhance insulin secretion, and reduce glucose production.

Considerations:

a. **Individualization**: Treatment plans should be individualized based on patient factors such as age, comorbidities, and adherence to therapy.

b. **Monitoring**: Regular monitoring of blood glucose levels, HbA1c, and renal function is necessary to assess treatment efficacy and adjust therapy as needed.

c. **Hypoglycemia and Hyperglycemia**: Management of hypoglycemic episodes and strategies to prevent hyperglycemia are critical aspects of diabetes care.

3. Adrenal Disorders

Clinical Applications:

a. **Adrenal Insufficiency**: Glucocorticoid replacement therapy (e.g., Hydrocortisone) is essential to manage symptoms of cortisol deficiency and prevent adrenal crisis.

b. **Cushing's Syndrome**: Medications (e.g., Ketoconazole, Metyrapone) or surgical interventions are used to suppress adrenal hormone production or remove adrenal tumors.

Considerations:

a. **Dosing**: Individualized glucocorticoid replacement dosing based on the severity of adrenal insufficiency and stress conditions.

b. **Adrenal Crisis**: Education of patients on recognizing and managing adrenal crisis, including the need for stress-dose steroids during illness or trauma.

4. Reproductive Health

Clinical Applications:

a. **Contraception**: Hormonal contraceptives (combination oral contraceptives, progestin-only pills, contraceptive patches, implants, and intrauterine devices) are used to prevent pregnancy.

b. **Menopausal Symptoms**: Hormone replacement therapy (estrogen-alone or combined with progestin) alleviates symptoms like hot flashes and vaginal dryness.

Considerations:

a. **Risk-Benefit Assessment**: Individual assessment of risks (e.g., thromboembolism with estrogen-containing contraceptives) versus benefits (contraception, menstrual cycle regulation, symptom relief).

b. **Patient Counseling**: Education on proper use, potential side effects (e.g., breakthrough bleeding, mood changes), and adherence to contraceptive methods or hormone replacement therapy.

5. Bone Health

Clinical Applications:

a. **Osteoporosis**: Bisphosphonates (e.g., Alendronate), PTH analogs (e.g., Teriparatide), and selective estrogen receptor modulators (e.g., Raloxifene) are used to increase bone density and reduce fracture risk.

Considerations:

a. **Long-term Use**: Monitoring bone mineral density and assessing fracture risk to guide treatment duration and selection of therapeutic agents.

b. **Adverse Effects**: Potential adverse effects such as gastrointestinal irritation (with bisphosphonates), hypercalcemia (with PTH analogs), and thromboembolic events (with estrogen-containing medications).

6. Pituitary Disorders

Clinical Applications:

a. **Acromegaly**: Somatostatin analogs (e.g., Octreotide), GH receptor antagonists (e.g., Pegvisomant) are used to suppress GH secretion and manage symptoms.

b. **Prolactinomas**: Dopamine agonists (e.g., Bromocriptine) normalize prolactin levels and shrink pituitary tumors.

Considerations:

a. **Monitoring**: Regular monitoring of hormone levels and tumor size via imaging studies to assess treatment response and adjust therapy.

b. **Adverse Effects**: Potential adverse effects include gastrointestinal disturbances (with somatostatin analogs), and neurological symptoms (with dopamine agonists).

7. Parathyroid Disorders

Clinical Applications:

a. **Hyperparathyroidism**: Calcimimetics (e.g., Cinacalcet) and surgical intervention are used to manage hypercalcemia by reducing PTH secretion or removing abnormal parathyroid tissue.

Considerations:

a. **Calcium Monitoring**: Regular monitoring of serum calcium levels to guide dosage adjustments of calcimimetics and assess treatment efficacy.

b. **Surgical Considerations**: Evaluation for surgical intervention in cases of refractory hyperparathyroidism or complications like nephrolithiasis.

8. Neuroendocrine Tumors

Clinical Applications:

a. **Carcinoid Tumors**: Somatostatin analogs (e.g., Octreotide) control hormone hypersecretion and tumor growth.

b. **Insulinomas**: Diazoxide inhibits insulin release to manage hypoglycemia in insulinoma patients.

Considerations:

a. **Multidisciplinary Care**: Collaboration with oncologists, surgeons, and endocrinologists for comprehensive management of neuroendocrine tumors.

b. **Symptom Management**: Focus on alleviating symptoms related to hormone hypersecretion (e.g., flushing, diarrhea) and tumor burden.

ANDROGENS AND ANABOLIC STEROIDS

Androgens and anabolic steroids are a class of drugs that mimic the effects of male sex hormones, primarily testosterone. These agents have significant therapeutic uses but also potential for abuse, especially in athletic contexts. This section explores the pharmacology, mechanisms of action, therapeutic uses, and potential adverse effects of androgens and anabolic steroids.

Androgens

Androgens are natural or synthetic steroid hormones that regulate the development and maintenance of male characteristics by binding to androgen receptors. The primary endogenous androgen is testosterone.

Key Endogenous Androgens:

Endogenous androgens are naturally occurring steroid hormones primarily responsible for the development and maintenance of male secondary sexual characteristics and reproductive function. Here are the key endogenous androgens involved in the endocrine system:

1. Testosterone

Role:

a. **Primary Androgen**: Testosterone is the primary male sex hormone and the most potent androgen.

b. **Development**: Stimulates the development of male secondary sexual characteristics during puberty, such as facial and body hair growth, deepening of the voice, and muscle development.

c. **Reproductive Function**: Essential for spermatogenesis and maintenance of male reproductive organs (testes).

Biosynthesis:

a. **Source**: Produced primarily in the Leydig cells of the testes in males and in small amounts by the adrenal glands in both sexes.

b. **Regulation**: Regulated by the hypothalamic-pituitary-gonadal (HPG) axis. Gonadotropin-releasing hormone (GnRH) from the hypothalamus stimulates the release of luteinizing hormone (LH) and follicle-stimulating hormone (FSH) from the pituitary gland, which in turn stimulate testosterone production in the testes.

Metabolism:

a. **Conversion**: Testosterone can be converted to dihydrotestosterone (DHT) via the enzyme 5-alpha-reductase in tissues such as the prostate gland, skin, and hair follicles.

b. **Inactivation**: Metabolized in the liver to inactive forms such as testosterone glucuronide and testosterone sulfate, which are excreted in urine.

2. Dihydrotestosterone (DHT)

Role:

a. **Potency**: More potent than testosterone in certain tissues due to higher affinity for androgen receptors.

b. **Functions**: Mediates androgenic effects in the prostate gland, skin, and hair follicles, contributing to male pattern baldness and prostate growth.

Biosynthesis:

a. **Conversion**: Derived from testosterone through the action of 5-alpha-reductase enzyme, primarily in target tissues rather than systemic circulation.

Metabolism:

a. **Inactivation**: Metabolized to 3-alpha and 3-beta diols, which are less active metabolites, and further conjugated to glucuronide and sulfate forms for excretion.

3. Androstenedione

Role:

a. **Precursor**: A weak androgen that serves as a precursor for testosterone and estrone in peripheral tissues.

Biosynthesis:

a. **Source**: Produced in the adrenal glands and gonads.

b. **Conversion**: Can be converted to testosterone in the gonads and to estrone in adipose tissue via aromatase enzyme activity.

Metabolism:

a. **Conversion**: Converted to testosterone in the testes under the influence of LH.

4. Dehydroepiandrosterone (DHEA) and Dehydroepiandrosterone Sulfate (DHEA-S)

Role:

a. **Precursor**: Serve as precursors for testosterone and estradiol synthesis.

b. **Adrenal Function**: Produced predominantly in the adrenal glands, with DHEA-S being the sulfated form, which is more stable and serves as a reservoir for DHEA.

Biosynthesis:

a. **Adrenal Production**: Synthesized in the zona reticularis of the adrenal cortex.

b. **Conversion**: Converted to androstenedione and testosterone in peripheral tissues.

Metabolism:

a. **Peripheral Conversion**: Converted to active androgens and estrogens in tissues expressing appropriate enzymes (e.g., 3-beta-hydroxysteroid dehydrogenase).

Clinical Relevance

Mechanisms of Action

Androgens and anabolic steroids are pharmacological agents that exert their effects primarily through interaction with androgen receptors (AR) in various tissues throughout the body. Understanding their mechanisms of action (MOA) is crucial for comprehending their physiological effects and therapeutic uses. Here's a detailed exploration of the mechanisms of action of androgens and anabolic steroids:

Mechanisms of Action of Androgens:

1. Binding to Androgen Receptors (AR):

a. **Location**: Androgen receptors are located in the cytoplasm of target cells.

b. **Activation**: Upon binding of androgens (such as testosterone) to the androgen receptor, a conformational change occurs.

c. **Translocation**: The androgen-receptor complex translocates into the nucleus.

2. Gene Transcription Regulation:

a. **Interaction with DNA**: In the nucleus, the androgen-receptor complex binds to specific DNA sequences known as androgen response elements (AREs).

b. **Transcription Activation**: This binding initiates transcription of specific genes involved in various biological processes, including:

   i. **Protein synthesis**: Especially in muscle tissue, leading to increased muscle mass and strength.

ii. **Bone growth**: Enhances bone mineral density and promotes bone growth.

iii. **Secondary sexual characteristics**: Induces development and maintenance of male characteristics (e.g., facial hair, deepening voice).

3. Non-Genomic Effects:

a. **Rapid Signaling**: Androgens can also exert rapid effects through non-genomic pathways, independent of gene transcription.

b. **Cellular Signaling**: Activation of intracellular signaling cascades, such as protein kinase pathways, leading to rapid responses in target tissues.

Mechanisms of Action of Anabolic Steroids:

Anabolic steroids are synthetic derivatives of testosterone designed to maximize anabolic effects (muscle growth) while minimizing androgenic effects (secondary sexual characteristics). They primarily exert their effects through similar mechanisms as endogenous androgens, but with some distinctions:

1. Androgen Receptor Activation:

a. **Similar to Endogenous Androgens**: Anabolic steroids bind to androgen receptors and activate similar downstream signaling pathways.

b. **Enhanced Anabolic Effects**: Some synthetic steroids have enhanced anabolic effects compared to testosterone, promoting protein synthesis and muscle growth.

2. Protein Synthesis Stimulation:

a. **Increased Nitrogen Retention**: Enhances nitrogen retention in muscle tissue, leading to increased protein synthesis and muscle hypertrophy.

b. **Reduction in Protein Catabolism**: Inhibits protein breakdown, preserving lean muscle mass.

3. Interaction with Growth Factors:

a. **Insulin-like Growth Factor (IGF-1)**: Anabolic steroids can increase IGF-1 production, which promotes muscle growth and repair.

b. **Growth Hormone**: Enhances sensitivity to growth hormone, further stimulating muscle growth.

Clinical Applications:

1. Medical Uses:

a. **Hypogonadism**: Testosterone replacement therapy for males with low testosterone levels due to hypogonadism.

b. **Delayed Puberty**: Stimulating puberty in adolescent boys with delayed puberty.

c. **Wasting Syndromes**: Counteracting muscle wasting in conditions like HIV/AIDS and cancer cachexia.

2. Performance Enhancement:

a. **Athletic Performance**: Illicit use by athletes and bodybuilders to enhance muscle size, strength, and endurance.

b. **Recovery**: Speeding up recovery from intense workouts or injuries.

Adverse Effects and Considerations:

1. Androgens:

a. **Virilization**: Development of male secondary sexual characteristics in females (e.g., deepening voice, facial hair growth).

b. **Cardiovascular Risks**: Increased risk of cardiovascular diseases, including hypertension and adverse lipid profiles.

c. **Liver Toxicity**: Potential hepatotoxicity, especially with oral preparations.

2. Anabolic Steroids:

a. **Androgenic Effects**: Potential for androgenic side effects such as acne, baldness, and gynecomastia (male breast enlargement).

b. **Psychological Effects**: Mood swings, aggression ("roid rage"), and dependence.

c. **Endocrine Disruption**: Suppression of endogenous testosterone production, leading to testicular atrophy and infertility.

Therapeutic Uses

Androgens and anabolic steroids have various therapeutic uses, primarily stemming from their ability to mimic or enhance the effects of endogenous testosterone. These pharmacological agents are utilized in both medical and non-medical contexts, each with specific therapeutic goals and considerations. Here's an in-depth look at the therapeutic uses of androgens and anabolic steroids:

Therapeutic Uses of Androgens:

1. Hormone Replacement Therapy (HRT):

    a. **Hypogonadism**: Androgens, such as testosterone, are administered to males with hypogonadism (low testosterone levels).

        i. **Clinical Indications**: Treatment aims to alleviate symptoms of testosterone deficiency, including fatigue, decreased libido, erectile dysfunction, and mood disturbances.

        ii. **Forms of Administration**: Can be administered via intramuscular injections, transdermal patches, topical gels, or buccal patches.

2. Delayed Puberty:

    a. **Boys**: Androgens may be prescribed to stimulate puberty in adolescent boys with delayed puberty.

        i. **Clinical Indications**: Initiates development of secondary sexual characteristics (e.g., facial and body hair growth, deepening of voice, growth of external genitalia).

        ii. **Forms of Administration**: Often administered intramuscularly or as transdermal patches.

3. Gender Dysphoria (Transgender Men):

    a. **Masculinization**: Androgens are used as part of hormone therapy in transgender men (female-to-male transition).

    i.   **Clinical Indications**: Induces masculine secondary sexual characteristics, such as voice deepening and increased muscle mass.

    ii. **Forms of Administration**: Tailored to individual needs and often involves testosterone injections or transdermal applications.

Therapeutic Uses of Anabolic Steroids:

1. Muscle Wasting Disorders:

a. **HIV/AIDS**: Anabolic steroids may be prescribed to counteract muscle wasting (cachexia) associated with HIV/AIDS.

    i.   **Clinical Indications**: Enhances lean body mass and muscle strength, potentially improving quality of life.

    ii. **Forms of Administration**: Typically administered orally or via intramuscular injection.

b. **Chronic Illness**: Used in patients with chronic diseases causing muscle wasting, such as cancer or renal failure.

    i.   **Clinical Indications**: Helps maintain muscle mass and strength, supporting overall physical function.

    ii. **Forms of Administration**: Varied, depending on patient condition and medical provider preferences.

2. Osteoporosis:

a. **Bone Health**: Anabolic steroids may aid in the treatment of osteoporosis by promoting bone mineral density.

    i.   **Clinical Indications**: Reduces fracture risk and improves bone strength.

    ii. **Forms of Administration**: Typically administered orally or via injection, often in combination with other therapies.

3. Anemia:

a. **Erythropoiesis**: In certain cases of anemia, anabolic steroids may stimulate erythropoiesis (red blood cell production).

i. **Clinical Indications**: Increases hemoglobin levels and improves oxygen-carrying capacity of blood.

ii. **Forms of Administration**: Usually administered as intramuscular injections.

Non-Therapeutic Uses (Non-Medical):

1. Performance Enhancement:

a. **Athletics**: Illicit use by athletes and bodybuilders to enhance muscle size, strength, and endurance.

  i. **Clinical Indications**: Improves physical performance and recovery from intense training.

  ii. **Forms of Administration**: Typically administered in supraphysiological doses, often illegally obtained.

2. Aesthetic Purposes:

a. **Bodybuilding**: Anabolic steroids are used to achieve a more muscular physique beyond natural potential.

  i. **Clinical Indications**: Increases muscle mass and reduces body fat percentage.

  ii. **Forms of Administration**: Often self-administered via injections or oral tablets, with potential health risks.

Considerations and Monitoring:

a. **Medical Supervision**: Proper administration and monitoring by healthcare providers are crucial to mitigate potential side effects and ensure therapeutic efficacy.

b. **Risk-Benefit Assessment**: The benefits of therapeutic use must outweigh potential risks, especially in non-medical contexts where misuse can lead to significant health complications.

c. **Adverse Effects**: Side effects include cardiovascular complications, hepatotoxicity, endocrine disruptions, psychiatric disturbances, and dependency issues.

Anabolic Steroids

Anabolic steroids are synthetic derivatives of testosterone, designed to enhance anabolic (muscle-building) effects while minimizing androgenic (secondary sexual characteristics) effects. They play a significant role in pharmacology, primarily in sports medicine and some medical conditions. Here's a detailed exploration of anabolic steroids in the context of pharmacology and their effects on the endocrine system:

Mechanism of Action:

Anabolic steroids exert their effects primarily through interaction with androgen receptors (AR) in various tissues throughout the body:

1. **Androgen Receptor Binding**:
    a. Anabolic steroids bind to androgen receptors in target tissues, such as skeletal muscle cells.
    b. This binding initiates a series of molecular events leading to increased protein synthesis and muscle growth.

2. **Protein Synthesis Stimulation**:
    a. By binding to androgen receptors, anabolic steroids enhance nitrogen retention and stimulate protein synthesis in muscle cells.
    b. This results in increased muscle mass, strength, and recovery ability, especially in combination with resistance training.

3. **Enhanced IGF-1 Production**:
    a. Anabolic steroids can increase the production of insulin-like growth factor 1 (IGF-1).
    b. IGF-1 promotes anabolic processes, including muscle hypertrophy and tissue repair.

Types of Anabolic Steroids:

Anabolic steroids can be classified into two main types based on their administration and metabolism:

1. **Oral Anabolic Steroids**:

a. Examples include methandrostenolone (Dianabol) and oxandrolone (Anavar).

b. These steroids are orally active and undergo hepatic metabolism, potentially leading to liver toxicity.

2. **Injectable Anabolic Steroids**:

a. Examples include testosterone esters (e.g., testosterone enanthate, testosterone cypionate) and nandrolone decanoate (Deca-Durabolin).

b. Injectables bypass first-pass metabolism and are administered via intramuscular injection.

Therapeutic Uses:

1. Medical Uses:

a. **Muscle Wasting Disorders**: Anabolic steroids are prescribed to treat conditions involving muscle wasting, such as HIV/AIDS-associated cachexia and certain types of cancer.

i. **Clinical Indications**: Help maintain lean body mass, improve strength, and enhance quality of life.

ii. **Administration**: Typically administered in low to moderate doses under medical supervision.

b. **Hypogonadism**: In cases of testosterone deficiency, anabolic steroids may be used as testosterone replacement therapy.

i. **Clinical Indications**: Corrects symptoms of low testosterone, including fatigue, reduced libido, and muscle weakness.

ii. **Administration**: Varied, depending on formulation (e.g., injectable testosterone esters, transdermal patches).

2. Non-Medical Uses:

a. **Performance Enhancement**: Anabolic steroids are widely misused in competitive sports and bodybuilding to gain a competitive edge and enhance physical performance beyond natural capabilities.

i. **Clinical Indications**: Increases muscle mass, strength, and endurance.

ii. **Administration**: Often administered in supraphysiological doses, obtained illicitly without medical supervision.

Adverse Effects:

Anabolic steroids, despite their potential benefits, carry significant risks and adverse effects, including:

a. **Cardiovascular Effects**: Increased risk of hypertension, cardiomyopathy, and myocardial infarction.

b. **Hepatic Effects**: Liver toxicity, potentially leading to jaundice, peliosis hepatis, and liver tumors.

c. **Endocrine Disruptions**: Suppression of endogenous testosterone production, testicular atrophy, and infertility.

d. **Psychiatric Effects**: Mood swings, aggression ("roid rage"), and dependency or addiction.

e. **Virilization**: Development of male characteristics in females, such as deepening voice and facial hair growth.

Legal and Ethical Considerations:

a. **Regulation**: Anabolic steroids are classified as controlled substances in many countries due to their misuse potential and adverse health effects.

b. **Sports Bans**: Prohibited in competitive sports under anti-doping regulations due to unfair advantage and health risks.

c. **Ethical Concerns**: Misuse of anabolic steroids raises ethical issues related to fairness, integrity in sports, and athlete safety.

Common Anabolic Steroids:

In pharmacology, anabolic steroids encompass a variety of synthetic derivatives of testosterone, each with specific pharmacokinetic profiles and varying degrees of anabolic and androgenic effects. These substances are widely used in both medical and non-medical settings, primarily for their ability to enhance muscle growth and performance. Here's an overview of some common anabolic steroids used today:

1. Testosterone and its Esters

a. **Description**: Testosterone is the primary male sex hormone and the prototype of all anabolic steroids.

b. **Forms**: Includes various esterified forms such as testosterone enanthate, testosterone cypionate, testosterone propionate, and testosterone undecanoate.

c. **Administration**: Administered via intramuscular injection (esters) or transdermal patches (testosterone gel).

d. **Medical Uses**: Treatment of hypogonadism, delayed puberty, and certain types of breast cancer in women.

e. **Effects**: Enhances muscle growth, strength, and bone density. Can also have androgenic effects like facial hair growth and deepening voice.

2. Nandrolone and its Derivatives

a. **Description**: Nandrolone is a synthetic derivative of testosterone with reduced androgenic properties.

b. **Forms**: Includes nandrolone decanoate (Deca-Durabolin) and nandrolone phenylpropionate (Durabolin).

c. **Administration**: Administered via intramuscular injection.

d. **Medical Uses**: Treatment of anemia, muscle wasting conditions, and osteoporosis.

e. **Effects**: Promotes muscle growth, increases red blood cell production, and enhances bone density with fewer androgenic side effects compared to testosterone.

3. Oxandrolone (Anavar)

a. **Description**: Oxandrolone is a synthetic derivative of dihydrotestosterone (DHT) with high anabolic activity and reduced androgenic effects.

b. **Administration**: Usually administered orally.

c. **Medical Uses**: Treatment of muscle wasting in chronic illness, promoting weight gain after surgery or trauma.

d. **Effects**: Enhances nitrogen retention, stimulates protein synthesis, and improves muscle strength without significant estrogenic effects.

4. Stanozolol (Winstrol)

a. **Description**: Stanozolol is a synthetic derivative of dihydrotestosterone (DHT).

b. **Forms**: Available in oral and injectable forms.

c. **Medical Uses**: Used in veterinary medicine to promote muscle growth in animals. Rarely used medically in humans due to hepatotoxicity.

d. **Effects**: Enhances muscle growth and strength, reduces SHBG (sex hormone-binding globulin) levels, and can improve athletic performance.

5. Methandrostenolone (Dianabol)

a. **Description**: Methandrostenolone is an oral synthetic derivative of testosterone.

b. **Administration**: Administered orally.

c. **Medical Uses**: Historically used for muscle wasting conditions, but now mostly discontinued due to hepatotoxicity and other side effects.

d. **Effects**: Rapidly increases muscle mass and strength, enhances glycogenolysis, and boosts nitrogen retention.

6. Trenbolone

a. **Description**: Trenbolone is a synthetic derivative of nandrolone with strong anabolic properties.

b. **Forms**: Available in various esters for injectable administration.

c. **Medical Uses**: Not approved for medical use in humans. Used in veterinary medicine to promote muscle growth in livestock.

d. **Effects**: Potent anabolic effects, enhances protein synthesis, and promotes muscle growth. Known for its ability to increase muscle hardness and vascularity.

Legal Status and Regulations:

Anabolic steroids are classified as controlled substances in many countries due to their misuse potential and adverse health effects. In medical practice, they are used cautiously under strict supervision to treat specific conditions. Outside medical use, their non-prescription use is illegal and subject to anti-doping regulations in sports.

Mechanisms of Action

Similar to natural androgens, anabolic steroids bind to androgen receptors, leading to enhanced protein synthesis, muscle growth, and overall anabolic effects. They also increase the retention of nitrogen, which is critical for muscle repair and growth.

Therapeutic Uses

1. **Wasting Syndromes**: Treatment of cachexia and muscle wasting associated with chronic diseases like HIV/AIDS and cancer.
2. **Severe Burns**: Promote muscle and weight gain in patients recovering from severe burns.
3. **Anemia**: Enhance erythropoiesis in certain types of anemia.

Adverse Effects

Androgens and anabolic steroids can have numerous adverse effects, especially when used in supra-physiological doses or for non-medical purposes such as performance enhancement.

1. **Cardiovascular**: Increased risk of cardiovascular diseases, including hypertension, myocardial infarction, and stroke.
2. **Liver Toxicity**: Hepatotoxicity, including liver tumors and peliosis hepatis, particularly with oral anabolic steroids.
3. **Endocrine**: Suppression of natural testosterone production, leading to testicular atrophy and infertility; gynecomastia (breast tissue development in men) due to aromatization of excess testosterone to estrogen.
4. **Psychiatric**: Mood swings, aggression, depression, and dependence.

5. **Musculoskeletal**: Premature epiphyseal closure in adolescents, leading to stunted growth.

6. **Metabolic**: Dyslipidemia, with decreased HDL (good cholesterol) and increased LDL (bad cholesterol).

Abuse and Legal Status

The non-medical use of anabolic steroids, particularly in sports and bodybuilding, is associated with significant health risks and is banned by most sports organizations. Anabolic steroids are classified as controlled substances in many countries due to their potential for abuse and adverse health effects.

ESTROGENS

Estrogens are a group of steroid hormones crucial for the development and regulation of the female reproductive system and secondary sexual characteristics. They also play significant roles in other body systems, including the cardiovascular, skeletal, and central nervous systems. In pharmacology, estrogens are used to treat various conditions related to estrogen deficiency or imbalance.

Key Endogenous Estrogens

1. **Estradiol (E2)**: The most potent and predominant estrogen in premenopausal women.

2. **Estrone (E1)**: Less potent than estradiol, predominates after menopause.

3. **Estriol (E3)**: The weakest estrogen, primarily produced during pregnancy.

Mechanisms of Action

1. **Receptor Binding**: Estrogens exert their effects by binding to estrogen receptors (ERs), which are nuclear receptors that regulate gene expression. There are two main types of estrogen receptors:

    a. **ER-alpha (ERα)**: Found in tissues such as the uterus, liver, and breast.

b. **ER-beta (ERβ)**: Predominantly found in the ovaries, prostate, and cardiovascular system.

2. **Genomic Actions**: Upon binding to ERs, the hormone-receptor complex translocates to the nucleus, where it binds to estrogen response elements (EREs) on DNA, modulating the transcription of target genes involved in cell growth, differentiation, and metabolism.

3. **Non-Genomic Actions**: Estrogens can also exert rapid effects through non-genomic pathways involving membrane-bound estrogen receptors and intracellular signaling cascades.

Therapeutic Uses

1. **Hormone Replacement Therapy (HRT)**: Used to alleviate symptoms of menopause such as hot flashes, vaginal dryness, and osteoporosis prevention.

   a. **Preparations**: Conjugated estrogens (Premarin), estradiol (oral, transdermal patches, gels), esterified estrogens.

2. **Contraception**: Combined with progestins in oral contraceptive pills, patches, and rings to prevent ovulation and pregnancy.

   a. **Examples**: Ethinyl estradiol, mestranol.

3. **Hypogonadism**: Treatment of estrogen deficiency in women with primary ovarian insufficiency or other conditions leading to low estrogen levels.

4. **Menstrual Disorders**: Management of dysfunctional uterine bleeding, amenorrhea, and polycystic ovary syndrome (PCOS).

5. **Osteoporosis**: Prevention and treatment of postmenopausal osteoporosis by maintaining bone density.

6. **Cancer Therapy**: High-dose estrogens have been used in the past for prostate cancer, though this is less common with the advent of more targeted therapies.

7. **Gender-Affirming Hormone Therapy**: Estrogens are used in transgender women and non-binary individuals assigned male at birth to induce feminizing changes.

Pharmacokinetics

1. **Absorption**: Estrogens can be administered orally, transdermally, intramuscularly, or vaginally. Oral estrogens undergo significant first-pass metabolism in the liver, reducing bioavailability.

2. **Metabolism**: Primarily metabolized in the liver through hydroxylation and conjugation, resulting in various metabolites excreted in the urine and bile.

3. **Half-Life**: Varies depending on the form and route of administration. For example, estradiol has a half-life of a few hours when taken orally, whereas transdermal patches provide more sustained levels.

Adverse Effects

1. **Thromboembolic Events**: Increased risk of deep vein thrombosis (DVT), pulmonary embolism (PE), and stroke, particularly in smokers and women over 35.

2. **Cardiovascular Risks**: Potential increase in the risk of myocardial infarction, particularly when combined with progestins in HRT.

3. **Breast Cancer**: Prolonged use of estrogens, especially in combination with progestins, has been associated with an increased risk of breast cancer.

4. **Endometrial Cancer**: Unopposed estrogen therapy (without progestins) increases the risk of endometrial hyperplasia and cancer. Adding a progestin mitigates this risk.

5. **Gallbladder Disease**: Increased risk of gallstone formation and cholecystitis.

6. **Other Effects**: Nausea, headaches, breast tenderness, and mood changes.

Drug Interactions

1. **CYP Enzymes**: Estrogens are metabolized by cytochrome P450 enzymes (e.g., CYP3A4). Drugs that induce or inhibit these enzymes can affect estrogen levels and efficacy.

   a. **Inducers**: Rifampin, phenytoin, carbamazepine.

   b. **Inhibitors**: Grapefruit juice, ketoconazole, erythromycin.

2. **Anticoagulants**: Estrogens can decrease the effectiveness of anticoagulants like warfarin, increasing the risk of clotting.

3. **Thyroid Hormones**: Estrogens can increase thyroid-binding globulin (TBG) levels, affecting thyroid hormone measurements and potentially requiring dosage adjustments of thyroid medications.

Clinical Considerations

1. **Individualized Therapy**: The choice of estrogen therapy, dose, and route of administration should be individualized based on the patient's health status, risk factors, and treatment goals.

2. **Monitoring**: Regular monitoring for side effects and efficacy is essential, including assessments of bone density, lipid profiles, and mammograms.

3. **Contraindications**: Estrogen therapy is contraindicated in patients with a history of estrogen-dependent cancers, active thromboembolic disorders, liver disease, and unexplained vaginal bleeding.

PROGESTERONE

Progesterone is a key hormone in the regulation of the menstrual cycle, maintenance of pregnancy, and development of secondary sexual characteristics. It is produced mainly by the corpus luteum in the ovary after ovulation and by the placenta during pregnancy. In pharmacology, progesterone and its synthetic derivatives (progestins) are used for various therapeutic purposes, ranging from contraception to hormone replacement therapy.

Mechanisms of Action

1. **Receptor Binding**: Progesterone acts primarily through binding to the progesterone receptors (PRs), which are nuclear receptors. There are two main isoforms of the progesterone receptor:
   a. **PR-A**: Involved in the regulation of gene expression and cellular responses.
   b. **PR-B**: Plays a role in the mediation of progesterone's effects in reproductive tissues.
2. **Genomic Actions**: Upon binding to its receptor, the hormone-receptor complex translocates to the nucleus, where it binds to progesterone response elements (PREs) on DNA, modulating the transcription of target genes involved in reproductive function, metabolism, and cell cycle regulation.
3. **Non-Genomic Actions**: Progesterone can also exert rapid effects through non-genomic pathways, involving membrane-bound receptors and signaling cascades, such as modulation of ion channels and activation of second messengers.

Therapeutic Uses

1. **Hormone Replacement Therapy (HRT)**: Used in combination with estrogens to alleviate symptoms of menopause and prevent endometrial hyperplasia caused by unopposed estrogen therapy.
   a. **Preparations**: Micronized progesterone (Prometrium), combined estrogen-progestin therapies.
2. **Contraception**: Used alone or in combination with estrogens in various forms, including oral contraceptives, injectables, implants, intrauterine devices (IUDs), and vaginal rings.
   a. **Examples**: Medroxyprogesterone acetate (Depo-Provera), norethindrone, levonorgestrel (Plan B), etonogestrel (Nexplanon).
3. **Menstrual Disorders**: Management of conditions such as dysmenorrhea, abnormal uterine bleeding, and amenorrhea.

a. **Examples**: Oral progesterone, medroxyprogesterone acetate, norethindrone.

4. **Assisted Reproductive Technology (ART)**: Used to support the luteal phase in women undergoing in vitro fertilization (IVF) and other assisted reproductive techniques.

    a. **Preparations**: Vaginal progesterone gel, intramuscular progesterone.

5. **Endometriosis**: Used to reduce endometrial tissue growth and alleviate pain associated with endometriosis.

    a. **Examples**: Dienogest, medroxyprogesterone acetate.

6. **Prevention of Preterm Birth**: Progesterone is used to reduce the risk of preterm birth in women with a history of spontaneous preterm delivery or with a short cervix.

    a. **Preparations**: Vaginal progesterone, intramuscular 17-alpha hydroxyprogesterone caproate.

Pharmacokinetics

1. **Absorption**: Progesterone can be administered orally, vaginally, intramuscularly, or via subcutaneous implants. Oral progesterone undergoes extensive first-pass metabolism, leading to low bioavailability.

2. **Distribution**: Progesterone is widely distributed in body tissues, with high levels found in fat tissues due to its lipophilicity.

3. **Metabolism**: Primarily metabolized in the liver to pregnanediol and other metabolites, which are excreted in the urine as glucuronide conjugates.

4. **Half-Life**: The half-life of progesterone is approximately 5 minutes when administered intravenously, but varies with other routes due to differences in absorption and metabolism.

Adverse Effects

1. **Mood Changes**: Progesterone can cause mood swings, depression, and irritability in some individuals.

2. **Weight Gain**: Fluid retention and increased appetite can lead to weight gain.

3. **Breast Tenderness**: Commonly reported side effect, especially in the initial phase of therapy.

4. **Menstrual Irregularities**: Changes in bleeding patterns, including spotting, breakthrough bleeding, or amenorrhea.

5. **Cardiovascular Risks**: Progestins, especially in combination with estrogens, can increase the risk of thromboembolic events and cardiovascular diseases.

6. **Other Effects**: Headaches, bloating, acne, and changes in libido.

Drug Interactions

1. **Cytochrome P450 Enzymes**: Progesterone is metabolized by CYP3A4, and drugs that induce or inhibit this enzyme can affect progesterone levels.

   a. **Inducers**: Rifampin, phenobarbital, carbamazepine.

   b. **Inhibitors**: Ketoconazole, erythromycin, grapefruit juice.

2. **Anticonvulsants**: Certain anticonvulsants can decrease the effectiveness of hormonal contraceptives containing progestins.

   a. **Examples**: Phenytoin, carbamazepine.

3. **Anticoagulants**: Progesterone can alter the effectiveness of anticoagulants, requiring monitoring and possible dose adjustments.

   a. **Examples**: Warfarin.

Clinical Considerations

1. **Individualized Therapy**: The choice of progesterone or progestin therapy, including the dose and route of administration, should be tailored to the individual's medical condition, health status, and risk factors.

2. **Monitoring**: Regular monitoring of treatment efficacy and side effects is essential, including assessments of menstrual patterns, mood, and cardiovascular health.

3. **Contraindications**: Progesterone therapy is contraindicated in patients with a history of hormone-sensitive cancers, active thromboembolic disorders, liver disease, and undiagnosed vaginal bleeding.

ORAL CONTRACEPTIVES

Oral contraceptives (OCs) are a widely used method of preventing pregnancy. They contain synthetic hormones that mimic the actions of natural estrogens and progestins to inhibit ovulation, alter the uterine lining, and modify cervical mucus. This section explores the pharmacology, mechanisms of action, therapeutic uses, and potential adverse effects of oral contraceptives.

Types of Oral Contraceptives

1. **Combined Oral Contraceptives (COCs)**: Contain both estrogen and progestin.

   a. **Estrogen Components**: Ethinyl estradiol, mestranol.

   b. **Progestin Components**: Norethindrone, levonorgestrel, desogestrel, drospirenone, norgestimate.

2. **Progestin-Only Pills (POPs)**: Contain only progestin.

   a. **Examples**: Norethindrone, desogestrel.

Mechanisms of Action

1. **Inhibition of Ovulation**:

   a. **Estrogens**: Suppress follicle-stimulating hormone (FSH) release from the pituitary, preventing follicular development.

   b. **Progestins**: Suppress luteinizing hormone (LH) surge, which inhibits ovulation.

2. **Alteration of Cervical Mucus**:

   a. **Progestins**: Thicken cervical mucus, making it less penetrable to sperm.

3. **Endometrial Changes**:

   a. **Progestins**: Induce changes in the endometrium, making it less suitable for implantation.

4. **Fallopian Tube Motility**:

   a. **Progestins**: May alter the motility of the fallopian tubes, hindering the transport of sperm and ova.

Therapeutic Uses

1. **Contraception**: Primary use is to prevent pregnancy. Highly effective when taken as prescribed.

2. **Regulation of Menstrual Cycles**: Helps regulate irregular menstrual cycles and reduce menstrual cramps.

3. **Management of Menstrual Disorders**: Used to treat menorrhagia (heavy menstrual bleeding), dysmenorrhea (painful menstruation), and premenstrual syndrome (PMS).

4. **Treatment of Acne**: Certain COCs can reduce androgen levels, thereby decreasing acne.

   a. **Examples**: COCs containing drospirenone, norgestimate.

5. **Polycystic Ovary Syndrome (PCOS)**: Helps manage symptoms by regulating menstrual cycles and reducing androgen levels.

6. **Endometriosis**: Reduces pain and suppresses the growth of endometrial tissue.

Pharmacokinetics

1. **Absorption**: Both estrogen and progestin components are well-absorbed from the gastrointestinal tract.

2. **Distribution**: Widely distributed in the body, binding to plasma proteins.

3. **Metabolism**: Metabolized in the liver via cytochrome P450 enzymes (CYP3A4).

4. **Excretion**: Excreted in urine and feces as metabolites.

Adverse Effects

1. **Cardiovascular Risks**: Increased risk of thromboembolic events (deep vein thrombosis, pulmonary embolism), myocardial infarction, and stroke, particularly in smokers and women over 35.

2. **Hypertension**: Can cause a slight increase in blood pressure.

3. **Breast Tenderness and Pain**: Common side effect, especially in the initial months of use.

4. **Nausea and Vomiting**: Particularly with higher estrogen doses.

5. **Weight Gain**: Some users may experience weight gain due to fluid retention or increased appetite.

6. **Mood Changes**: Can cause mood swings, depression, or anxiety in some users.

7. **Hepatic Effects**: Rarely, can cause liver dysfunction or benign liver tumors.

8. **Other Effects**: Headaches, dizziness, and changes in libido.

Drug Interactions

1. **CYP450 Enzyme Inducers**: Drugs that induce CYP3A4 can decrease the effectiveness of OCs.

    a. **Examples**: Rifampin, phenobarbital, carbamazepine, phenytoin.

2. **Antibiotics**: Some antibiotics can reduce the efficacy of OCs by altering gut flora.

    a. **Examples**: Rifampin.

3. **Anticonvulsants**: Some anticonvulsants can decrease OC effectiveness.

    a. **Examples**: Phenytoin, carbamazepine.

4. **Antiretrovirals**: Certain antiretrovirals used for HIV can affect OC metabolism.

    a. **Examples**: Efavirenz.

Clinical Considerations

1. **Patient Selection**: Not all women are suitable candidates for OCs. Thorough medical history and assessment of risk factors are essential.

2. **Contraindications**: Absolute contraindications include a history of thromboembolic disorders, stroke, coronary artery disease, breast cancer, liver tumors, and unexplained vaginal bleeding.

3. **Monitoring**: Regular follow-up is necessary to monitor blood pressure, manage side effects, and ensure compliance.

4. **Counseling**: Patients should be counseled on the importance of adherence, potential side effects, and what to do in case of missed pills.

DRUGS ACTING ON THE UTERUS

Drugs acting on the uterus are used to manage a variety of conditions related to uterine function, including labor induction, abortion, control of postpartum hemorrhage, and treatment of uterine atony. These drugs can stimulate or relax the uterine muscles and are integral in reproductive health management. This section details the pharmacology, mechanisms of action, therapeutic uses, and potential adverse effects of these drugs.

Categories of Uterotonic and Uterorelaxant Drugs

1. **Uterotonics**: Stimulate uterine contractions.

    a. **Oxytocics**: Oxytocin, ergot alkaloids, prostaglandins.

2. **Uterorelaxants (Tocolytics)**: Inhibit uterine contractions.

    a. **Beta-agonists**, calcium channel blockers, NSAIDs, magnesium sulfate, oxytocin receptor antagonists.

Uterotonic Drugs

Oxytocin

Mechanism of Action:

1. **Receptor Binding**: Oxytocin binds to oxytocin receptors on the uterine smooth muscle, causing an increase in intracellular calcium, which leads to muscle contraction.

2. **Effect on Labor**: Induces labor by stimulating uterine contractions and is used to augment labor and manage postpartum hemorrhage by promoting uterine involution.

Therapeutic Uses:

1. **Induction of Labor**: Used to induce labor in women at term or when labor is delayed due to medical reasons.

2. **Augmentation of Labor**: Enhances contractions in cases of weak or insufficient uterine contractions.

3. **Postpartum Hemorrhage**: Prevents and controls bleeding after childbirth by contracting the uterus.

Adverse Effects:

1. **Uterine Hyperstimulation**: Can lead to excessive contractions, fetal distress, or uterine rupture.

2. **Hyponatremia**: Prolonged use can cause water retention and hyponatremia.

3. **Hypotension**: Rapid infusion can cause hypotension and tachycardia.

Ergot Alkaloids (e.g., Methylergonovine)

Mechanism of Action:

- **Smooth Muscle Contraction**: Acts on smooth muscles of the uterus by binding to serotonin and alpha-adrenergic receptors, causing sustained uterine contractions.

Therapeutic Uses:

1. **Postpartum Hemorrhage**: Used to control bleeding by promoting sustained uterine contraction.

2. **Post-Abortion Hemorrhage**: Prevents and manages excessive bleeding after abortion.

Adverse Effects:

1. **Hypertension**: Can cause severe hypertension and should be used cautiously in patients with preexisting hypertension.

2. **Nausea and Vomiting**: Common gastrointestinal side effects.

3. **Vasospasm**: Can lead to vasospasm and peripheral ischemia.

Prostaglandins (e.g., Misoprostol, Dinoprostone)

Mechanism of Action:

1. **Receptor Binding**: Prostaglandins bind to receptors on the uterine smooth muscle, increasing intracellular calcium and causing muscle contraction.
2. **Cervical Ripening**: Promote cervical ripening by remodeling collagen in the cervix.

Therapeutic Uses:

1. **Induction of Labor**: Used for cervical ripening and induction of labor.
2. **Medical Abortion**: Used in combination with mifepristone for medical abortion.
3. **Postpartum Hemorrhage**: Used to control bleeding by contracting the uterus.

Adverse Effects:

1. **Gastrointestinal Symptoms**: Nausea, vomiting, diarrhea.
2. **Fever**: Transient fever can occur.
3. **Uterine Hyperstimulation**: Risk of excessive uterine contractions and potential rupture.

Uterorelaxant Drugs (Tocolytics)

Beta-Agonists (e.g., Terbutaline)

Mechanism of Action:

- **Beta-2 Adrenergic Receptor Activation**: Relaxes uterine smooth muscle by increasing cyclic AMP, which decreases intracellular calcium.

Therapeutic Uses:

1. **Preterm Labor**: Used to delay preterm labor by inhibiting uterine contractions.

Adverse Effects:

1. **Cardiovascular Effects**: Tachycardia, palpitations, hypotension.
2. **Hyperglycemia**: Can cause elevated blood glucose levels.
3. **Pulmonary Edema**: Risk of pulmonary edema with prolonged use.

Calcium Channel Blockers (e.g., Nifedipine)

Mechanism of Action:

1. **Inhibition of Calcium Influx**: Blocks calcium channels in the uterine smooth muscle, reducing intracellular calcium levels and causing muscle relaxation.

Therapeutic Uses:

1. **Preterm Labor**: Effective in delaying preterm labor.

Adverse Effects:

1. **Hypotension**: Can cause low blood pressure.
2. **Tachycardia**: May lead to increased heart rate.
3. **Headache and Dizziness**: Common side effects.

Non-Steroidal Anti-Inflammatory Drugs (NSAIDs) (e.g., Indomethacin)

Mechanism of Action:

1. **Prostaglandin Synthesis Inhibition**: Inhibits cyclooxygenase enzymes, reducing the production of prostaglandins that induce uterine contractions.

Therapeutic Uses:

1. **Preterm Labor**: Used as a short-term tocolytic to delay labor.

Adverse Effects:

1. **Fetal Complications**: Risk of premature closure of the ductus arteriosus in the fetus.
2. **Maternal Gastrointestinal Symptoms**: Nausea, vomiting, gastritis.
3. **Oligohydramnios**: Reduced amniotic fluid levels.

Magnesium Sulfate

Mechanism of Action:

1. **Calcium Antagonism**: Competes with calcium at cellular binding sites, reducing muscle contractility.

Therapeutic Uses:

1. **Preterm Labor**: Used as a tocolytic to delay preterm labor.

2. **Neuroprotection**: Provides neuroprotection for the fetus in preterm labor.

Adverse Effects:

1. **Respiratory Depression**: High doses can cause respiratory depression.

2. **Hypotension**: Can lead to low blood pressure.

3. **Flushing and Sweating**: Common side effects.

Oxytocin Receptor Antagonists (e.g., Atosiban)

Mechanism of Action:

1. **Oxytocin Receptor Inhibition**: Blocks oxytocin receptors in the uterine smooth muscle, reducing contractions.

Therapeutic Uses:

1. **Preterm Labor**: Used to delay preterm labor.

Adverse Effects:

1. **Nausea and Vomiting**: Common side effects.

2. **Headache**: Can cause headaches.

3. **Injection Site Reactions**: Pain or inflammation at the injection site.

Clinical Considerations

1. **Patient Selection**: The choice of uterotonic or tocolytic therapy should be based on the specific clinical scenario, considering the patient's health status and potential risks.

2. **Monitoring**: Regular monitoring is necessary to assess the effectiveness and side effects of therapy, including uterine contractions, fetal heart rate, and maternal vital signs.

3. **Contraindications**: Each drug has specific contraindications that must be considered to avoid adverse outcomes.

MCQs Based on the Provided Context:

1. What is the primary function of GnRH agonists like Leuprolide?

   A) To reduce bone density

B) To stimulate the production of LH and FSH initially, then reduce their secretion

C) To increase glucose uptake

D) To directly inhibit GnRH receptors

2. Which hormone is primarily responsible for the regulation of metabolism, growth, and development in the thyroid gland?

A) Cortisol

B) Thyroxine (T4)

C) Insulin

D) Prolactin

3. Somatropin is used to treat which of the following conditions?

A) Diabetes insipidus

B) Growth hormone deficiency

C) Hyperthyroidism

D) Prostate cancer

4. Which drug is a synthetic version of thyroid hormone used to treat hypothyroidism? A) Methimazole

B) Levothyroxine

C) Octreotide

D) Pegvisomant

5. Flutamide is classified as what type of drug?

A) Glucocorticoid

B) Mineralocorticoid

C) Anti-androgen

D) GH antagonist

6. Progesterone is mainly produced by which part of the body?

A) Adrenal cortex

B) Pancreas

C) Corpus luteum in the ovary

D) Pituitary gland

7. What is the primary action of anabolic steroids on muscle tissue?

    A) Decrease protein synthesis

    B) Stimulate rapid muscle growth

    C) Inhibit nitrogen retention

    D) Promote fat deposition

8. Insulin glargine is used to treat which type of diabetes?

    A) Type 1 diabetes mellitus

    B) Type 2 diabetes mellitus

    C) Gestational diabetes

    D) Both A and B

9. Which medication is used to treat severe hypoglycemia?

    A) Metformin

    B) Glucagon

    C) Somatostatin

    D) Glyburide

10. Estrogens and progestins are used together in which of the following?

    A) Treating prostate cancer

    B) Hormone replacement therapy

    C) Diabetes management

    D) Bone density improvement

11. Which hormone is involved in the fight-or-flight response?

    A) Cortisol

    B) Aldosterone

    C) Epinephrine

    D) Oxytocin

12. What is the primary therapeutic use of Tamoxifen?

    A) Treating diabetes

    B) Reducing high blood pressure

C) Breast cancer treatment

D) Treating osteoporosis

13. Methimazole is used to treat:

A) Hypothyroidism

B) Hyperthyroidism

C) Diabetes mellitus

D) Growth hormone deficiency

14. Which drug is a common treatment for Cushing's syndrome?

A) Ketoconazole

B) Levothyroxine

C) Insulin

D) Somatropin

15. What is the mechanism of action of GH agonists like Somatropin?

A) Blocks GH receptors

B) Mimics endogenous GH

C) Inhibits insulin secretion

D) Increases cortisol production

16. Which drug is used to induce labor and control postpartum hemorrhage?

A) Vasopressin

B) Oxytocin

C) Bromocriptine

D) Cetrorelix

17. Which hormone is responsible for regulating calcium and phosphate metabolism?

A) Insulin

B) Thyroxine (T4)

C) Parathyroid hormone (PTH)

D) Growth hormone (GH)

18. What is the primary function of anti-estrogens like Tamoxifen?

A) To stimulate estrogen production

B) To block estrogen receptors

C) To promote estrogen release from the ovaries

D) To inhibit progesterone receptors

19. Which is NOT a use of glucocorticoids?

A) Treating inflammation

B) Promoting fluid retention

C) Treating diabetes insipidus

D) Treating adrenal insufficiency

20. How does Metformin work to treat type 2 diabetes mellitus?

A) Increases insulin secretion

B) Directly reduces blood glucose levels

C) Decreases hepatic glucose production

D) Blocks glucagon receptors

Short Answer Type Questions:

1. What is the primary role of GnRH agonists in the treatment of prostate cancer?

2. How do somatostatin analogues like octreotide function in the management of acromegaly?

3. Describe the main adverse effect of dopamine agonists used in the treatment of hyperprolactinemia.

4. What is the mechanism of action of thyroid hormone replacements like levothyroxine in treating hypothyroidism?

5. Explain the use of vasopressin analogues in the treatment of diabetes insipidus.

6. What is the clinical significance of PTH analogues in treating hypoparathyroidism?

7. How do glucocorticoids like prednisone alleviate symptoms in inflammatory conditions?

8. What are the key functions of insulin in the management of diabetes mellitus?

9. How do anti-estrogens like tamoxifen work in the treatment of breast cancer?

10. What role does testosterone play in the treatment of hypogonadism?

11. Describe the adverse effects associated with the use of anabolic steroids.

12. How do mineralocorticoids like fludrocortisone function in the management of Addison's disease?

13. What is the therapeutic use of somatostatin analogues in treating hormone-secreting tumors?

14. Discuss the mechanism by which GnRH antagonists prevent premature LH surge in IVF treatments.

15. Explain how oral hypoglycemic agents like metformin manage type 2 diabetes mellitus.

16. What are the risks associated with the long-term use of glucocorticoids?

17. How do progestins function in hormone replacement therapy?

18. Discuss the role of catecholamines in the management of cardiac arrest.

19. What are the clinical uses of estrogens in managing menopausal symptoms?

20. Describe how progestin-only pills prevent pregnancy.

Long Answer Type Questions:

1. Discuss the pharmacological effects of insulin analogues like insulin glargine in diabetes management and compare them with traditional human insulin.

2. Explain the role of hormone replacement therapy using estrogens and progestins in post-menopausal women, including benefits and risks.

3. Outline the mechanisms of action and clinical uses of thyroid hormone replacement therapies in the management of different thyroid disorders.

4. Discuss the use of bisphosphonates in the treatment of osteoporosis, including their mechanism of action and potential adverse effects.

5. Analyze the role of GnRH agonists and antagonists in the management of reproductive health disorders, highlighting their mechanisms and clinical outcomes.

6. Explain the therapeutic applications and safety considerations of using glucocorticoids in autoimmune diseases.

7. Detail the pharmacodynamics and clinical applications of catecholamines in emergency medicine, including their effects on cardiovascular and respiratory systems.

8. Discuss the role and mechanism of action of androgen and anabolic steroids in the treatment of muscle wasting diseases and their potential misuse in sports.

9. Provide a comprehensive overview of the pharmacological management of diabetes mellitus, including a comparison of different classes of drugs used.

10. Describe the role of mineralocorticoid therapy in managing electrolyte imbalances in adrenal insufficiency, discussing the effects on sodium and potassium homeostasis.

Answer Key:

1. B) To stimulate the production of LH and FSH initially, then reduce their secretion

2. B) Thyroxine (T4)

3. B) Growth hormone deficiency

4. B) Levothyroxine

5. C) Anti-androgen

6. C) Corpus luteum in the ovary

7. B) Stimulate rapid muscle growth

8. D) Both A and B

9. B) Glucagon

10.B) Hormone replacement therapy

11.C) Epinephine

12.C) Breast cancer treatment

13.B) Hyperthyroidism

14.A) Ketoconazole

15.B) Mimics endogenous GH

16.B) Oxytocin

17.C) Parathyroid hormone (PTH)

18.B) To block estrogen receptors

19.C) Treating diabetes insipidus

20.C) Decreases hepatic glucose production

CHAPTER – 7

BIOASSAY

A bioassay (biological assay) is a scientific method used to measure the concentration, potency, or biological activity of a substance by observing its effects on living organisms, tissues, cells, or biochemical systems. The primary goal of a bioassay is to assess the impact of a substance on a biological system, often comparing it to a standard or control to determine its efficacy, toxicity, or other biological properties.

Bioassays are essential tools in biological and medical research, providing critical data for the safe and effective use of various substances in healthcare, environmental management, and other fields

Key Components of a Bioassay

1. Test Substance: The material or compound being evaluated for its biological activity.

2. Biological System: The living organism, tissue, cell culture, or biochemical system used to assess the test substance's effects.

3. Standard or Control: A reference substance with known activity, used for comparison to ensure accuracy and reliability of the results.

4. Response Measurement: The specific biological response observed and measured, such as enzyme activity, cell proliferation, behavior changes, or physiological effects.

5. Dose-Response Relationship: The relationship between the dose of the test substance and the magnitude of the observed biological response, often plotted as a dose-response curve.

Others Types of Bioassay

1) In Vivo Bioassays:

   a) Animal Models: Use whole animals to observe the effects of a substance on the entire organism. Commonly used in toxicity testing.

   b) Plant Bioassays: Use plants or plant tissues to study the effects of substances like herbicides or growth regulators.

2) In Vitro Bioassays:

   a) Cell Culture Assays: Use cultured cells to examine the effects of substances on cell viability, proliferation, and function.

   b) Tissue Culture Assays:Use specific tissues or organ slices to assess more complex interactions than cell cultures.

3) Biochemical Bioassays:

   a) Enzyme Assays: Measure the activity of enzymes in the presence of a substance to determine its inhibitory or stimulatory effects.

   b) Receptor Binding Assays: Assess the binding affinity of a substance to its receptor, often used in pharmacology to study drug-receptor interactions.

Applications of Bioassays

1. Pharmaceutical Industry:
2. Drug development and quality control.
3. Medical Diagnostics:
4. Measuring hormones, enzymes, and other biomarkers.
5. Environmental Science:
6. Detecting and quantifying pollutants and toxins.
7. Agriculture:
8. Evaluating the effects of pesticides, herbicides, and fertilizers.
9. Toxicology:
10. Assessing the toxicity of chemicals and substances.

Principles of Bioassay

1. Biological Activity Measurement: Bioassays are used to measure the concentration or potency of a substance (such as a drug, hormone, or toxin) by its effect on living cells or tissues.

2. Dose-Response Relationship: The effect of a substance is related to its dose, and bioassays often involve creating a dose-response curve to determine the effective dose (ED) or lethal dose (LD).

3. Standardization: Bioassays require a standard or reference substance to compare the test substance's effects, ensuring consistency and accuracy.

4. Reproducibility and Sensitivity: Assays must be reproducible, with minimal variability, and sensitive enough to detect small changes in biological activity.

BIOASSAY OF INSULIN

Overview:

Insulin bioassays are conducted to determine the potency and biological activity of insulin preparations. These assays are crucial for ensuring the efficacy and safety of insulin used in diabetes treatment.

Types of Insulin Bioassays:

1. In Vivo Bioassays:

   Rabbit Blood Sugar Test:

- Measures the hypoglycemic effect of insulin by monitoring blood glucose levels in rabbits after insulin administration.

- Mouse Convulsion Test:

- Assesses insulin potency by observing the time taken for mice to exhibit convulsions after insulin injection, which indicates hypoglycemia.

2. In Vitro Bioassays:

   Adipocyte Glucose Uptake:

- Measures the uptake of glucose by cultured adipocytes in response to insulin, reflecting insulin's ability to stimulate glucose transport.

- L6 Myoblast Assay:
- Uses cultured L6 myoblasts (muscle cells) to assess insulin's effect on glucose uptake and glycogen synthesis.

Procedure for a Typical In Vivo Rabbit Blood Sugar Test:

1. Preparation: Fast the rabbits overnight to stabilize baseline blood glucose levels.
2. Administration: Administer a known dose of insulin subcutaneously to the test rabbits.
3. Monitoring: Measure blood glucose levels at regular intervals (e.g., 0, 30, 60, 90, 120 minutes) post-insulin administration.
4. Comparison: Compare the glucose levels to those of a standard insulin preparation to determine the test sample's potency.

Importance:

- Ensures the consistency and reliability of insulin used in clinical settings.
- Helps in the development and approval of new insulin formulations.
- Monitors the stability and activity of insulin during storage and after production.

BIOASSAY OF OXYTOCIN

Oxytocin is a hormone involved in various physiological processes, including childbirth and lactation. Bioassays for oxytocin are crucial for determining its potency and ensuring its quality for clinical use.

Principles of Oxytocin Bioassay

1. Biological Activity Measurement: The primary goal is to measure the biological activity of oxytocin by observing its specific physiological effects on a biological system.

2. Standardization: A standard or reference preparation of oxytocin is used to compare the test sample's activity, ensuring consistency and accuracy.

3. Dose-Response Relationship: The response is proportional to the dose within a certain range, allowing the determination of the effective concentration of oxytocin.

Procedure for Oxytocin Bioassay

Common Bioassay Methods:

1. Uterine Strip Assay (Rat or Mouse): Measures the contraction of uterine muscle strips in response to oxytocin.

2. Milk Ejection Assay (Lactating Rats): Observes the milk ejection response in lactating rats as an indicator of oxytocin activity.

Uterine Strip Assay

Materials:

- Uterine strips from non-pregnant rats or mice
- Physiological saline solution
- Oxytocin standard solution
- Test oxytocin sample
- Organ bath setup with recording devices

Procedure:

1. Preparation:
   a. Dissect uterine strips from rats or mice.
   b. Suspend the strips in an organ bath containing a physiological saline solution, maintained at 37°C, and aerated with a mixture of oxygen and carbon dioxide.

2. Baseline Recording:

3. Administration of Oxytocin:

   a. Allow the tissue to equilibrate and establish a baseline contraction pattern.

3. Administration of Oxytocin:

   a. Add increasing concentrations of the oxytocin standard solution to the organ bath.

   b. Record the amplitude and frequency of uterine contractions at each concentration.

4. Test Sample Analysis:

   a. Replace the saline solution and repeat the process with the test oxytocin sample.

   b. Compare the contraction responses to those obtained with the standard oxytocin solution.

5. Data Analysis:

   a. Plot the dose-response curves for both the standard and test samples.

   b. Determine the concentration of the test sample that produces a response equivalent to a known concentration of the standard.

Application of Oxytocin Bioassay

1. Pharmaceutical Quality Control: Ensures the potency and efficacy of oxytocin formulations used in clinical settings, such as for inducing labor or controlling postpartum hemorrhage.

2. Research: Studies the physiological and pharmacological effects of oxytocin, contributing to the understanding of its role in various biological processes.

1. 3. Regulatory Compliance: Meets the standards set by regulatory authorities for the approval and release of oxytocin products.

3. Veterinary Medicine: Assesses the potency of oxytocin used in veterinary practices, particularly in managing reproductive health in animals.

Bioassay of Vasopressin:

Vasopressin, also known as antidiuretic hormone (ADH), plays a crucial role in regulating water balance in the body by promoting water reabsorption in the kidneys. Bioassays for vasopressin are essential for determining its potency and ensuring the quality of pharmaceutical preparations.

Principles of Vasopressin Bioassay

1. Biological Activity Measurement: The primary goal is to measure the biological activity of vasopressin by observing its specific physiological effects on a biological system, such as its antidiuretic action.

2. Standardization: A standard or reference preparation of vasopressin is used for comparison to ensure consistency and accuracy in measuring the test sample's activity.

3. Dose-Response Relationship: The response is proportional to the dose within a certain range, allowing for the determination of the effective concentration of vasopressin.

Procedure for Vasopressin Bioassay

Common Bioassay Methods:

1. Rat Antidiuretic Assay: Measures the reduction in urine output in rats in response to vasopressin.

2. Blood Pressure Assay (Vascular Smooth Muscle): Observes the vasopressor effect (increase in blood pressure) induced by vasopressin.

Rat Antidiuretic Assay

Materials:

- Male rats (water-deprived to increase sensitivity to vasopressin)
- Vasopressin standard solution
- Test vasopressin sample

- Metabolic cages for urine collection
- Graduated cylinders or tubes for measuring urine volume

Procedure:

1. Preparation:
    a. Deprive rats of water for 12-24 hours to increase the sensitivity to vasopressin.
    b. Place the rats in metabolic cages to allow for separate collection of urine.
2. Baseline Measurement:
    a. Collect and measure the baseline urine output over a specified period (e.g., 1 hour).
3. Administration of Vasopressin:
    a. Inject a known dose of the vasopressin standard solution subcutaneously or intravenously.
    b. Collect and measure urine output at regular intervals (e.g., every 30 minutes) for a specified period.
4. Test Sample Analysis:
    a. Replace the standard solution with the test vasopressin sample and repeat the process.
    b. Compare the reduction in urine output caused by the test sample to that of the standard solution.
5. Data Analysis:
    a. Plot the dose-response curves for both the standard and test samples.
    b. Determine the concentration of the test sample that produces a response equivalent to a known concentration of the standard.

Application of Vasopressin Bioassay

1. Pharmaceutical Quality Control: Ensures the potency and efficacy of vasopressin formulations used in clinical settings, such as for treating diabetes insipidus or managing bleeding disorders.
2. Research: Studies the physiological and pharmacological effects of vasopressin, contributing to the understanding of its role in water balance, cardiovascular function, and other biological processes.
3. Regulatory Compliance: Meets the standards set by regulatory authorities for the approval and release of vasopressin products.
4. Clinical Diagnostics: Assists in the diagnosis of conditions related to vasopressin deficiency or excess by measuring its biological activity.

BIOASSAY OF ACTH

Adrenocorticotropic hormone (ACTH) is a peptide hormone produced by the anterior pituitary gland that stimulates the adrenal cortex to release cortisol. Bioassays for ACTH are important for determining its potency and ensuring the quality of pharmaceutical preparations.

Principles of ACTH Bioassay

1. Biological Activity Measurement: The primary goal is to measure the biological activity of ACTH by observing its specific physiological effects on a biological system, such as its ability to stimulate cortisol production.
2. Standardization: A standard or reference preparation of ACTH is used for comparison to ensure consistency and accuracy in measuring the test sample's activity.
3. Dose-Response Relationship: The response is proportional to the dose within a certain range, allowing for the determination of the effective concentration of ACTH.

Procedure for ACTH Bioassay: Common Bioassay Methods:

a. In Vivo Assay (Rat or Mouse): Measures the increase in plasma cortisol levels in response to ACTH administration.

b. In Vitro Assay (Adrenal Cell Culture): Observes the stimulation of cortisol secretion in cultured adrenal cells.

In Vivo Assay (Rat or Mouse): Materials:

- Rats or mice
- ACTH standard solution
- Test ACTH sample
- Blood collection tubes
- Centrifuge for plasma separation
- Cortisol assay kit (e.g., ELISA)

Procedure:

1. Preparation:
   a. Acclimate the animals to the testing environment.
   b. Fast the animals overnight to stabilize baseline cortisol levels.
2. Baseline Measurement:
   a. Collect a baseline blood sample from each animal to measure initial cortisol levels.
3. Administration of ACTH:
   a. Inject a known dose of the ACTH standard solution intraperitoneally or subcutaneously.
   b. Collect blood samples at regular intervals (e.g., 15, 30, 60 minutes) after administration.
4. Test Sample Analysis:
   a. Replace the standard solution with the test ACTH sample and repeat the process.

      b. Measure the cortisol levels in the collected blood samples using an appropriate assay kit.

5. Data Analysis:

      a. Plot the time-response curves for both the standard and test samples.

      b. Determine the concentration of the test sample that produces a response equivalent to a known concentration of the standard.

Application of ACTH Bioassay

1. Pharmaceutical Quality Control: Ensures the potency and efficacy of ACTH formulations used in clinical settings, such as for diagnosing adrenal insufficiency or treating certain medical conditions.

2. Research: Studies the physiological and pharmacological effects of ACTH, contributing to the understanding of its role in stress response, adrenal function, and other biological processes.

3. Regulatory Compliance: Meets the standards set by regulatory authorities for the approval and release of ACTH products.

4. Clinical Diagnostics: Assists in the diagnosis of conditions related to ACTH deficiency or excess by measuring its biological activity.

BIOASSAY OF D-TUBOCURARINE:

d-Tubocurarine is a naturally occurring alkaloid and a muscle relaxant that acts as a competitive antagonist at nicotinic acetylcholine receptors. It is historically significant as the active component of curare, used in anesthesia to induce muscle paralysis.

Principles of d-Tubocurarine Bioassay

1. Biological Activity Measurement: The bioassay aims to measure the potency and efficacy of d-tubocurarine by observing its effect on muscle

contraction, particularly its ability to induce muscle relaxation or paralysis.

2. Standardization: A standard or reference preparation of d-tubocurarine is used to compare the test sample's activity, ensuring consistency and accuracy.

3. Dose-Response Relationship: The response is proportional to the dose within a certain range, allowing the determination of the effective concentration of d-tubocurarine.

Procedure for d-Tubocurarine Bioassay: Common Bioassay Methods:

1. In Vivo Assay (Animal Models): Measures the degree of muscle relaxation or paralysis in response to d-tubocurarine administration.

2. In Vitro Assay (Isolated Tissue Preparations): Observes the inhibition of electrically induced muscle contractions in isolated tissues, such as frog rectus abdominis or rat diaphragm.

In Vitro Assay (Isolated Frog Rectus Abdominis Muscle): Materials:

- Isolated frog rectus abdominis muscle preparation
- Physiological saline solution
- d-Tubocurarine standard solution
- Test d-tubocurarine sample
- Organ bath setup with electrical stimulator and recording devices

Procedure:

1. Preparation:
   a. Dissect the rectus abdominis muscle from a frog and suspend it in an organ bath containing physiological saline solution at room temperature, aerated with oxygen.
2. Baseline Recording:

a. Apply regular electrical stimulation to the muscle and record the baseline contractions.

3. Administration of d-Tubocurarine:

    a. Add increasing concentrations of the d-tubocurarine standard solution to the organ bath.

    b. Record the changes in muscle contraction amplitude at each concentration.

4. Test Sample Analysis:

    a. Replace the saline solution and repeat the process with the test d-tubocurarine sample.

    b. Compare the muscle relaxation responses to those obtained with the standard d-tubocurarine solution.

5. Data Analysis:

    a. Plot the dose-response curves for both the standard and test samples.

    b. Determine the concentration of the test sample that produces a response equivalent to a known concentration of the standard.

Application of d-Tubocurarine Bioassay

1. Pharmaceutical Quality Control: Ensures the potency and efficacy of d-tubocurarine formulations used in clinical settings, such as for inducing muscle relaxation during surgical procedures.

2. Research: Studies the pharmacological effects of d-tubocurarine, contributing to the understanding of neuromuscular transmission and the development of new muscle relaxants.

3. Regulatory Compliance: Meets the standards set by regulatory authorities for the approval and release of d-tubocurarine products.

4. Clinical Diagnostics: Assists in the diagnosis of neuromuscular disorders by evaluating the responsiveness of muscle tissue to d-tubocurarine.

Bioassay of Digitalis:

Digitalis is a group of compounds derived from the foxglove plant (Digitalis purpurea and Digitalis lanata) that have potent cardiac effects, primarily used to treat heart conditions such as atrial fibrillation and heart failure. The primary active components are cardiac glycosides like digoxin and digitoxin.

Principles of Digitalis Bioassay

1. Biological Activity Measurement: The bioassay aims to measure the potency and efficacy of digitalis compounds by observing their specific physiological effects, such as increasing the force of cardiac contraction and altering heart rate.

2. Standardization: A standard or reference preparation of digitalis (e.g., digoxin) is used to compare the test sample's activity, ensuring consistency and accuracy.

3. Dose-Response Relationship: The response is proportional to the dose within a certain range, allowing the determination of the effective concentration of digitalis.

Procedure for Digitalis Bioassay: Common Bioassay Methods:

1. In Vivo Assay (Animal Models): Measures the effect of digitalis on heart rate, force of contraction, and electrocardiographic changes in animals like cats or pigeons.

2. In Vitro Assay (Isolated Heart Preparations): Observes the effect of digitalis on isolated heart tissues, such as guinea pig atria or frog heart.

In Vivo Assay (Pigeon Digitalis Assay): Materials:

    a. Pigeons (preferably healthy adult birds)

    b. Digitalis standard solution (e.g., digoxin)

    c. Test digitalis sample

    d. Syringes for drug administration

e. Electrocardiograph (ECG) for monitoring heart rate and rhythm

Procedure:

1. Preparation:
    a. Acclimate the pigeons to the testing environment.
    b. Fast the pigeons for several hours before the experiment to stabilize baseline physiological conditions.
2. Baseline Measurement:
    a. Record the baseline heart rate and rhythm using an ECG.
3. Administration of Digitalis:
    a. Administer a known dose of the digitalis standard solution intravenously or intramuscularly.
    b. Monitor the heart rate and rhythm continuously, recording the onset of any arrhythmias or changes in heart rate.
4. Test Sample Analysis:
    a. Replace the standard solution with the test digitalis sample and repeat the process.
    b. Compare the cardiovascular responses to those obtained with the standard digitalis solution.
5. Data Analysis:
    a. Plot the dose-response curves for both the standard and test samples.
    b. Determine the concentration of the test sample that produces a response equivalent to a known concentration of the standard.

Application of Digitalis Bioassay

1. Pharmaceutical Quality Control: Ensures the potency and efficacy of digitalis formulations used in clinical settings, such as for treating heart conditions.

2. Research: Studies the pharmacological effects of digitalis, contributing to the understanding of its mechanisms of action and the development of new cardiac drugs.

3. Regulatory Compliance: Meets the standards set by regulatory authorities for the approval and release of digitalis products.

4. Clinical Diagnostics: Assists in the diagnosis and management of digitalis toxicity and monitoring therapeutic levels in patients receiving digitalis therapy.

BIOASSAY OF HISTAMINE:

Histamine is a biogenic amine involved in various physiological functions, including immune response, gastric acid secretion, and neurotransmission. Bioassays for histamine are essential for determining its potency and activity in biological systems.

Principles of Histamine Bioassay

1. Biological Activity Measurement: The bioassay measures the potency and efficacy of histamine by observing its specific physiological effects, such as contraction of smooth muscles or stimulation of gastric acid secretion.

2. Standardization: A standard or reference preparation of histamine is used for comparison to ensure consistency and accuracy in measuring the test sample's activity.

3. Dose-Response Relationship: The response is proportional to the dose within a certain range, allowing the determination of the effective concentration of histamine.

Procedure for Histamine Bioassay: Common Bioassay Methods:

4. In Vivo Assay (Animal Models): Measures the physiological effects of histamine, such as changes in blood pressure or bronchoconstriction in animals like guinea pigs or dogs.

5. In Vitro Assay (Isolated Tissue Preparations): Observes the effect of histamine on isolated tissues, such as guinea pig ileum or rat uterus.

In Vitro Assay (Isolated Guinea Pig Ileum): Materials:

- Isolated guinea pig ileum preparation
- Physiological saline solution
- Histamine standard solution
- Test histamine sample
- Organ bath setup with recording devices

Procedure:

1) Preparation:
   - Dissect the ileum from a guinea pig and suspend it in an organ bath containing physiological saline solution at 37°C, aerated with oxygen.

2) Baseline Recording:
   - Allow the tissue to equilibrate and establish a baseline contraction pattern.

3) Administration of Histamine:
   - Add increasing concentrations of the histamine standard solution to the organ bath.
   - Record the amplitude and frequency of ileum contractions at each concentration.

4) Test Sample Analysis:
   - Replace the saline solution and repeat the process with the test histamine sample.

- Compare the contraction responses to those obtained with the standard histamine solution.

5) Data Analysis:

- Plot the dose-response curves for both the standard and test samples.
- Determine the concentration of the test sample that produces a response equivalent to a known concentration of the standard.

Application of Histamine Bioassay

6. Pharmaceutical Quality Control: Ensures the potency and efficacy of histamine preparations used in clinical and research settings.

7. Research: Studies the pharmacological effects of histamine, contributing to the understanding of its role in allergic reactions, gastric acid secretion, and neurotransmission.

8. Regulatory Compliance:Meets the standards set by regulatory authorities for the approval and release of histamine products.

9. Clinical Diagnostics: Assists in the diagnosis of conditions related to histamine imbalance, such as allergies and mast cell disorders.

10. Drug Development:Used in the development and testing of antihistamines and other drugs targeting histamine receptors.

Bioassay of 5-HT (Serotonin):

5-Hydroxytryptamine (5-HT), commonly known as serotonin, is a neurotransmitter that plays a crucial role in regulating mood, appetite, sleep, and other physiological processes. Bioassays for serotonin are essential for determining its potency and activity in biological systems.

Principles of 5-HT Bioassay

1. Biological Activity Measurement: The bioassay measures the potency and efficacy of serotonin by observing its specific physiological effects,

such as contraction of smooth muscles or modulation of neurotransmission.

2. Standardization: A standard or reference preparation of serotonin is used for comparison to ensure consistency and accuracy in measuring the test sample's activity.

3. Dose-Response Relationship: The response is proportional to the dose within a certain range, allowing the determination of the effective concentration of serotonin.

Procedure for 5-HT Bioassay: Common Bioassay Methods:

1. In Vivo Assay (Animal Models): Measures the physiological effects of serotonin, such as changes in blood pressure or behavioral responses in animals like rats or cats.

2. In Vitro Assay (Isolated Tissue Preparations): Observes the effect of serotonin on isolated tissues, such as rat fundus strip or guinea pig ileum.

In Vitro Assay (Isolated Rat Fundus Strip): Materials:

- Isolated rat fundus strip preparation
- Physiological saline solution
- Serotonin (5-HT) standard solution
- Test serotonin sample
- Organ bath setup with recording devices

Procedure:

1. Preparation: Dissect the fundus strip from a rat and suspend it in an organ bath containing physiological saline solution at 37°C, aerated with a mixture of oxygen and carbon dioxide.

2. Baseline Recording: Allow the tissue to equilibrate and establish a baseline contraction pattern.

3. Administration of Serotonin:
   a. Add increasing concentrations of the serotonin standard solution to the organ bath.
   b. Record the amplitude and frequency of fundus strip contractions at each concentration.
4. Test Sample Analysis:
   a. Replace the saline solution and repeat the process with the test serotonin sample.
   b. Compare the contraction responses to those obtained with the standard serotonin solution.
5. Data Analysis:
   a. Plot the dose-response curves for both the standard and test samples.
   b. Determine the concentration of the test sample that produces a response equivalent to a known concentration of the standard.

Application of 5-HT Bioassay

1. Pharmaceutical Quality Control: Ensures the potency and efficacy of serotonin preparations used in clinical and research settings.
2. Research: Studies the pharmacological effects of serotonin, contributing to the understanding of its role in mood regulation, gastrointestinal function, and other physiological processes.
3. Regulatory Compliance: Meets the standards set by regulatory authorities for the approval and release of serotonin products.
4. Clinical Diagnostics: Assists in the diagnosis of conditions related to serotonin imbalance, such as depression, anxiety, and irritable bowel syndrome.
5. Drug Development: Used in the development and testing of serotonergic drugs, including antidepressants and antiemetics.